Praise for Aidan Higgins

"The ferocious and dazzling prose of Aidan Higgins, the pure architecture of his sentences, takes the breath out of you. He is one of our great writers."

—Annie Proulx

"Higgins writes with genuine Irish bitter poetic intensity. . . . He reminds me of novelists who used to write for the sake of writing, to achieve what Nabokov called 'aesthetic bliss.' Higgins helps to revive language."

—*Spectator*

"*Scenes from a Receding Past* is ironic and tender, like *Langrishe, Go Down*, and equally informative about love."

—*New Statesman*

"*Langrishe, Go Down* is clearly the best Irish novel since *At Swim-Two-Birds* and the novels of Beckett."

—*Irish Times*

"*Dog Days*—a bloody marvelous book."

—Harold Pinter

Other Books by Aidan Higgins

Asylum & Other Stories
Balcony of Europe
A Bestiary
Bornholm Night-Ferry
Flotsam & Jetsam
Helsingør Station & Other Departures
Images of Africa
Langrishe, Go Down
Lions of the Grunewald
Ronda Gorge & Other Precipices
Scenes from a Receding Past

Windy Arbours
collected criticism

AIDAN HIGGINS

Dalkey Archive Press
NORMAL · LONDON

Library of Congress Cataloging-in-Publication Data:

Higgins, Aidan, 1927–
    Windy arbours / by Aidan Higgins.— 1st Dalkey Archive ed.
        p. cm.
    ISBN 1-56478-400-2 (cloth : alk. paper) — ISBN 1-56478-391-X (paper : alk. paper)
    1. Fiction—20th century—History and criticism. I. Title.

PN3324.H54 2005
809.3'04—dc22

                                                                    2004063476

        Partially funded by a grant from the Illinois Arts Council, a state agency.

        Dalkey Archive Press is a nonprofit organization whose mission is
        to promote international cultural understanding and provide a forum
                        for dialogue for the literary arts.

                            www.dalkeyarchive.com

        Printed on permanent/durable acid-free paper, bound in the United States of America,
                and distributed throughout North America and Europe.

For Jonathan Williams
Dredger of dross

Contents

Part I: Ilium Falling

1. Below Memphis Junction   3
2. Ilium Falling   7
3. *Liebestod*   11
4. Djuna   15
5. Kin   18
6. Railroads   20
7. Blacklist   24
8. Wing Shot   26
9. Gonzo   29
10. Lunar   31
11. Barthelme   33
12. Dandy   35
13. Privilege   38
14. Americana   40
15. Bonafides   43
16. Tosh   45
17. Los Angeles Dick   47
18. Voice from the Bronx Laundry   50
19. Boz & Co.   53
20. The Heavy Bear   55
21. Gigantic Knockers   59
22. Seeing Big   62
23. Hope Deferred   65
24. Doctored Letters   68
25. Peanuts   70
26. A Whispering Gush   73
27. In the Land of Glut   76
28. Tales from the Killing Ground   78

29. The People of the Spirit   81
30. Natchez Trace   84
31. In the American Grain   86
32. Lynching in the Everglades   88
33. Fresh Horrors   90
34. Narco   92

Part II: Recurring Refrain

35. Down the Line   97
36. Outlandish Places   100
37. Loot   102
38. By the Damascus Stream   104
39. Dark Rites   108
40. Yangtze Bends   110
41. Dinner at Lipp's   112
42. Soldiers' Pay   115
43. The Vapours   118
44. Dry Thoughts in a Dry Season   120
45. Twilight in the *Saal*   123
46. Sappho & Co.   126
47. That Swine Hardcastle   128
48. Down There in Bohemia   131
49. Non-Lives   133
50. How Utterly Maddening!   136
51. Connubial Bliss   138
52. Glowing Cinders   140
53. Malignant Crabs   142
54. Cyril & Co.   145
55. On Storm King Mountain   149
56. The Faceless Creator   150
57. The Bombing Analyst   156
58. Copping Out   158
59. Lengthening Shadows   160
60. Pinter's Proust   162
61. Gnarled Oak   165
62. Eighty Years On   167

63. Zones of Insecurity 169

64. Grocer's Wine 172

65. Vinegar Dressing 174

66. Frothy Apophthegm 176

67. Infernal City 179

68. Anthony Burgess at the London Savoy 181

Part III: The Small Neurosis

69. Fire in the Hills 187

70. Fires from Gehenna 189

71. Cantraps of Fermented Words 192

72. Uric Acid 194

73. Stratafiction 196

74. A Purple Glow 199

75. The Blackrock Cosmology 202

76. The Bosky Dew 205

77. Glencree *Knackwurst* 210

78. The Corn Is Green 212

79. Blood Brothers 214

80. Buck Mulligan 217

81. Recurring Refrain 220

82. Cark 222

83. Poolbeg Flashers 223

84. Paradiddle and Paradigm 226

85. Old Porn and Corn-Plasters 229

Part IV: From Numina to Nowhere

86. Dream-Zoo 235

87. Our Hero, after Babel 238

88. Tellers of Tales 243

89. Tintin 248

90. Torquemada 252

91. Hallucinations 254

92. Kundera 256

93. Bore-Holes   258
94. Marx-Time   260
95. Gasoline   262
96. The Regimented Numbers Flow   264
97. Black Mischief   266
98. Sinewy Dreams   268
99. Blood in the Morning   270
100. In the Polluted Desert   273
101. Cautionary Tales   275
102. *Es muss sein* . . .   277
103. In the Land of the Bitter Macaroon   279
104. In Old Trieste   280
105. Period Effects   283
106. The Haunted Wood   285
107. Reality's Dark Dream   287
108. Glass Bead Games   290
109. Stuffed Grouse   292
110. 1990   294
111. Rising Fever   297
112. Culture on the Rocks   299
113. *Lebensraum*   302
114. Prophylactic Laughter   305
115. The Corpse in the Vault   307

I

Ilium Falling

An unsavoury America begins to emerge.

1

Below Memphis Junction

Joseph Blotner (ed.), *Uncollected Stories of William Faulkner* (Chatto & Windus)

'Man is circumstance,' wrote Faulkner; 'our virtues are usually by-products of our vices.' Chronicler of a land despoiled, he had a keen nose for liars and the fix; space was his chosen theme, the wilderness, the human heart at odds with itself. Firearms figure much in his fiction, after game and retribution; General Grant had just left off burning down Jefferson and gone riding away.

Language itself was a strategy, syntactical warfare; the words shuffled forward, assembling before they entered into the strategic line of a phrase—a phrase generally of impatience—massing for the attack.

He created a large cast of talkers and movers, no-goods and wasters, parasitic white and black trash. Garrulous lawyer Gavin Stevens is a rustic Maecenas, a Mississippian private eye in the mould of Philip Marlowe, with tireless volubility unraveling base and hidden motives, implacable foe of the proliferating Snopeses in and around Frenchmen's Bend and down the mean streets of Memphis. And if Chandler had the 'City of Angels' (L.A.) under bailiwick, Faulkner had Memphis and its brothels, Sutpen's Hundred.

It took him some time to discover his true metier, get into his stride, come into his true patrimony; but when at last he found it he never lost it, became sole owner and proprietor of Yoknapatawpha County down there below Memphis Junction. The hand-drawn map he boldly affixed to the prelims of *The Mansion* was by his own hand; the unrolling record of foul deeds and murders—where Wash Jones slew Sutpen, where Popeye murdered Tommy, there the jail where Godwin was lynched.

Nothing was straightforward with Faulkner, least of all his syntax; fifteen and even thirty-line sentences and their attendant sub-clauses went meandering off, the long-winded parenthesis were as tracks through the Mississippian wilderness, its swamps and bayous, levee and huge river bottom; a ten-page digression (within brackets) can end abruptly on a semi-colon, to indicate where the path ends or authorial breath—or patience—gave out. He had a proclivity for the bracket, the enclosure, asides spoken from the corner of the mouth, not for ladies' ears; for he was nothing if not a true Southern gentleman.

Jefferson may have been gutted and the men defending it surrenderd to the Yankees but the ladies had never surrendered. Mr. Faulkner's great ladies are garrulous as himself, which is saying something, formidable females of forbidding volubility, telling it as they knew it.

The men who rode into Jefferson came from no discernible past; the ruthless gambler on horseback who rode in with his French architect in chains and a retinue of wild enslaved blackmen. The big woods twenty miles from Jefferson was an area near a hundred miles deep.

The antithetical clauses coil upon themselves, backtracking, probing for motive. He made a high style of hyperbole, the gossip of a small place, a puff of steam from the stack. Here he is on the subject of Sam Fathers, grandson of old Chief Ikkemotubbe who was called Doom:

> Sam Fathers would be there; if he was glad to see us he did not show it. If he regretted to see us depart again he did not show that. Each morning he would go out to my stand with me before the dogs were cast.

Or again:

> We rode for about an hour, through the gray and unmarked afternoon where the light was little different from what it had been at dawn and which would become darkness without any gradation.

Or again:

> There was the soaring and sombre solitude in the dim light, there was the thin whisper of the cold rain, which had not ceased all day; then, as if it had waited for us to find our positions and become still, the wilderness breathed again.

He always had plenty of words when he wanted them—too damn many, some would say. But he worked on a large scale, as Whitman and Melville before him, venturing alone into that vastness and vacancy that was American space, pushing on from where Mark Twain and Sherwood Anderson had left off. When Bill Faulkner launched himself into one of his tall tales there weren't nara man alive knowed where it might end; he was sole owner and proprietor of Yoknapatawpha County as Crusoe was lord and master of his desert island:

> He had an affable and penetrating volubility, a gift for anecdote and gossip. He never forgot names and he knew everyone, man, mule and dog, in fifty miles. He was believed to be well fixed.

Affability apart, the description might fit Mr. Faulkner himself, rather than his creature V. K. Ratliff, sewing-machine salesman, trader in land and livestock, pie-jawer extraordinaire whom Faulkner had re-named thrice, hardly crediting what he was creating.

Prosperity came late for the most distinguished author on the Random House list, the Nobel Prizeman airing his views on the human condition in Stockholm.

Faulknerean cadences and pyrotechnics have been put into service in French by Claude Simon, Nobel-prizeman-to-be operating on the fringe of the *nouvelle vague*, those new French novels emanating from *Editions de Minuit*; few others would have had the nerve.

Faulkner's women are an exceedingly odd lot. The listless overweight child Eula Varner is carried to school but grows up to be a raging beauty to whom Gavin Stevens loses his heart; to be later enraptured by the daughter, Linda, a replica of the mother who married Flem Snopes. Deaf after a shell-burst in the Spanish Civil War, Mrs. Eula Snopes ends up spouting sententious twaddle just like the lawyer, quacking like a duck, conveying messages on a little pad.

Here then are forty-five stories extracted from three novels and three collections of stories, with thirteen hitherto unpublished stories thrown in for good measure. It's as good a way as any to discover Faulkner, ranging from early work to late; for were you to enter his world by the wrong door (*A Fable*), you might not care to proceed any further. When he turned from Mallarmé and the notion of himself as a dandy young poet, he began to find himself with the jocks and the low life drifters of *New Orleans Sketches*. Here it is dirt cheap at £13 give or take a few lousy nickels. 'The Hound,' 'The Bear' and 'The Old People' could stand comparison with Count Tolstoy himself.

Reading him is akin to laying your finger on the pulse of the Southern past, still warmly aflutter there on the page; telling of men going armed into the darkness, of Negroes passing into the night, singing, trying to catch up with the Yankee Army and become free.

Hibernia, 2 October 1980

2
Ilium Falling

Joseph Blotner (ed.), *Selected Letters of William Faulkner* (Scolar)

'Between grief and nothing I will take grief,' he wrote, paraphrasing Baudelaire. But even the immortals have their moments of weakness, their human foibles: Diogenes with half his hair shaved off practicing rhetorical effects for six weeks underground in a cave; Papa Hemingway, praise from Berenson (another Great Cod) gone to his head, composing letters to his admirer in Homeric strain; Malcolm Lowry's rhapsodies: the alcoholic ravings of the Consul, dire monologues from that ill-named pair, Plantaganet and Sijbjørn Wilderness—three great asses of presumptive literature. Or, at a more fundamentally absurd level: Homer nodding off, Pound's long silence, when at last released from durance vile; a silence as deafening as his torrential speech.

Nor was William Cuthbert Faulkner free of such absurdity amid the lucidity and insight, in the razzmatazz of his justly famous prose effects; as a reading of the *Selected Letters* and a re-reading of *The Wild Palms* (now arranged as the author had originally intended and making some sense at last) bears testimony. Faulkner's absurdities, his excess baggage, become endearing; if you like the work you forgive the man everything. The public man who spoke of two truths and advised caution on matters of Civic Rights at the time of Little Rock was the same man who spoke of upholding liberty and the vigilance required to the cadets of West Point. Obedience, honour, duty and responsibility, he upheld these virtues. For the State Department he traveled to Japan and Greece, Venezuela; as a good citizen was proud to serve his President, Ike. General W.C. Westmoreland was the officer in charge of the academy on the occasion of Faulkner's visit just a month prior to the fatal heart attack in 1962; and Westmoreland was Ike's man in South Korea.

The letters, over 450 pages of them, will be of abiding interest to all those who admire Faulkner's work. Perhaps mercifully less prolix than the tumultuous fiction (hot with a new novel he speaks of 'coming in under the wire,' winning the race, meeting the deadline) and reveal a shrewd businessman in the management of his own affairs, a loyal friend, a discreet lover. Faulkner was a Southern gent before he was anything else. Beethoven is said to have had love affairs in order to correspond about them; Faulkner puts little or nothing down on paper, the secrets are safe with him, though heavy hints are dropped by editor Blotner, the former B-17 bomb-aimer.

When putting in stints at script-writing in Hollywood (*The Big Sleep*), which he hated, the list of dependants are as extensive as Issac Babel's when he was scripting Soviet propaganda movies, collaborating with Eisenstein on 'Bezhin Meadow' until it was denounced. The Hollywood hack Harry Kurnitz was probably wrong to impute drunkenness to Faulkner when the Nobel Prizeman was carried past him on a stretcher, having flown in with a broken back following a tumble when riding to hounds. He changed publishers thrice, was difficult with his agents; there were tax troubles in the late 1940s after the affluent Hollywood years when he was earning big money at 'Warner's saltmine.' From that affluence to the indignity of having to borrow from his mother to pay outstanding grocery bills and the cook, must have been galling. Success neither surprised him nor changed him much; he seemed amazed at his own talent, as well he might. That the bullying Hemingway considered him 'a good skate' pleased him; he put down the uppity Mailer, ever presumptuous, in a few devastating lines. He was not a literary man, spoke scathingly of 'a kind of jail corridor of literary talk.' Mencken impertinently wished to trim one of his rambling yarns (Maugham entertained the grandiose notion of cutting Proust). Not for him *Life* and *Time* coverage ('Tell the bastards nothing'); to them he was not at home. He detested smugness, fanaticism, meddling; he had a daughter, who only lived for five days—Alabama. A rakehell Grandfather had owned slaves.

At his beguiling best (*As I Lay Dying*) Faulkner was a great wonder; at his worst (*A Fable*) intolerable. He doubted the goodness of people but kept an open mind: 'Human beings are terrible. One must believe well in man to endure him, wait out his folly and savagery.'

Endure was always a strong word with him; he refused most honours, hunted with the Keswick and Farmington Hunts, shot quail, was pestered by trophy hunters and rubbernecks, not to mention poor relations who called uninvited and were summarily turned away. 'Dar he be, a-writin!' (The discreet tapping of a distant typewriter). He changed houses, lived in some splendour.

His letter on the doomed child who died of cancer at the age of ten is the most affecting in the collection. There are references to a favourite pipe mislaid, dingy pigskin gloves, a suit that must be found. He worried about formality of dress in Japan; he who had kept the hoop skirt and plug hat out of his writing on the Deep South.

A French Professor thought he had discovered a vein of puritanism in the *oeuvre*; one wouldn't have to look too far. He was rarely guilty of malevolence; even if Jonathan Cape is 'the Limey with the teeth.' Some royalties had been lost when Cape & Smith went into liquidation and in these changeovers the author always loses out.

He created one of the truly great bores of Literature—perhaps the only one in the same league of long-windedness as Dostoevesky's Father Zossima—stand-up lawyer Gavin Stevens, incorrigible bachelor and Heidelberg graduate who represented the silly snobbish side of Faulkner, the failed poet of New Orleans, not the gay blade who refers to 'switch-tail nigger whores.' He feared the gross flesh, the 'dark precipice' with a truly Baptist fatalism, being much addicted to moralising. Certainly the lust and folly are laid on thickly in places.

His great years were 1929-1936, the time of:

As I Lay Dying (1930)
The Sound & the Fury (1929)
Sanctuary (1931)
These Thirteen (1931)
Light in August (1932)
Absalom, Absalom! (1936)

And later towards the end:

The Mansion (1959)
The Town (1957).

These two coupled with *The Hamlet* (1940) constitute a trilogy hard to match. His best books took least time; seven months for *The Wild Palms* (originally *If I Forget Thee, Jerusalem*, for a good Baptist is always *au fait* with his Bible), six weeks for *As I Lay Dying* (written on a wheelbarrow through the nights when employed in a power station), and what is arguably his worst novel, *A Fable*, which took 'ten good years' of his life. Another dud work, *Requiem for a Nun*, gave much trouble.

Titles were changed about: *Absalom, Absalom!* was once *The Dark House*; *The Hamlet* was once *The Peasants*, *The Sound and the Fury* was once *Twilight*; as *Sartoris* was once *Flags in the Dust*. Everything changed, everything improved, nothing wasted.

Faulkner himself was unsure whether or not *The Wild Palms* was 'drivel' or even 'absolute drivel.' He wrote to the editor at Random:

> It was just as if I had sat on one side of a wall and the paper was on the other and my hand with the pen thrust through the wall and writing not only on invisible paper but in pitch blackness too, so that I could not even know if the pen still wrote on the paper or not.

But then again it was a bad time all over—summer 1938 and the dictators growing fractious. By 1956 (The Nobel Prize had come in 1949) he feared that he had shot his bolt and 'all that remains now is the empty craftsmanship—no fire, force, passion anymore in the words and sentences.'

Well he was surely wrong there; for if bad Faulkner gets worse with time, good Faulkner gets even better.

Hibernia, 21 December 1989

3

Liebestod

Djuna Barnes, *Nightwood* (Faber & Faber)

One cup poured into another makes different water; tears shed by
one eye would blind if wept into another eye. The breast we strike
in joy is not the breast we strike in pain; any man's smile would
be consternation on another's mouth. Rear up, eternal river, here
comes grief!

She belongs by right to that very rare group of female expatriate writers
who passed through Paris in the 1920s. Paris—Joyce called it 'a lamp lit for
lovers in the wood of the world'—itself became her subject-matter and she is
now the sole survivor, old and frail and living in Patchen Place, Greenwich
Village. Her work is little known, much of it out of print. Thanks to Faber
her stories are again available; *Spillway & Other Stories* being a somewhat
modified version of *A Night Among the Horses* (1929), itself a modification of
the earlier *A Book* (1923), both with title changes and rewritten passages
that are not always an improvement; both from Boni and Liveright.

The novel *Ryder*, as odd as odd can be, has never been published on
this side of the Atlantic. No student of the recondite has made a study of
her work, to the best of my knowledge; though her name crops up here
and there in the records of the time. A formidable presence either forbid-
dingly silent or delivering some devastating put-down. She has a feminist
following, mainly for *Nightwood*.

I came upon it in a Dublin bookshop in the early 1950s, led to it by a
quotation in a review from a magazine now defunct (Pearse Hutchinson
in *Envoy*, Dublin). If the prose seems somewhat high for the occasion we
must not forget that her preoccupations were singular and archaic for her
time. On a first reading it would seem to be uninfluenced by any other
writer male or female, living or dead—none, that is, easily detectable—an
impossible achievement. The divines Jeremy Taylor and John Donne are

invoked, Cibber as well as Rops and Bosch, Schumann and Bach, Morgenrot and Rutbief, Prince Arthur Tudor and the Grand Duke Alexander of Russia, an exotic crew.

Few have attempted that theme from that particular angle, dealing with the psychopathology of love, and fewer still have brought it off, since Petronius and Catullus; or Proust and Genet in our time. Miss Barnes's fiction constitutes a sort of abridgement to the labours of Proust. Her manner recalls Webster, in its intent to shock, its moral fervour, its astringency—rare for a woman. There is something of Congreve in her style, though her sympathies would seem to lie with Catholics rather than with Protestants, with the destitute rather than the ownership class. She *detested* Jane Austin.

The archaisms were always deliberate, derived from wide reading; and if the subject matter was French or Austrian, the flair and nerve could only be American; only exceeded by the wilful excesses of Faulkner's syntactical warfare. The delayed verb placements being resoundingly Germanic, while the high manner contrived to be a mixture of painter and musician: Bosch and Buxtehude, Robert Schumann and the Viennese Secession.

That some of her characters talk and think alike we must not complain of, since their thinking and talking is remarkable by any standards ('thinking about something you know nothing about does not help'). When Nora Flood finds the Doctor abed, got up as a woman in wig and gown, she thinks:

> He dresses to be beside himself, he who is so constructed that love, for him, can only be something special; in a room that, giving back evidence of his occupancy, is as mauled as the last agony.

The piling on of metaphor and simile succeed, as the laying down of light artillery fire; the archaic imagery is pre-Copernican and the long shadow of the wily Dr. Freud never intrudes; no panaceas are offered, for the patient's condition (life) is incurable; the manner is perhaps impossible to emulate. She has no imitators. Kay Boyle comes closest (*The White Horses of Vienna*, 1936); not Jean Rhys, never Nin. Perhaps roughneck Genet in French?

Much that passes for fiction comes in the form of loosely strung together sequences of well-intentioned faux-pas; much of its (faked) dramatic action quite static, even when something is happening; and conducted as a private 'debate' that involves entanglements of 'plot' fabricated by the all-knowing, much-troubled narrator's conscience and the world out there, the forbidden ground; an area where problems are resolved, from the fake prehistoric past of William Golding's *The Inheritors* to the faked present of William Boyd's *Brazzaville Beach*. Fowles and Julian Barnes follow on.

'Only the scorned and ridiculous make good stories,' she wrote edgily, and 'Part the diamonds and you will find slug's meat' (pure Webster). The preface by T. S. Eliot has been much admired and imitated—see Guerard and Fiedler on Hawkes or some good heart pushing the claims of the tendentious Jerry Bumpus (*The Anaconda* secured in empty tar barrels before delivery, at horrific length, to his publisher).

Rhapsodic treatment of inversion, in this instance lesbian love, as presented from the inside by a woman, has been attempted by few female writers since Sappho. Djuna Barnes herself denied being of that sisterhood ('I'm not a lesbian, I just love Thelma').

Radclyffe Hall's old shocker, *The Well Of Loneliness*, has its unintended grotesqueries and is difficult to get through without the suppressed snigger or outright guffaw. A bullfinch warbling 'O Tannenbaum,' conversation with a horse.

Nightwood, as *Ulysses* and Proust's masterpiece, is, among other things, a record of its time. That time and that place; Vienna's inner city, the lost freedom of European Jewry, Berlin and then Paris again and Vienna in the 1920s; one of the main characters in all three works being Jewish. Ripe speculation on the nature of Catholicism features throughout *Nightwood*, much of it unorthodox: 'The joy and safety of the Catholic faith which, at a pinch, covers up the spots on the wall where the family portraits take a slide.' The Irish race is affectionately described as 'common as whale shit on the bottom of the ocean.'

The Baron's preoccupations and obsessions are possibly the writer's own; as some of Bloom's less savoury obsessions were doubtless Joyce's; as there was undoubtedly something of Jupien and Baron Charlus hidden in Proust.

Rapid geographical and topographical changes throughout—leaps from Europe into a curiously derelict and weedy America, to Cornwall-on-Hudson and the ruins of a church, a glimpse of the-shit-house-on-a-distant-hill—impart a dreamlike or better nightmarelike impetus and foreshortening effect; you get pulled in.

The incident of the cow and the Dublin Mick during the bombing raid, the encounter with the Czar's brother-in-law, are Godalmighty strange. The sepia matter, supposed to be dead and gone years ago, stirs a little and the past comes eerily back to life.

Reality itself, whatever that may be, is observed with a very beady eye. The meeting of Robin and Nora:

> The great cage for the lions had been set up, and the lions were walking up and down out of their small strong boxes into the arena. Ponderous and furred they came, their tails laid down across the floor, dragging and heavy, making the air seem full of withheld strength. Then as one powerful lioness came to the turn of the bars, exactly opposite the girl, she turned her furious great head with its yellow eyes afire and went down, her paws thrust through the bars and, as she regarded the girl, as if a river were falling behind impassable heat, her eyes flowed in tears that never reached the surface.

No other writer, Proust apart (describing homosexual love), has revealed the sorry plight of lovers, whether they be normal or not, with such exuberant tenderness and malignancy. Love is the rediscovery of the Self through the other; death is 'intimacy walking backward.'

This is a timely reissue of the 1950 second edition casebound. Try it, gentle skimmer. A most curious personalised version of European history as a servant-girl sharpening knives; *pâté de foie gras* stuffed with cyanide. If there is such a thing as a modern classic this must be it.

Hibernia, 15 October 1979

4

Djuna

Alyce Barry (ed.), *I Could Never Be Lonely Without a Husband:*
Interviews by Djuna Barnes (Virago)

'The past exudes legend' (Malamud); all biography is ultimately fiction. And fiction, a form of autobiography?

Djuna Barnes's fiction was as odd as her life, from the Chaucerian novel *Ryder* (1928), the Jacobean novel *Nightwood* (1936), *The Antiphon* (1958) a play that embarrassed T. S. Eliot, written in Shakespearean iambic pentameters to confuse the groundlings.

Both paternal grandparents wrote, as did the maternal grandmother Zadel Barnes; a novel was published in Boston in 1871 with the curious title *Can the Old Love?* There was Methodism in their madness.

Discarding strict Methodism, Djuna's father followed a loose form of Mormonism, changed surname and *prenomen* at will (he made up Djuna from Prince Djalma in *The Wandering Jew*) and always carried a damp sponge on his saddle to wipe himself with after any chance intercourse that might come his way.

His mistress was the opera singer Amelia d'Alvarez, caught on the rebound from Oscar Hammerstein. One of Djuna's distant female relatives had been hung as a witch in Hartford, Connecticut. The parents had met in Shepherds Bush in London. The priapic progenitor appears in all her work, and is the hero or villain of *Ryder*.

She herself had mixed feelings about America and Americans, 'the fierce sadistic race crouching behind radiators.' The 40 odd interviews in this collection of near 400 pages appeared originally in the *New York Press*, *Bruno's Weekly*, *New York Morning Telegraph*, *New York Sun*, *Vanity Fair*, *Charm*, *McCalls*, *Theatre Guild Magazine*, *Physical Culture* and *Unmuzzled Ox*.

The interviews were culled from the files of newspapers in the days when Diamond Jim Brady, Flo Ziegfeld, Jess Willard, Jack Dempsey,

Nazimova, Yvette Guilbert, Rachel Crothers, Coco Chanel and James Joyce were still alive.

'My roots, my affinities are with England,' she once admitted.

It took a pushy American, Emily Coleman, to get another reticent American, T. S. Eliot, to get *Nightwood* into print. It is still very much alive and kicking in the Faber list. Virago is to be commended for continuing on from where the Sun & Moon Press left off.

Andrew Field's somewhat vulgar biography of 1983 from Secker & Warburg offered biographical details of the Barnes ménage at Cornwall-on-Hudson that makes *Ryder* less baffling. It is still unpublished in England, though out with Christian Bourgeois in France. A window-cleaner in Oakley Street told her he'd read *Nightwood*—just published—but preferred Rabelais. Where have all those well-read window-cleaners gone?

One mot directed against Tom Eliot does not make any sense, a verbatim witticism mis-transcribed perhaps? To the effect that he 'kept his Auden in the church.' The late Bertie Rodgers told it to me otherwise in the Sign of the Zodiac: 'The trouble with you, Eliot, is that you keep your organ in the cathedral.' Not one of her wittier sallies.

She belonged in her own peculiar way to the past. Her best work (*Nightwood*, 1936) had echoes of Cibber and Webster, Donne and Marlowe; her worst (*The Antiphon*, a verse-play in the 17th century mode, retelling the story of her family already told in the novel *Ryder*, 1928) cockeyed with Elizabethan metaphor and simile, was flatulent as Nashe; and Kyd was lurking there too, in the shadows (' "What is beauty" saith my suffering, then').

The interviews with the now famous dead tell more about the interviewer than those interviewed. Here is James Joyce in a fancy waistcoat seen approaching the Deux Magots one April day in 1922, a month after the publication of *Ulysses*:

> Sitting in the café of the Deux Magots, which faces the little church of St. Germain des Pres, I saw approaching me out of the fog and damp, a tall man with head slightly lifted and slightly turned, giving to the wind an orderly distemper of red and black hair, which descended sharply into an out-thrust chin.
>
> He wore a blue-gray coat—too young it seemed, partly because he had thrust its gathers behind him, partly because the belt which circled lay two full inches above the hips.

He sits down opposite her, ordering a white wine. She resumes:

His hands, peculiarly limp in the introductory shake, and peculiarly pulpy—running into a thickness that the base gave no hint of—one on the stem of the glass, the other, forgotten, palm out, on the most delightful waistcoat it has ever been my happiness to see. Purple with alternate doe and dog heads. The does, tiny scarlet tongues hanging out over blond lower lips, downed in a light wool, and the dogs no more ferocious or on the scent than any good animal who adheres to his master through the seven cycles of change. He saw my admiration and he smiled. 'Made by the hand of my grandmother for the first hunt of the season.'

The Guardian, 15 June 1985

5

Kin

The Collected Stories of Caroline Gordon (Faber & Faber)

Her work is infested with ghosts:

> Once I saw a man ahead of me in a boat, drifting along, not fishing.
> He looked like Bob Reynolds but I don't think it could be; he'd said
> himself he could hardly make it down to the river.
>
> *One More Time*

> Before him a vista seemed to open, a tunnel, whose low arched side
> oozed dark mist. At the far end, a stooping shawled figure slowly
> raised a clumsy, bandaged hand.
>
> *The Presence*

One half of America seems to regard the other half as alien, as if
North and South were still divided by the bitterness of Civil War.

Two lads of fifteen years exhume Yankee skeletons from a frozen
December battlefield of 1864 and the Government contractor divides up
the remains into coffins so that he can 'git paid double':

> In a large family connection such as ours every member, no matter
> how remotely related or however unimportant, had his place and a
> sort of record in memory. We all sit here under the trees all after-
> noon and talk about people we used to know: Cousin Owen, who
> walked from house to house, carrying his teeth in a basket . . .
> Cousin Henry Hord, who was deafened by cannonading in the
> Civil War and lost all his property by ill-advised investments and
> had to live with any of the kin who would put up with him.

Her world is southeast Kentucky, along the Tennessee line; the revolutionary grant land chopped up generation by generation, despite the

device of cousinly marriages mentioned by Robert Penn Warren in his introduction. Six lane highways and urban development sprawl have taken over from the pasture land and grazing cattle.

These stories first began appearing in *Scribner's* and *The Yale Review*, *Sewanee Review* and the *Maryland Quarterly* in the 1930s. Caroline Gordon was private secretary to Ford Madox Ford, and married the poet Allen Tate. Her first story was published in 1929. Max Perkins took her first novel, *Penhally*, two years later; eight more have appeared since, with a gap after 1963 when she was occupied writing *The Narrow Heart*.

Her work has qualities peculiar to itself, found only in the very best of American writing: the family unit invoked as a strength, perhaps under threat (as in Bellow's work), but behind it all a largeness of heart not found elsewhere. Not for her the remorselessly rustic buttonholing manner of Mark Twain. Time moves on; Dan and Jerry Lout change their loves about.

These stories belong to a later America; the terrain of Faulkner, Eudora Welty, Djuna Barnes, Katherine Anne Porter. She is very good on light in human eyes, that troubled regard, 'I watched Aunt Zilphy set the big bowl of steaming burgoo down in front of me. There "ain't nothing like it."'

Behind it all the big plantations, the song of slaves, bad conscience. Not even Faulkner could write convincingly of the native Redskins, the cruel old gods. And ain't Alabama infested with cousins?

Hibernia, 23 January 1979

6

Railroads

Paul Theroux, *The Old Patagonian Express: By Train Through the Americas*
(Hamish Hamilton)

No better firsthand account of travel in out-of-the-way places has come our way this year, from Boston to Patagonia by rail, matching in *éclat* Theroux's *Great Railway Bazaar* ('By Train through the Asias'). Definitely for steam-men. This hefty book (340 pp.) is, by any standards, a most compulsive read; I couldn't put it down. Kerouac, after all, only made it as far as New Jersey before hurrying home to mother.

Never as permanently unwell as Graham Greene in Godless Mexico or Darwin on the Beagle, Theroux has his fair share of misfortune—his eardrums burning with pain coming down to steamy Veracruz from the heights of Orizaba. 'The passengers' faces were set in frowns.'

The formal politeness of his translation of Spanish speech gives the text an added dignity and flavour. Sinister characters abound, encountered in low dives in the early hours: Dibbs the 300-pound Texan ex-cop with a passion for hookers; there is an interrogation on semantics from some Rinso salesmen on a train somewhere in Central America. Since the epistolary art is dying or dead, published travel journals such as these provide a pleasing alternative to good long gossipy letters. The essay-type narrative opens a wide net, and many curious fish are trapped. Theroux, a most grumpy traveller, has all the right prejudices.

'Travel at its best is a solitary enterprise.' he concedes:

> Traveling on your own can be terribly lonely. What is required
> is the lucidity of loneliness to capture the vision which, however
> banal, seems in my private mood to be special and worthy of inter-
> est. There is something in feeling abject that quickens my mind and
> makes it intensely receptive to fugitive impressions.

Other world-besotted travellers have been there, or thereabouts, before him. Colombus touched at Limon in Costa Rica, Aldous Huxley came, saw, was patronising: All seekers after the inscrutable magnetisms of the exotic. Lone Germans travel in order to save money, and get up Theroux's nose; they notice nothing, might just as well have remained in Bremen. The Japanese fellow asks 'Where is the rest of your team?' The slanted world viewed through the moving windows is in many ways a nauseating place, if not terrifying. Deep gorges open up four hundred feet below the flying wheels, condors soar below, cities are perched miles high, and, Mr. Thornberry sits opposite Theroux, gets on his wick as annoyingly as the character in *Moby-Dick* who makes everything banal.

Tunnels entered unexpectedly in Central America produce 'exalted yells' from alarmed passengers. To further excite and stimulate his senses he reads Poe's *Narrative of Arthur Gordon Pym*—'an experience of pure terror.' He travels without a camera. Reality is just as *outré*: the long lava beach at Rio Matina, the crazed black man ('I am the Son of God!'), vultures wheeling over Limon:

> Limon looked like a dreadful place. It had just rained and the town stank. Even Salvadoreans, with their little-country loyalism and their violent nationalism, agree Cutuco was a hole.
>
> Visitors to Guayaquil are urged to raise their eyes, for on a clear day it is possible to see the snowy hood of Mount Chimborazo from the humid streets of this stinking city; and, if you look down, all you will see is rats.

You must not judge people by their country, a lady advises him. In South America it is always advisable to judge people by their altitude. Meanwhile the skittish Puntarenas woman is pinching the ticket collector's arse.

Conrad put in at Guayaquil. Aracataca, seen in passing, was the birthplace of G. G. Marquez, his 'Maconda,' as Guayaquil was Conrad's 'Sulaco.' The Canal Zone has the most geriatric tourists in the world ('travel was part of growing old').

On the Quindo Pass, rushing through clouds in the fastness of the Andes, he suffers from the bends, cannot even read Boswell. A boastful Frenchman, ill with tonsillitis, bound for the Amazon, annoys him worse than Mr. Thornberry, but 'it takes more than tonsillitis to prevent a Frenchman from boasting':

> The mournful countenance of Bogota's antique buildings is pure Spanish, but the gloom of its setting is Andean and all its own.

Over a mile high, the streets induce the staggers.

La Paz, another high place, is suffering from a sort of urban gangrene: 'a city of cement and stale bread, of ice storms that produced a Bulgarian aroma of wet tweeds.' A demented lady from Denver searches for her tubercular lost love in a park at midnight in Veracruz as the Mexican Navy Band plays Elgar and Webern, a Rossini overture. Human excrement steams under the stationary train near the Guatemala border. A blind dwarf climbs aboard as Theroux reads Bierce's *Devil's Dictionary,* makes notes ('ninety degrees heat all day'), suffers from stomach-cramps.

Times are so bad in Peru, that even the anchovy have left their waters and swum away. In Santiago de Estero, in the misty dusk, 'the cane trees and orange groves were richly green, like Ireland in twilight.' He never gives up, everything reminds him of something else, somewhere else; his mind is so rich it's always wandering. Rosario (birthplace of Che Guevara) passes—'a glimpse of a hawk steadying itself in the sky.' In Buenos Aires he dines with blind Borges in a restaurant on Good Friday. They take to each other. Theroux is given a guided tour of the blindman's bookshelves; Borges is especially proud of his copy of *Johnson's Dictionary,* sent from Sing-Sing Prison by an anonymous inmate.

He is given a conducted tour of the Gorgas Mortuary in Panama City. The 'happy people of Colombia' are found to be far from happy. Santa Ana, the most Central American of Central American towns, is full of half-breeds practicing a kind of Catholicism based on 'tactile liturgy.' A nocturnal soccer-match at San Salvador produces a semi riot:

> The mob was propelling me forwards towards the stadium where the roar of the spectators inside made a sound like flames howling in a chimney.

Travel is pointless without taking certain risks. Never was encountered such good-natured misanthropy; never a dull moment in this free-associating account of strenuous train-rides with our world-besotted traveller.

Hibernia, 27 September 1979

7

Blacklist

Lillian Hellman, *Scoundrel Time* (Macmillan)

The blaring trumpets of 16-foot pseudo-angels up on lofty rostrums, hotel elevator-shafts that reveal warehouses packed with bananas behind their glass walls, political rallies that go on all night, graft and the fix, cock-fights, a gorilla that grunts on the telephone and is thought to be the President, criminal activities of all kinds, hazardous undertakings and the lovelorn looking for peace and security and not finding much of either, while a Negro collects grunion in a bucket on the Californian shore—the America made familiar to us from *Day of the Locust*, *Last Tycoon* and Dr. Kafka's *Amerika* can hardly be less farfetched, less striking, than the original ground, the huge incoherent landmass stretching between the Tropic of Cancer and the Arctic Circle—judging from *Scoundrel Time*, a long-pondered work from the disenchanted liberal Lillian Heilman.

This brief, heavily leaded diatribe presents a mighty eerie picture of the Land of the Free during the McCarthy witch-hunt period. High-mindedness goes with low dealing, the purple gas of political rhetoric, as the champions of democracy renege on their own associates: Bogart, Edward G. Robinson, the 'pious shit' Kazan, Schulberg, Odets and others. Gary Cooper was just plumb puzzled, as well he might; and the way is open for the clever publicity-seeking lawyer Nixon.

The organs of the liberal left (*Partisan Review* and *Commentary*) were silent throughout the proceedings. Charles Laughton, who had been a close friend of Brecht's, on being invited by the East German government to attend his old friend's memorial service, took the precaution of immediately contacting Hoover to say he had received the cable but it wasn't his fault and should not be counted against him.

The lovely neo-Georgian house on East 82nd Street is sold; ways of earning are blocked for both of them, her lover Hammet sent to jail for refusing to testify. Korda, anchored in a yacht off Antibes, continues to make sharp deals.

The Rosenbergs are condemned to death, and blue-jowled Nixon is already on his way to the White House. Lillian Hellman's movie earnings sink from $140,000 to $10,000. Henry Wallace gives her a present (a sack of manure); Spyros Skouras tries to pass a curious contract; subpoenas fly.

Meanwhile the abominable Cohn of Columbia Pictures lives on cold chicken, sandwiches and white wine; and an unsavoury America begins to emerge, in a time of fear-induced trance. Its image will be bolstered up by turncoats like Kazan and Schulberg and their lying movies—*Gentleman's Agreement, Pinky, On the Waterfront.*

It comes as no surprise that a senior editor of *Time* might be capable of perjury and public lies—'youthful psychotic inventions,' in Miss Hellman's sometimes turbulent syntax. 'Truth made you a traitor as it often does in time of scoundrels.' She names names: Senators McCarthy and McCarran, Representatives Nixon, Walter and Wood. Nixon holds up the camera as irrefutable proof of Alger Hiss's guilt; but the planted 'evidence' has turned rotten in the pumpkin.

The corn may be as high as an elephant's eye but it was perilous stuff to find yourself in the thick of; better to dine with the Devil than with Chaplin and Gertrude Stein (surely an uncomfortable dinner-party?). Irish servants are prepared to go to jail; a goodhearted stagehand (Irish, redheaded) offers her a double bourbon to steady her nerves before a public reading.

Digesting this I thought of what cynic Céline had said of the proletariat, having none of the Communist sympathy for it as such: that there is no such thing as 'the people' in the touching sense of the word; only the exploiters and the exploited. And every victim of exploitation wishes to exploit in turn; the heroic egalitarian proletariat does not exist, for every proletarian is a failed bourgeois:

> To many intellectuals, the radicals had become the chief, perhaps the only enemy . . . Not alone because the radical's reasons were suspect but because his convictions would lead to a world that deprived the rest of us of what we had. Very few people were capable of admitting anything so simple. But the antiradical camp contained the same divisions: often they were honest and thoughtful men, often they were men who turned down a dark road for dark reasons.

Hibernia, 3 December 1976

8

Wing Shot

The Stories of John Cheever (Cape)

'Decorum is a mode of speech as profound and connative as any other' he says in his Preface, 'differing not in content but in syntax and imagery. The constants that I looked for in this sometimes dated paraphernalia are a love of light and a determination to trace some moral chain of being.'

This Episcopal-Calvinist part of him, however, gets killed off in the very first story, one of the best in this strong collection; Cain and Abel enjoy a sabbatical by the seaside and relish the 'rediscovery of inexhaustible goodwill.'

In quest of what he calls 'the indecipherable collision of contingencies,' producing exaltation or despair (elsewhere referred to as the 'preposterous chain of contingencies'), giving back the radiance that he had known when he was younger, the urbane Mr. Cheever finds incongruous evidence just about everywhere.

Two retrievers run, one barking in joy and the other in terror. An old American poet living in a hill village outside Rome, on hearing a waterfall, recalls a Sunday afternoon in Vermont when he was a boy and sat on a hill above a pool:

> While he was there he saw an old man, with hair as thick and white as his own now, come through the woods. He had watched the old man unlace his shoes and undress himself with the haste of a lover. First he had wet his hands and arms and shoulders and then he had stepped into the torrent, bellowing with joy. He had then dried himself with his underpants, dressed, and gone back into the woods and it was not until he had disappeared that Bascomb had realised that the old man was his father.

In a pool below Monte Giordano, Bascomb 'stepped naked into the torrent, bellowing' like his father.

26

When Mr. Cheever writes of 'the inestimable greatness of the race' he may be referring to the human race; the 'harsh surface beauty of life' belongs to his own background—Vermont, New Hampshire, Connecticut, Long Island. Born 67 years ago in Quincey, Massachusetts, John Cheever has been moderate in his output; four novels and six collections of short stories, five of which are included here.

Of the novels I knew only *The Wapshot Chronicle* (1958 National Book Award) and a Hollywoodised version of 'The Swimmer' with Burt Lancaster. The stories became rougher as the century advanced ('the lash of frustration was laid on and the pain stunned'); then the themes of earlier poverty are left behind for themes of later prosperity, the manner still urbane, never hard-bitten.

> Then two cars that seemed to be racing down Sunset Boulevard pulled up at a traffic light under my window. Three men piled out of each car and began to slug one another. You could hear the blows land on bone and cartilage. When the light changed, they got back into their cars and raced off. The fight, like the loop of light I had seen from the plane seemed like the sign of a new world, but in this case an emergence of brutality and chaos.

He presents his evidence without much heat; the manner is careful not to draw attention to itself. Shadows come over a beach and the people are departing; the dancers leave a dance floor at the end of a set. 'I saw in these gentle departures the energies and the thoughtlessness of life itself.' And again 'We seem to be dancing on the grave of social coherence.'

Two stories about Irish elevator operators, Clancy and Leary, fail; one, concerning the superintendent of a block of flats, succeeds—an extraordinary image of the river seen from the penthouse. The superintendent is thought to be the janitor. In another story a man of wealth is pushed into the service elevator, since he carries a box under his arm and must be the deliveryman. Characters make off, vanish from the story; in Soviet Russia even Khrushchev disappears.

The Italian stories continue the theme of life as a perilous adventure, as the world changes its boundaries and becomes less and less comprehensible. ('We began a journey in Italy to a clap of thunder and a sky nearly black with swallows'). There is an extraordinary description of a storm over Assisi. Waterholes, swimming pools, lakes, rivers, seas, oceans, bodies of water still or flowing, excite him—is he Piscean? A fine picture of a landfall at Lisbon: 'The immemorial smell of inshore water like my grandfather's bathing shoes.' The sound of summer rain transports him. The hands of his characters tremble with thirst and lechery. The wives are burning the dinners, longing to be away, to be free.

Sad, heavyhearted, 'caught up in those streams of feeling that never surface,' the adulteress takes the adulterer into her arms, to cry 'Oh my love, why are you so bitter?'

Cartoonist Giles managed to convey a good idea of austere Britain after the war, the emerging welfare state two decades after. These stories spanning the period 1946-1978 give a fair notion of East Coast middle-strata America, the legion of wage-earning ghosts that haunt midtown Manhattan, 'dreaming of this new life in Madrid, Dublin or Cleveland.' Their chronicler is this slippery author for whom the stern terms 'mannerly' and 'probity' mean something; for he is an implacable opponent of humbug. One must search back behind Mailer and his dirty games, behind Leonard Michael's deliberate fouling, the fulminations of Philip Roth, to a more balanced overall view of America, once best typified by Edmund Wilson.

Cheever is the chronicler of watersheds and of that enormous stratum of the middle class that is distinguished by its ability to recall better days. He perceives the rampant filth of the Land of the Free as but temporary encampments and outposts of the civilisation that America must build; and sanguine hope in the throes of 'a gruelling melancholy'; our external life has the quality of a dream:

> Thinking of peaceable things, I noticed that the black ants had conquered the red ants and were taking the corpses off the field . . .

He has one final rhetorical question:

> Which of us is not suspended by a thread above carnal anarchy, and what is that thread but the light of day?

Hibernia, 11 January 1979

9

Gonzo

Hunter S. Thompson, *The Great Shark Hunt: Strange Tales from a Strange Time* (Picador)

Dr. Hunter S. Thompson is an intemperate fellow and makes no attempt to disguise it. Here the undisputed Gonzo champion is smoking reefers and tossing off crude bursts of language: Gig, gonzo, mojo, dex, wild turkey, raptures of the deep. Go, man, go!

The trick in Gonzo journalism—much of it hearsay reporting—is to delete none of the expletives and let your wind go free; the hard-bitten manner recalling Chandler ('It was almost midnight when Pat Patterson got off the elevator and headed down the corridor towards 905, his room next door to the Champ's'), or the self-promotional antics of Mailer (*Advertisements for Myself*), though lacking the former's shrewd eye for grim terrain and the fix, or the latter's moral temper and occasional self-mockery. The deadline crunch and the word-count tend to produce, as often as not, gobbledygook.

As a sportswriter he is inferior to Mailer or McIllvanney. Both Jean-Claude Killy and Muhammad Ali try to avoid him, but he is not easily repulsed, even among such sharks as DeLorean of Chevrolet, Mark McCormack the sports impresario, former President Nixon ('a cheap, demented little fascist punk'), the decadent rich. He seems happier with his talent in savage places, when not baying too hard after subjective truth, before he went Gonzo. As Puerto Estrella's first ever tourist; or in Cuzco, Peru.

Exacerbated sensibilities are all very well, but the head must be given time to cool. Bennies, black beauties, 100 milligrams of pure speed sends him raging on his way. He is a buddy of Warren Beatty; tapes a *six-hour* interview with President Carter, feels exalted when confronted with a transcript of the President's Law Day address. At Cozumel the gullible natives are half mad with excitement to have a real honest-to-God *Playboy* writer in their midst, flown in to cover the international fishing contest. An alcoholic party ensues—'a living caricature of white trash run amuck on foreign shores.' Time spent with the dull President Carter sends the Gonzo man into ecstasies. Unknown names crop up—William O. Douglas, Benton L. Becker, among the famous, the demoted, the out-of-favour, the disgraced, with a good word for Stew Alsop of *Newsweek* and the bombastic William Shirer. Stevenson is told to his face that he is a professional liar, film star George Hamilton dismissed as 'a stinking animal ridiculed even in Hollywood'; while the disgraced Nixon is said to be 'sinking deeper and deeper into the quicksands of his own excrement.'

The best thing in this long (635 pp.) wordy compilation is an account of the Kentucky Derby in the company of the English cartoonist Ralph Steadman. More mud (and worse) bespatters the rich folk of Texas. While somewhere in South America a white man is thoughtfully driving golf balls down into the darkened city below. Warhol is dismissed as 'a witless phoney.' Graft is rife. A chilling account of Edwards Air Force Base, with test-pilots flying over the Mojave Desert north of Los Angeles. And once again the tiresome Watergate business; falsehood in high places, the plant, the cover-up, public lies. Nixon is now 'that pompous, plastic little fart.' Hunter runs for Sheriff of Aspen.

The sportswriting does not differ all that much from the sassy political commentary: 'They would be pushed over the brink that was already just a few steps in front of them—and no "comeback" would be likely, or even possible'—this is not Armageddon but the Muhammad Ali camp after defeat by Leon Spinks. Ali had come from St. Louis, hometown of William Burroughs, Martha Gellhorn, as had Ezra Pound and the Gonzo champ himself; all much acclaimed garrulous, self-destructive talents, all such pushful fellows.

The Gonzo stuff comes steaming hot as excreta from the presses of *Rolling Stone* and *Playboy*.

Hibernia, 17 December 1976

10

Lunar

John Hawkes, *Lunar Landscapes: Short Stories and Novels, 1949-1963*
(Chatto & Windus)

Chatto & Windus, erstwhile publishers of Beckett's *More Pricks Than Kicks*
(1934), are in the process of bringing out the 'deucedly odd' work of the
American writer John Hawkes, that 'fastidious and frightening' novel-
ist, using New Directions blocks or photo-offsets, following the intrepid
Neville Spearman who published handsome editions of *The Cannibal* and
The Lime Twig in 1962.

'One of the most admired American writers of his generation,' boldly
affirms the blurb. For 'admired' read 'unread'; he is one of the Great
Unknowns. In San Francisco they prefer Mailer the hammer-hurler, the
show-off. Hawkes has had a sour press on this side of the Atlantic; Irving
Wardle in the *Observer* (January 1966) thought that *Second Skin* was 'tough
going.' Tough is the word. Tough and knotty, like Burton or Cibber? 'His
is a slanted and limited vision, perhaps,' muttered the perplexed Paul
Bailey (*Observer*, May 1970) of the title under review. 'Perhaps' is rich.

Susan Sontag, whose first book had been praised by Hawkes, failed to
return the compliment. She found the work 'fragmentary'; as did Christopher Ricks in a long and perceptive review in the *New Statesman* in
1966.

'I wanted to try and create a world, not represent it. The need is to
maintain the truth of the fractured picture,' the author himself said in
an interview. *Second Skin* ran Bellow's *Herzog* close for the 1965 National
Book Award, which Bellow had already won eleven years previously
with *The Adventures of Augie March*.

Hawkes's background is as odd as his fiction: a Morgan-supported
father in Juneau, childhood in Alaska ('an incredible experience'), a bad
first semester at Harvard. He drove an American Field Service ambulance
in Italy towards the end of World War II, into Belgium and Germany

('everything came down then'), saw books burning in the street. While on a working vacation in Montana he began writing *Charivari* when not labouring on Fort Peck irrigation dam. A worker slipped and was buried in the dam's mountain of dirt and never found ('I got to think of him as swimming around in the sea of mud'). He returned to Albert Guerard's creative writing class at Harvard and in 1949, when he was twenty-four, New Directions published his extraordinary first novel, *The Cannibal*, written at Guerard's class after reading an alleged account of German cannibalism in *Time*: 'I thought I was telling a perfectly straight story.'

The novella *Charivari* appeared in a New Directions anthology. He was feeling his way towards the later hermetically sealed off style of *The Lime Twig*, and *Second Skin*. Before that came *The Beetle Leg* (1951), *The Goose Grave* (1954) ('an attempt to expunge horrors carried back from war and only partly exorcised in *The Cannibal*'); but neither these nor *The Owl*, nor *Charivari* were successfully realised:

> I wanted to show what was on the opposite side of the nightmare. I deliberately lifted up the log to see the soft seamy side underneath.

Life was a series of private disasters; reality a tortured form of imagination. After seven years silence *The Lime Twig* was published in 1960 ('transformations of stuff already remote'), by New Directions, followed by Spearman in 1962 and by Chatto and Windus in 1968. The racing tipster Sidney Slyter was an inspired addition when publisher James Laughlin complained that the plot was impossible to follow. *Second Skin* was written on Grenada on the Windward Isles and came out in 1964.

He had begun unravelling his scrambled texts. Life wasn't going to end on this planet after all; through creation more astonishing than representation of reality, he catches the rhythm of our secret processes; history, the slow return of the repressed.

In 1967, he wrote me that he was 'trying to direct' a freshman writing experiment at Stanford University, after a year as writer-in-residence. A Ford Foundation Fellowship spent at the Actors' Workshop in San Francisco produced *The Innocent Party*, four one-act short plays. *Lunar Landscapes* brings together material from magazines, going back to the days when he wrote while soaking his blistered feet in chemicals.

Hibernia, 10 December 1976

11

Barthelme

Donald Barthelme, *Forty Stories* (Secker & Warburg)

All that is not literature bores me, including conversations about literature.

Franz Kafka

'Winding-sheets were unwound and things best forgotten were remembered,' writes Barthelme who lives in New York and teaches in the University of Houston, Texas, where the grackles rattle. We are back in the Land of Plenty:

> Pia was chopping up an enormous cabbage, a cabbage big as a basketball. The cabbage was of an extraordinary size. It was a big cabbage.
> 'That's a big cabbage,' Edward said.
> 'Big,' Pia said
> They regarded the enormous cabbage God had placed in the world for supper.
> [. . .]
> 'Well' he says to Christie, are you hungry?'
> 'Yes,' she says, 'I am.'
> 'We just ate,' Harry says. 'You can't be hungry. You can't possibly be hungry.'
> 'Hungry, hungry, hungry,' she says, taking Bishop's arm, which is, can you believe, sticking out.

Later in Bishop's apartment, he is putting slices of duck in bean water while Christie watches *The Adventures of Robin Hood* with Errol Flynn and Basil Rathbone. At the same time Hank Williams, Jr. is singing on the FM.

'I like a place where I can take my shoes off,' she says, as Errol Flynn throws a whole dead deer on the banquet table.

We are as remote from Musil & Co. as it is possible to be, but perhaps not so far from Cervantes. In the land of plugs, of opportunity (and its opposite), Faulkner, Saroyan, the suicide Brautigan, the land of gripe, where all is possible, hear this.

From a story called 'The Wound': the Bishop of Valencia enters with attendants:

> The bishop is a heavy man with his head cocked permanently to the left—the result of years of hearing confessions in a confessional where the right-hand box is said to be inhabited with vipers.

He would have made Frank O'Connor sit up. 'The Temptation of St. Anthony' is calculated to make a griffin grin. Years ago I read *The Dead Father* but it seemed to pass me by. These forty stories possess that curious quality of hope found in old Hollywood movies and most conspicuous by its absence today. Cf. 'Sinbad,' 'Bluebeard,' 'Captain Blood.'

The stories themselves are short, their implications far-reaching.

Hibernia, 10 November 1976

12

Dandy

Alistair Cooke, *Six Men* (Bodley Head)

In a time of tele-pundits, tele-moralists, tele-nuns, tele-frontsmen, tele-fun-nymen, tele-tattlers of all stripes, professional axe-grinders and profes-sional charmers of one sort or another, the ghastly David Frost, how pleasant to encounter Mr. Alastair Cooke, late of the *Manchester Guardian*, who seems to have all the time in the world to call his shots. His is a deceptively leisured style, like Ben Hogan's swing. It is a style that never became mannered. His BBC Radio 4 broadcast 'Letter from America' has been going out now for more than thirty years.

When all were baying for blood in the Angela Davis case, who coun-selled moderation? Herewith his short-list of significant twentieth-century men from all walks of life who in their various ways 'sounded tocsins':

> Mencken tolled the bell on the genteel tradition; [Bertrand] Russell expected, single-handed, to cleanse the establishment; Bogart was the first anti-hero; [Adlai] Stevenson, with a noble naïveté, hoped to render obsolete the American party political machine; Chaplin did much to anachronise the tradition of the gentleman by parodying it on behalf of the dispossessed; and in the ordeal of Edward VII we may hear the death-rattle of kingship.

Mr. Cooke wittily describes the first official engagement of the last-named in 1932, when Prince of Wales. The Prince and young Alastair are togged out in identical double-breasted houndstooth tweeds, and Alastair has the misfortune to be a dead-ringer for the Prince's own brother. The Prince stares hard at him. The bafflement of one who had everything and lost it all is marvelously well caught, as the 'bulging mournful stare' (Hanoverian-Saxe-Coburg-Windsor) gives way to 'the wistful, baffled expression' of later days—'a Levine caricature of jet-set boredom.'

Or again the young Princeling is hurried into a darkened cinema with Mrs. Simpson, both in high spirits, for a screening of the Astaire-Rogers *Top Hat;* after all, it's their story.

The falling graph of our allegiance to authority, matching a profound shift in social values, is touched in with deft strokes; the trenchant sentence, the moral injunction, now as Prosecutor, now Defendant, is his to command. On the subject of collective hysteria—Rock fans at an airport, awaiting the arrival of their idols—he is cool:

> I have seen them as a congregation of dolls, bobbing behind the customs barrier at Tokyo, waiting for the Rolling Stones to wing in from Seattle or Hawaii.

He can be amusing on any subject; not for him the thuggery of a Mailer or the two-fisted punching of James Baldwin. He once had ambitions to write Coward-type comedies of manner and behaviour. Woolcott and Lippman are mentioned in passing, the divine Max, but Alastair Cooke is far wittier than Beerbohm.

A train journey with Bertrand Russell from Penn Station to Washington in 1950 shows the philosopher rebuffed by one of the station staff. Cooke worked on a script for a Chaplin movie that was never made—Chaplin as Napoleon on St. Helena. Mencken's slob eating habits and eccentric typing come under scrutiny; Adlai Stevenson ('the noble cat's paw') goes on the campaign trail, hopelessly; Lord Russell, 'the towering malcontent, the last of the Whigs,' speaks in Glasgow; Bogart is dying of cancer, his spirit still unbroken, skeleton thin.

All these subjects are studied with a lizard's eye; the dead spring to life again—Paulette Goddard on Chaplin's yacht is 'trim and shiny as a trout.' There is trouble with a scene in *City Lights*.

A famous amateur cricketer, C. Aubrey Smith, yclept 'Round-the-Corner Smith,' is bowling at a cricket match in Hollywood, watched closely by Cooke:

> He was a bowler with a peculiar run-up to the wicket that has not, as far as I know, been imitated since: starting at eight o'clock, he ran down and around a fish-hook curve up to one o'clock and then delivered the ball. Since, from the batsman's point of view, he started way right of the umpire and then suddenly appeared close

to his left side, Smith offered the menacing illusion of being two bowlers instead of one.

The author of *Garbo and The Nightwatchman* has himself a deceptively easy style that requires close watching. The book is dedicated to John Ford's longstanding scriptwriter Nunnally Johnson and is as witty as anything written by Preston Sturges. An older voice speaks here for rational values everywhere, and makes for amusing reading. One thing is for sure; no ghost wrote it.

Hibernia, 18 November 1977

13

Privilege

James Salter, *Light Years* (Bodley Head)

This is James Salter's fourth novel, praised by Saul Bellow and Graham Greene ten years after *A Sport and a Pastime*; it has been well received in the United States. The spendthrift life is well recorded as possibilities slip out of the hands of the protagonists and into the unsafe hands of their grown-up children, to pass from there God knows where. Salter himself is none too sanguine.

It reads oddly, with the Hudson flowing both ways; the tarnished dream half a century on recalling Gatsby. With property and privilege found to be oppressive, the American Dream continues to darken, as surfeit sickens and apathy replaces plenty. The mansion—a replica of Fitzgerald's 'huge incoherent failure'—changes hands, new and more ruthless developers move in.

In this unnamed mansion in its grounds by the Hudson live Vladimir (Viri) Berland, a New York architect of Jewish extraction, with his ('beautiful and intelligent') wife Nedra and their two beautiful children Franca and Diane (Danny), with Jamaican maid Alma, Hadji the pedigree pup, Ursula the pony, and a tortoise that will outlive them all. A large cast of raconteurs and *bon vivants* are assembled; advanced fringe-theatre people, a painter who will become famous; their conversation and many meals are recorded, under the Chagall, before the coffee and Grand Marnier.

Cuckoldings ensue, inevitably; the seasons fly by. Life and ill health—the terms here seem synonymous—decimate bosom friends, the talkers are buried, the mansion sold. Yellow construction machines open the earth for new foundations; apartments rise. Among the pure and innocent, only two grandchildren and the tortoise will survive.

Summer is the noontime of devoted families . . . Pure, empty days. The dog barking on the shore.

Places, rooms, objects, pets, all are contaminated by the narrator's moods, lose their lustre and first allure. The record of the good life reads like the advertising columns of *The New Yorker*: dinners beneath the great trees, summers at Amagansett. But then the mood darkens, melancholy becomes pervasive; the mugged victim's stopped wristwatch has the eerie quality of the dead dashboard clock in the abandoned Delarge in *A Sport and a Pastime.*

Tenses change within a line, main verbs are omitted in a manner reminiscent of certain cinema techniques by the more subtle European practitioners: Kluge's humour, the girl in the bath; Herzog's swift elisions and awe before mystical nature. Salter has an eye as sharp as Bellow's own for rotting urban terrain; objects 'glistening like evidence' as the metropolis continues to expand and befoul itself. America the Bountiful has become America the Bloated, 1975-style. Salter goes on from Alfred Hayes; a poet of the automobile and the fleeing couple, neither guilty nor much blamed; European hotels at what Germans call the little-shepherd-hour and the Spaniards call siesta. 'What passes between them, this couple, in the mindless hours of consort?' The earlier novel with its Paris and French rural background gives way to a sharper focus; there are some acid home truths in this, while the good life goes on. Iced vodka with pernod (White Nights) at the Sherry-Netherland, the Russian Tea Room, Zabars and Bendels, *Swan Lake* at the Philharmonic, luncheon at the Toque and l'Etoile, picnics in summer. 'A Jew without money is like a dog without teeth.' The last third loses coherence and would require more space, or a Proust, to develop it:

> He had travelled, he had dined, he discussed hotels with the affection one usually reserves for women and beasts.

At the end the architect has re-married and now lives in Rome. 'The hours passed quickly. The mist was forming, the brandy gone.'

Hibernia, 25 September 1975

14

Americana

Leonard Michaels, *I Would Have Saved Them if I Could* (Faber & Faber)
Larry Woiwode, *Beyond the Bedroom Wall: A Family Album* (Faber & Faber)

A second collection of stories, a second novel, both from authors unknown
on this side of the Atlantic, appear under the joint imprint of Faber and
Farrar. One, of undoubted talent, of Polish Jewish background, is caustic
and brief: Leonard Michaels. His fellow American Larry Woiwode comes
from a German background, with an expansive heart, torrents of wild
and whirling words from the pushy fellow who once phoned Cheever in
the middle of the night.

To take the best first: here are thirteen stories or 188 well-leaded pages
from Michaels sketching in Bellevue and the muggers who make life a
misery there. The attack is ferocious, savage as Bellow's crazed venom-
spewers, the manner deliberately vile. In Lower Manhattan in the abyss
of 42nd Street subway lesbians are discussing Jung in creepy whispers,
their teeth like knives. In the Metropolis of Total Excitement life goes on;
at a rich dinner-party two men, naked above the waist, fight as a black
waiter urinates into the coffee urn ('Servants are the price elegance pays
to pain.') Is the grubby philosopher Sartre? Stories of 'suspected Jews'
recur; 'Trotsky's Garden' is very fine:

> Ikstein played harpsichord music on the phonograph and opened
> a bottle of wine. I said, 'Let's be frank, Ikstein. There's too much
> crap in the world.'
> He said 'Sure.'

The title comes from Lord Byron's account of a public beheading of
three robbers in Rome. One would hope that his first collection of stories,
Going Places (1969) is listed among the four titles promised.

I drove a Chevy Bel Air eighty-five miles per hour on a two-lane blacktop. It was a nightmare. Intermittent thick white fog made the headlights feeble and diffuse. Four others in the car sat with the strict, silent rectitude of catatonics. If one of them didn't admit to being frightened, we were dead. A Cadillac, doing a hundred miles per hour, passed us and was obliterated in the fog. I slowed down.

* * *

To have to live family life can be bad enough at times; to read about those bad times is intolerable. The German emigrants brought their Sousa marches with them, their pumpernickel, their expansive hearts, *ach mein Gott!* Son Charles is employed as a voice-over in beer commercials, married to a girl who advertises soft drinks. Gaping at television has replaced pinochle as a pastime; whether or not irony is intended is not clear. Larry Woiwode's first novel won the William Faulkner Foundation Award for the most promising first novel of 1969.

This long (619 pp.) family saga followed, charting the trials and tribulations of the Neumillers of Stustud County ('Mrs. Martin Neumiller had a 7lb 10oz baby boy on Sunday, May 21st, at the McCallister Hospital'); their departure from Hyatt, North Dakota, to Forest Creek, Illinois.

The manner throughout is relentlessly longwinded, as if size alone could pull the matter down; there is something in it of *Winesburg, Ohio*, way back in the past. The button-holing manner of town bores, the clotted goo of small-town rectitude; the whole aspiring towards the early toughness of Steinbeck, the punch of Mark Twain, when he was good.

Despite quadrupled-layered narrative and truncated chronology, true Faulknerian qualities fail to appear. The gritty homegrown Baptist wisdom is missing; dialogue is stilted and bookish. Family sagas can be tedious (Galsworthy, Hamsun's *Growth of the Soil*): here the gush of a Harper Lee, the roseate hue of *Margery Morningstar*. And behind the alfalfa and vetch rises a more insidious growth: Ars Poetica.

> Then he's chewing bubble-gum. His jaws move from side to side in a soft, erotic cowlike mastication. He's home again, in bed, asleep yet not asleep: his eyelids are transparent gems. 'Tell us about Granda Jones and the billy goat.'

The buffalo grounds are no more, the wilderness already shrinking in *Go Down, Moses* has virtually disappeared. The fishing trip is fine; elsewhere the vigour of the line is diluted with breathy qualifications. A long windy novel in the manner of Gaddis's *J. R.*

Hibernia, 4 March 1977

15

Bonafides

J. P. Donleavy's Ireland in All Her Sins and in Some of Her Graces
(Michael Joseph/Rainbird Publishing)

The convivial chronicler of imbroglios and gross misunderstandings in and around Dublin (not to mention the ultra eccentric atmosphere of your usual Anglo-Irish house, as recorded in his frolicsome fiction) has here produced a sort of *tabula rasa* for our amusement.

He follows a well-trodden path along which such luminaries as William Trevor, Ben Kiely, Edna O'Brien, not to mention Heinrich Böll and the winsome Uris twosome, have preceded him in rendering fit homage to the Old Sow.

Some illustrious dead again go carousing through the streets and stews of Dublin, the quads of Trinity, the purlieus of County Wicklow. Rip-roaring Brendan Behan and prototypal Gainor Crist are there; up from Annamoe and the bulb farm comes Ralph Cusack; assorted black sheep are discovered underground in the fabled Catacombs (here 'Charnelchambers'), admitted by doorman Basil the queer stark naked with permanent erection.

The 'figures aswirl' are exhumed rather as a magician will produce, with a flourish, rabbits and doves from his tall hat, though all belong to the Donleavy Bestiary. Ever-boggish Paddy Kavanagh is doling out rude abuse in the offices of the defunct Envoy at No. 39 Grafton Street above Ryan's Monument Creamery; Con Leventhal signs chits in his ground floor office in Front Square, and the Legion of Decency are again on the march. It's the start of the Michaelmas term of 1946 and Professor W. B. Stanford, Regius Professor of Greek, encounters the science undergraduate whom he is supposed to tutor, over on a G.I. Bill of Rights.

Thwarted erotic desires ('the crut') hardly feature here; nor does the cunning hand of the self-promotional shaman reveal itself, the acerbic tone being quite distinctive, Donleavy's own, whether dispensing homage

or unleashing abuse. Emolument is slow to arrive; but the giving hand
never wavers. Jammet's doors are thrown wide open, large meals consumed and much fine wine quaffed, as long-gone Dublin landmarks
spring up again like conjuring tricks: the Red Bank, The Royal Hiber-
nian Hotel, Jury's snuggery off Anglesea Street, the restaurant of the
Grafton Picture House, the Monument Creamery and Findlater's; Mrs.
Ryan's chauffeur-driven Daimler is pulling out with a party of inebriated
gents as is only right and proper in a world of 'the rich and prosperous
and the purely Irish Irish' against whom our author from the Bronx has
vented his spleen before now.

The racketing manner invokes *The Ginger Man,* and here is the young
author in a rough and ready studio in Kilcoole of all places, already
engaged upon the novel that will make his fortune. A stark naked Behan
brandishes his member at a trainful of alarmed commuters leaving
Gorey behind them, Josie the barber is trimming the hair of corpses in
Greystones, and the British accent being used 'like a blow torch to cut a
social swathe through all that was Irish.'

The style is frankly bellicose; you either take to him or you don't.
The very prim and proper Miss O'Flaherty of Parson's Bookshop on
Baggot Street bridge wouldn't tolerate a dirty Donleavy title amid her
clean stock.

London Magazine

16

Tosh

Deborah Tall, *The Island of the White Cow* (Deutsch)

Glance now, if you would, to the North-West: *The Island of the White Cow* concerns itself with life on Inishboffin ('rigidly asexual'), as seen by a female graduate of a Midwestern American campus. After the caperings of Donleavy in the 'drinking and thinking world' he likes to frequent—Dublin and environs become a sort of lower Mississippi basin with its retinue of seedy eccentrics—his preference for mayhem and profligacy, and his researches into whatever will spur him into further frolics and misdeeds; lo and behold we now find ourselves back in the Land of Nice Tints, in Deb's mellifluous account of a sabbatical spent on Inishboffin as the putative spouse of a man twenty years her senior, a rising star of the Dublin dramatic firmament, thinly disguised as 'Owen.'

One dislikes carping, but the authenticity of the record is somewhat marred by the manner of the telling, which the name of Lawrence Durrell under the opening epigraph does nothing to dispel. Fat bees are not like helicopters, and the verbs are in terrible shape; as witness, Ann mutters, Catrina burbles, Rosie croons (and 'waxes'), the Postmistress gurgles (when not 'crooning goodwill'); whereas Richard reiterates, while Sean intones, barks (when not 'bubbling with eventfulness'), prior to suicide (understandable enough) in the cold Atlantic.

Fresh out of Yaddo, educated (well, graduated at least) and assertive, yet at a loss in a very American way, the writer must have thought Philadelphia very far away, as viewed from this austere landfall known to the Blessed Bede and St. Colman. 'A beautiful man was in love with me and he wanted to steal me away.'

The islanders (males) sit or stand about in 'an awed stupor'; faces are 'flushed with drink or virginity.' No matter, presently colour TV, that rough beast, its hour come round at last, will be off the quayside and into every home. After which intrusion life on the island will never be the same again; and the young blades may have their way with obliging female visitors from overseas, as a pleasant alternative to haymaking.

One knows some of these Atlantic islands, and they are not happy places, but pervaded with paranoia; the smaller the island the bigger the neurosis. Atlantic islanders as a rule are unhappy people, what with the incessant Ocean pounding, the interminable winters, the smallness of the community, the bitchery, the dullness of the diet, the closed-in nature of the life there, which must induce something akin to madness, the malady that Roethke succumbed to; those islanders live a stunned sort of existence in a veritable ecstasy of regressiveness. When such misery becomes so ingrown, suicide seems the only way out.

A husband and wife team of anthropologists, the Messengers (appropriately named) have studied the misery of Aran, and found it a sad place. Poet Heaney has fixed his seal of approval on the text here streaming away from under us. *Kleinvieh macht auch Mist*, croaked the raven.

London Magazine

17

Los Angeles Dick

Miriam Gross (ed.), *The World of Raymond Chandler* (Weidenfeld & Nicholson)
Frank McShane (ed.), *The Notebooks of Raymond Chandler* (Ecco)

A drunken and violent father appeared throughout the *oeuvre* in the guise
of lawbreaker and psychopath; the vile bitches stood in for his disappointed love, for he had married a woman some twenty years older than
himself. He was not quite what he seemed; the former Dulwich College
classical scholar was to be the only survivor from a shelled platoon in
1918. The parents had separated when young Raymond was but seven;
and when his wife Cissy died, he began to go to pieces.

Towards the end he wanted to return to London but feared the Inland
Revenue. He was somewhat racist ('the fat greasy sensual Jew with the tall
stately bored showgirl'), fairly laid on the horrors with brilliant adjectival
clauses. He was a master of metaphor and simile, the unexpected adjective,
the acid verb ('Darkness ate me up'), his work was permeated with the
harsh smell of cordite, he drank too much, but he was not the hard man he
pretended to be. Chandler's puritan background was Quaker Irish; early
injuries done to his spirit, injuries caused by a broken home, these left
their traces. The persona of the tough guy with the gun and a conscience,
the loner in a criminal milieu, was all bluff, a protective disguise:

> His later years were not happy; he said that Americans were still
> Frontiersmen in spirit, not well protected by laws that the cops
> themselves found hard to enforce. He began writing in middle age,
> following a stint with the Black Mask mob in L.A. George Grosz
> himself could hardly have bettered the grim details: 'A case of false
> teeth hung on the mustard-coloured wall.'

Fleming, Deighton and Le Carré seem shoddy by comparison; Erle
Stanley Gardner merely flatulent. For Ross McDonald, Ed McBain or

Travis McGee I cannot answer. Poe, Wilkie Collins and Conan Doyle seem closer in spirit, angst-activated, driven writers.

But was our hardboiled dick a . . . faggot?

All those swell broads pushing themselves at him, those murderous lovelies; Marlowe tearing daybeds apart, just vacated by some hot strumpet. Then consider the fussy style of dress, the domestic neatness, the bachelor quarters almost Trappist in its austerity, if you overlook the gats, the hard-boiled manner, the Scotch.

Some here are of the opinion that Chandler was as fruity as they come; but aspersions are also cast on the two buddies of *Double Indemnity*, the chums of Graham Greene's *The Third Man*, all suspect bonding. But then again, who would credit such theories coming from a schmuck by the name of Gershon Legman? Come in, Captain Gregarious, Moses Maglashan, Moose Molloy, Joseph B. Toad, all regular guys.

Billy Wilder annoyed Chandler by brandishing a leather-thonged malacca cane under his nose while they were co-scripting *Double Indemnity*. More likely the Kraut's compulsive 'laying' of starlets was a worse provocation. The scene in the gas chamber was omitted.

Of the essays here, Clive James is excellent on Chandler's diction; the Wilder interview is the most illuminating:

> Chandler's great strength was a descriptive one. There are very few people who can get the flavour of California. It's very peculiar, you know, that the only person who caught the Californian atmosphere in prose was an Englishman—Chandler. And the only person who caught it on canvas was also an Englishman by the name of Hockney. No one else can paint California.

The shamans (and shams) are out with hue and cry after the shamus. Los Angeles private eye Philip Marlowe is 'studied in piquant retrospective' by Frank McShane, whom I seem to recall exalting the wild and whirling words of one Jerry Bumpus, or (in transcript) as an acolyte's voice putting questions to Borges. Here he goes again, editing out the contents of two loose-leaf notebooks, all that survive of those salvaged from a San Diego refuse dump.

What exact relevance Jack Woodford's 'Rules for Writing a Novel' might have in this mighty loose compendium is anybody's guess. Or, for that matter, the contributions from James Grant Still, Mary Roberts

Rinehardt, James S. Pollak, Philip K. Schever and the more modestly named Frank Gruber. The novella *English Summer* (Chandler's Folly) reads as oddly as *The Well of Loneliness*: the scene in the garden when the lesbians come together illustrated by Gorey in a blurred style worthy of Ardizzone—Lady Lakenham of Lakeview sits astride a black stallion. The siren fluffs out her hair tempestuously in a manner favoured by the screen vamps of the 1940s, throws hat, gloves and whip onto a bench, prior to seducing John Paringdon ('a nice sturdy name'). But Constable Tressider and Inspector Knight, following a walking tour in Devon ('fields of drowsy cattle'), collar him in London, come from consorting with Russell Street trollops.

Now that he is safely dead these two-score years, how has Time, that final arbitrator, treated Chandler's work? Long after Edgar Wallace, Dorothy L. Sayers, Chesterton's winsome Fr. Brown, Philo Vance, Agatha Christie, Dashiell Hammett or Ellery Queen ('two guys named Fred Dannay and Manfred B. Lee'), his effects linger.

Beginning in his forties, as Joseph Conrad before him, he sent out into the world *The Big Sleep* (1939), *Farewell, My Lovely* (1940), *The High Window* (1942), *The Lady in the Lake* (1943), *The Little Sister* (1949), *The Long Goodbye* (1953), *Playback* (1958) of which the first is thought to be the best and the last the worst, my own preferences being undecided as between the second and the fifth.

He died at La Jolla, California, in March 1959, aged seventy. There may never be another like him. Ever heard of Frank Gruber? *The Notebooks* are a rip-off; I know what Lash Camino would do with them. Chandler said in an interview:

> My theory has always been that the public will accept style, provided that you do not call it style either in words or by, as it were, standing off and admiring it.

Hibernia, 2 February 1979

18

A Voice from the Bronx Laundry

Maxine Hong Kingston, *The Woman Warrior: Memoirs of a Girlhood Among Ghosts*
(Allen Lane)

For life in changing China just before Chairman Mao, during Mao and immediately after, consult Joshua Horn's *Away from All Pests* or Joan Robinson's *The Cultural Revolution in China*, or (for the bare foot doctor scheme) William Hinton's *Fan Shen*.

For the pre-Revolution past, see Han Suy-In's works, if you can plough through them; all are in favour of change, all praise Mao.

Now comes a dissenting voice. A Berkeley graduate, Maxine Hong Kingston, lives in Honolulu with husband and small son, teaching English and creative writing at a private school. *The Woman Warrior* is her first published book, a pseudo-autobiography with the myths of a martial and cruel Chinese past presented as dreams, communes derided, Chinese Communism also, as a five-thousand-year-old tradition ends, the Revolution less than thirty years old. In the Hundred Years' March, culture is marked 'Not Wanted on Voyage.'

The highly disdainful manner is not unlike Nabokov's lordly dismissal of all things rancidly Soviet and thick-eared. The tone is almighty high for beginnings so humble; for the father was a gambler and the mother ran a dairy. A dead Imperial China (still alive in Maxine Ting Ting Hong Kingston's bright mind) is reflected as in a burnished mirror from Sacramento, the Bronx, San Francisco, Chinatown. The manic minutiae observed so coolly, recalls another cynic, Saul Bellow, the chronicler of the morally diseased cities of America.

Eccentricities of conduct abound; her mother slits her tongue, she cannot speak but quacks like Eula Snopes. But the voice from the Bronx laundry cannot be silenced:

> To make my waking life American-normal, I turn on the lights before anything untoward makes an appearance. I pushed the

deformed into my dreams, which are in Chinese, the language of
impossible dreams, stories . . .

   Those in the emigrant generations who cannot reassert brute sur-
vival died, young and far from home. Those of us in the first American generations have had to figure out how the invisible world the
emigrants built around our childhood fit in solid America . . .

   My mother left China in the winter of 1939 and arrived in New
York Harbor in January 1940. She carried the same suitcase she
had taken to Canton, this time filled with seeds and bulbs. On Ellis
Island the officials asked her, 'What year did your husband cut off
his pigtail?' and it terrified her when she could not remember.

That rational philosopher Confucius would have been dumbfounded
by her adopted language so free with Chink, Gook, What an asshole!
Dog vomit! Tit and ass, but, the caustic vernacular of the Big City is on
everyone's tongue, becomes habitual, though such abrasive slang reads
oddly in the body of this disdainful text.

   Korea, Vietnam, Laos and Cambodia are mentioned *en passant*; LBJ
puts in another million men, the 'fool half ghosts' (Ball, Bundy, Warnke)
are thickly plotting; Fulbright is dubious. The diction of high rhetoric
again recalls Bellow. The meeting of the ageing sisters (Brave Orchard
and Moon Orchard) is very weird and saddening, as much else in this
extraordinary book.

   The father, white shirt sleeves rolled up, smiles in front of a wall of
clean laundry. In the spring he wears a new straw hat cocked at a Fred
Astaire angle. His daughter watches the movies in her own head; a door
opens, out come an old man and woman carrying bowls of rice and soup
and a leafy branch of peaches. Mao would not have approved. Let Mrs.
Kingston have the last word:

   'So this is the United States,' Moon Orchard said. 'It certainly looks
   different from China. I'm glad to see the Americans talk like us.'
      Brace Orchard was again startled at her sister's denseness. 'These
   aren't the Americans. These are the overseas Chinese.'

And then the clincher:

Chinese-Americans, when you try to understand what things in
you are Chinese, how to separate what is peculiar to childhood,

to poverty, insanities, one family, your mother who marked your growing with stories, from what is Chinese tradition and what is in the movies?

Not all defects could be explained so congenially.

Hibernia, 4 November 1977

19

Boz & Co.

Frederick Busch, *The Mutual Friend* (Harvester)

As with Joyce, all was turning into words. 'Did the place in his brain which made his books so real, and his characters to actually walk the stage before the awed, persuaded eyes, finally burn him with the heat which overwhelmed his sense of what was true?' asks Professor Busch of Colgate University with a fine rhetorical flourish.

The subject here is Charles Dickens on a reading tour in America; the peerless chronicler of London low-life (V. S. Pritchett's 'cocksure, bitter city') is in a bad way himself. Like purblind Joyce composing *Finnegans Wake* and laughing hysterically behind locked doors, Dickens rehearsed Sykes's murder of Nancy, was Nancy, was Sykes, was the dog; the murder had to be repeated over and over to packed houses, and women swooned. The left side of his face went rigid, his wrists became thin and ropey, 'the pulse beneath beat like bone at the skin of a drum.' The pulse rate rose from 72 to 96 for *Copperfield*, and was up to 114 for *Dombey*, the murder towards the end registered as high as 118, even 124. He fortified himself with eggs beaten up in sherry before the readings; gave sixteen a month and women fainted regularly at the murder of Nancy:

> When he declaimed he had as many faces and voices and tones as
> a church-choir in their highest public ecstasies.

It had happened not much more than a hundred years ago. The insomniac who had no appetite and at times couldn't eat, took laudanum tincture for relief of 'frostbite'—the foot wrapped in a black silk bandage—was afraid to travel in trains, suffered horribly in the Flying Scotsman. He wore gutta-percha overshoes, a pink silk waistcoat, 'could not tolerate awfully much of this world.' He had seduced Ellen Ternan when she was eighteen; later, as Mrs. George Robinson, she perjured herself to keep his good name.

As with Hitler, Dickens both loved and despised his public, needed their admiration, adored fire, had a touch of the sanctimonious about him. He disapproved of giving Negroes the vote, complained about Irish waiters (he preferred Negroes, the true servitude), 'mounted the stage as if it were a cliff he dared look down from'; and was equally harsh about the godlessness of the Pre-Raphaelite Brethren, although Professor Busch omits to mention it. His boyhood in the blacking factory had marked him for life; later he needed money and lots of it, drew up sharp contracts, was not easily put-upon, except by the owner of Baggs Hotel in Utica.

Extraordinary description of the dead sheep in the Mohawk Valley floods ('Horrible, Dolby. Ghastly to look at. Look!'). As with Hemingway with the dead dog run over by the roadside, crouching and taking notes; Dickens could not avert his eyes. He took rich American friends on excursions into the lower depths of London, the city he had known too well when he was very poor, entering the Ratcliffe Highway opium dens escorted by a large policeman.

In Albany he had a near-fatal accident, another in the Rotunda in Dublin; somewhere else his train jumped the tracks; the heat made him faint, he was too ill to taste food, he was taking terrible punishment. His marriage had gone wrong; his son Plorn had his own misfortunes; another son was a miserable failure in business, nursing a papermill gone bankrupt. His attitude to whores was ambiguous. Lean villainous Bealpost began to behave worse than one of his own characters outside the law. Boz attempted to reason with him; it was too late.

A fine description of Mold in Wales: low talk, the smell of rum and the sharp taste of ale and sausages. The return to health was short-lived; one is tempted to weep at the last reading. As a walker he was the equal of Wordsworth in his prime, or Lamb, but a *nocturnal* walker. One Christmas day in Paris he took young Wilkie Collins to visit the morgue.

There is an affecting scene with the ghost of Dolby's da sneaking a pint in The George, watched by his son, aghast, come half-cut from the Boot and Flogger; and a powerful scene in the workhouse; 'the desperate deep snores of the ill and the very exhausted.' Dickens did truly hate the abyss in which the poor must dwell.

Hibernia, 8 February 1979

20

The Heavy Bear

Delmore Schwartz, *In Dreams Begin Responsibilities & Other Stories*
(Secker & Warburg)
James Altas, *Delmore Schwartz: The Life of an American Poet* (Faber & Faber)

Delmore Schwartz, as Thomas Wolfe before him, was strong on titles, weak on content. Too prone to bully and bluster, he eventually talked himself empty, dying alone in a midtown Manhattan hotel in 1966, leaving behind him no unfinished masterpieces.

For the unwanted son of immigrant Romanian parents, the father hot and unfaithful, the mother cold and unforgiving, both presently divorced, life could not be easy. 'In love with art, ashamed of the habits and values of his parents, and full of the most serious and childish pretensions,' he wrote; but did not always write so honestly about himself. Of the emigrant Jews:

> He reflected upon his separation from these people, and he felt in every sense he was removed from them by thousands of miles, or by a generation . . . whatever he wrote as an author did not enter into the lives of these people, who should have been his genuine relatives and friends, for he had been surrounded by their lives since the day of his birth, and in an important sense, even before them.
>
> 'America! America!'

From Thoreau on, American cracker-barrel philosophers interested in the history of thought and with an eye for what the witless Atlas calls 'existential theory' (the ravings of Pound or the deliberations of Charles Olson), tended to come to wretched ends, and Delmore Schwartz proved no exception to the rule.

Of his own nearer contemporaries, Berryman and Jarrell committed suicide, Roethke was certified insane in Ireland, Van Wyck Brooks was brainwashed by a nervous breakdown, Lowell dispatched by a heart-attack in a taxi. Not all were latterly reduced to the rustic vernacular or the lisping baby-talk favoured by Uncle Ez or hirsute Papa, *los Malcontentos* gone ape in their latter years. Some Jewish-American writers became rich and famous, struggling in a most public way with their Jewishness (Bellow and Singer), but under that oppressive burden the Heavy Bear sank. Perhaps the estranged parents were to blame; Schwartz was not wanted in the world; not even by those best qualified to know and love him, before drugs and booze had laid him low.

If there is nothing quite like Jewish good taste (Heine, Proust, Kafka), then neither is there anything quite like Jewish bad taste (Mailer). From his mother he had inherited gaucheness and a lack of understanding of human nature, despite loud contrary claims in Foreword and Introduction by Irving Howe and James Atlas respectively, the latter revealing too little of Schwartz and rather too much of his plots; like Lowry pickled in gin, he hadn't wanted to be born; we have John Davenport's word on it.

On that theme—why must it seem so essentially Jewish?—that our desires will not be richly satisfied, he has his good and bad days. It was necessary, he figured, to belong to a circle of friendship, if one is to be present at the wedding which is the world; and the world is first of all the wedding of God and nature; *we* come in later. But what happens if one has no such circle? One does not belong.

In awe of his peers, first Eliot and Pound, later Berryman and Bellow; and then spiteful against them, he was far from easy to get along with. Only Mark Van Doren and Shorer would be safe from his spleen, for their mediocrity offered no threat. Dr. Benjamin Sieve, his eccentric and well-named physician, fed him a tissue of very flattering lies that were instantly swallowed. It suited Schwartz to believe those lies; had he not been telling himself useful lies all his life?

> Deep in the unfriendly city
> Delmore lies
> And cannot sleep

wrote someone more talented than he. He was very touchy; those who attempted to criticise him would never be forgiven. He was sleeping around with the Boston wives when their menfolk were overseas fighting for Uncle Sam. *In Dreams Begin Responsibilities* was first published in 1938 and very favourably received. But West (*A Cool Million*, 1934, *The Dream Life of Balso Snell*, 1931) and Faulkner (with *Sartoris*, 1929 and *Sanctuary*, 1931) had already produced better work.

Delmore Schwartz was to attain a dubious posthumous fame as 'Von Humboldt Fleischer' in Saul Bellow's bloated bestseller *Humboldt's Gift*, a Bildungsroman as unpleasant in its carefully planned way as Nabokov's earlier *Pale Fire*, and almost as pretentious.

Alfred Kremborg published a verse drama, before megalomania took over. The Heavy Bear had Tartar blood coursing through his veins, fouled up with a lethal daily intake of Nembutal and Seconal, twenty Dexedrine—he was swallowing them like candy. The depression induced by this, the sense of futility, produced ill-tempered harangues, insomnia; there was a tendency for memory to rot as invention flagged and then failed, 'even if he still enjoyed periods of apparent lucidity.' In the end he was not too far from outright raving, and death, when it came, must have been a merciful deliverance.

Biographer Atlas is no Boswell; but there again Schwartz was no Dr. Johnson. Prolix, free with opinions (not always his own), he stops just a fraction short of plain vulgarity, the overly familiar chummy references to 'Delmore' not helping his case: 'While Delmore languished in his apartment at Washington Square Park, his literary career advanced on its own.' This is Ellmann's *James Joyce* put out for *Reader's Digest*: all eyewash, replete with pseudo-references (to urination, p. 63) and a new and more baleful probe: the telephone interview, the cone interview.

Time staffers are quoted with reverence and evident approval (ever hear of Kimon Friar?); the whole presented in a congested style a fit match for the thickening sensibilities of its unfortunate suffering subject; ('running up and down the hills and dirt roads of sensibility'), replete with neologism and solecism ('his rumpled suits and urban pallor contrasted oddly with the physical beauty of rural Ohio').

This type of peeping and botanising is much favoured by Atlas with some of his very own botanical metaphors thrown in for good measure ('complaints and lawsuits blossomed forth'). The critical acumen displayed is pathetic: a detail of a ghastly verse play 'anticipates Beckett,' reviewers roundly declare Schwartz 'Chaplinesque,' others favouring 'Audenesque,' and pretty soon 'Delmore' is taking 'a Danteesque' view of Harvard centenary proceedings and being introduced by Dwight MacDonald as the new Hart Crane. Publisher Laughlin plumps for 'the

American Auden,' notable for a . . . 'Yeatsian' preoccupation with, er, masks, while attempting to conquer 'Prufrockian' hesitancies in himself. A lame yarn, 'Screeno,' is 'full of Kafkaesque' incidents.

I have gone several times very carefully around 'Oh mother forsaken your son' (telephone interview with Victoria Bay Knight, 1975), allegedly a deliberate misquote from *Finnegans Wake* (this is rich), but can make no sense of it, unless it be a line from Joyce's poem 'Ecce Puer': 'Oh father forsaken, forgive your son.' And George Lanning should read George Lamming; but of nothing else in this sorry compilation can one be certain, except that Delmore Schwartz's bad luck continues beyond the grave.

Hibernia, 11 January 1979

21

Gigantic Knockers

Erica Jong, *How to Save Your Own Life*, (Secker & Warburg)
Loveroot: Poems by Erica Jong (Secker & Warburg)

The first thing I always do is to kick off my shoes, strip naked, and open the mail. I read my fan mail in the nude—one form of nakedness greeting another.

I see. When champion cocksmen and self-publicists like Mailer or Roth boast of their abilities between the sheets it seems as natural as any other body-contact sport, taken into the bedroom; but when dishy blond Erica, the sexual tease, boasts of *her* abilities it is somehow . . . distasteful. After all, Shakespeare's ladies affected not to hear or understand when their men spoke bawdy and were no less feminine on that account, and this in a century rougher far than ours, before go-go dancers at breakfast diners, topless Texan bars, full frontals, drive-in porn cinemas where porn is sold as casually as topping up your tank.

To her two previous books of poetry—*Fruits & Vegetables* (1971) and *Half-Lives* (1973)—Erica Jong has added *Loveroot*, and a sequel to her bestselling novel *Fear of Flying*, published in 1973. Sufficient to say that her vainglory is unabating and unstoppable, the equal of the ghastly Nin—'Pictures of me covered the walls.' Who put them up? Who admires them? Me; mememe. ME!

Plot: After eight unfruitful years of wedlock to a Chinese Freudian analyst beset with an unresolved Oedipus Complex, while gainfully employed as institutional psychiatrist in Noo York, our heroine Isadora White Wing (32), a 'nice' Jewish girl from the Upper West Side, lights out on Thanksgiving Day in search of climax, and lots of it. There follows a modernised and sanitised metropolitan American *Fanny Hill*. Sessions follow with her analyst Abigail Schwartz, there are flashbacks to Heidelberg and an account of her erring husband's infidelity at a famous Alpine ski-resort; sessions (oh God!) with Frankfurt analyst Dr. Happe, then *Kaffee mit Schlag mit*

Chuck and Ricey, a right pair of gobshites. The husband is seen at tennis, followed by Bach cantatas; then its back to Noo York and into the awful present with the nice Jewish girl, her problems still unsolved.

Then Stolichnaya vodka and Ovulindex thermometer, nightcaps at the Algonquin, cunnilingus with Jeffrey Ruder, M.D. (seen 'striding towards me along Park Avenue'), followed by madcap pranks (fellatio) with Jeffrey Roverts forty blocks downtown ('now I am striding into Jeffrey's office'); no sooner out than love-bouts with Rosanna Howerd, a rich ex-seminar student got up as Mick Jagger with Cartier jewellery, followed by ill-advised trip to California and *trout meuniere* with Britt Goldstein, encounters with Spinoza and Dante, two fixers, sport in the Jacuzzi pool, Vitabath shower followed by some home truths from Viennese pornographer Hans, hard upon sodomy *mit Gruppensex,* new use found for curly-lip Dom Perignon bottle by ravening Rosanna, who shows up again, tireless, before eager Erica-Isadora encounters (wait for it) Henry Miller, King of Priap, spouting interminable twaddle ('Do you wanna cut the balls off the English langwidge?'), then *more* Mouton-Cadet with the insatiable Rosanna; and always chit-chat, more chit-chat.

Two hundred and eighty-six or so painful pages on and our heroine has met Mr. Right in the rough and ready personage of one Josh Ace, a bluntspoken ('I don't give a shit about immorality, I just love ya') banjo-playing blockhead some six years her junior.

The overheated terrain common to the distaff side would be familiar trampled ground for those who have already dipped into Doris Lessing's *The Golden Notebook.* Much yelling and awful verbal intimacies occur between 'the cosmic crash of cock and cunt' (note nice alliteration) as the insatiable demands of the body electric are satisfied; which leads Isadora-Erica (purporting to be authoress of best-selling *Candida Confesses*) into more unpretty scrapes and additional boasting. 'Man or woman, vibrator or shower spray, I come in three minutes flat.'

Soon now she is spouting Freudian talk all over the Szechuan food and here comes Anaïs Nin (Gawd!) in person, and the self-endorsement and self-engrossment has come full circle:

'You're gonna be the most famous woman writer of our generation,'
Hope said to me, looking up.

As a self-confessed Spokesperson for the Feminist Movement she speaks out stoutly:

'There was a great upheaval of the female half of the species, the buried lives of women were suddenly surfacing . . .'

August names are brazenly invoked from Whitman to Colette, though the gushing manner suggests more Helen Gurley Brown or Xavier Hollander, the Happy Hooker herself. The *subido, subido* manner can get tiresome: 'Then Kirsten of the gigantic knockers appeared and pre-empted me in the breast department.' We have heard of pre-emptive strikes and body-bags, American Army euphemisms for bombing raids and stiffs; but I have never encountered it in this disgusting guise.

The companion volume of poems is a little more restrained, some of them brazenly dedicated to the great dead: Mary Wollstonecraft Godwin, Mary Shelley, Colette of course, fashionable suicides Anne Sexton and Sylvia Plath, Keats and Whitman with Pablo Neruda—all the good guys.

Some of these verses contrive to raise themselves above the general rut; one poem dedicated to the beluga whale that died gravid in Coney Island Aquarium. She is less sound on humans. A deal of shrewd calculation can be detected behind the girlish gush, the cultivated guilelessness and quintessential silliness. She is not quite as silly as she seems. To be Jewish and female, successful and attractive in Noo York must inflate the ego mightily.

Louis Untermeyer preferred the happier verse. Fulsome praise comes from lechers Updike and Miller for her first novel, banned in Ireland. For the rest, it's the chauffeur-driven Rolls, bright chat about the dead Roethke; Coke bottles serve as dildoes, green plastic vibrators are imported from Japan, all pour into the Capital of Conspicuous Waste. What would the Earl of Rochester have made of all this buggery, the huggermuggery, the piggery, the two-beast-backery?

> The sperm-smell of the
> mango
> reminds me of how long
> it's been
> since a man opened me up
> and sucked my juice . . .

Hibernia, 18 January 1979

22

Seeing Big

Vickey Goldberg, *Margaret Bourke-White: A Biography* (Heinmann)

In biography perhaps the trick is not to be awestruck before the subject. Great biographers require great subjects; Ellmann on Joyce and not George Moore, George Painter on Proust and not Alain-Fournier, Chateaubriand on himself, Stendhal on Beyle. Keep it cool.

A cool manner lends credibility to findings and sharpens analysis. The brisk explicatory manner here deployed—a dreadful mix of William L. Shirer and Gordon Thomas—does little to reassure.

A critical admirer, one of the very few critical in this interminable and somewhat vulgar record of Margaret Bourke-White's life and career, spoke of a certain chill: 'Those eyes—I can't understand the eyes. . . . They are stern, there is no expression in them.'

Dom Moraes as a lad encountered her; recalls a tough handsome woman in her forties, smart in slacks, who addressed him as 'honey.' She had made her way in the world, had clout and used it. The startling feminist effigy here designated 'Margaret' and even 'Peg' is another story, more fit for a Mills & Boon romance.

Her 5 x 7 Corona View on its tripod recorded horrors: the pig-slaughter factory, 70,000 dead on a Soviet battlefield, vultures gorging on mutilated Hindus after a Calcutta riot, the Hooghly River awash with bloody corpses. 'The beauty of the past belongs to the past.'

She had a weakness for top American brass, became intimate with Brigadier General J. Hampton Atkinson, CO of the 97th Bomb Group, and Major Jerry Papurt of Counterintelligence, Colonel 'Ros' Rosengreen of Army PRO, flew on a combat mission against a Nazi airfield in Tunis, in a war atmosphere 'charged with desire and longing.'

'The war lurched forward in spurts,' sententiously declares our biographer, 'as humanity sank to new depths'; so too this biography, ever adept at combining the soignée and the ridiculous. A memo from Hitler to Bormann as chapter-head; a note to her sister-in-law's dog.

> In Tiflis MBW photographed Stalin's mother; the tyrant's Babush-
> ka had never understood what her son was up to, had packed him
> off to study under the Jesuit Fathers, wanted him to be a priest. The
> darker secret was that MBW was herself part Jewish on her Polish
> father's side and never has acknowledged it, kept it to herself.

An English-Irish grandmother is mentioned in *Portrait of Myself*, the
1963 autobiography, but no word of grandfather Weiss or the Polish-
Jewish past.

Something cold and reserved in her nature prevented her from making
much of human subjects. The Buchenwald inmates of 1945 caged in
their compound seemed posed as male window-dummies, mere effigies.
Korean mother and defector son embracing, coy as a cereal advertise-
ment; only the eyes of the Soviet tanksmen or the youthful factory
workers at Tractorstroi give something away. Man Ray and the always
invisible Cartier-Bresson in a Paris brothel were her masters there.

She responded to gigantic scale: the Terminal Tower in Cleveland, the
Otis Steel Plant, a PWA irrigation scheme in the Columbia River Basin,
Fort Peck Dam, American gigantism. She has a studio sixty-one stories
up on the Chrysler Building, where two pet alligators, Pyro and Hypo,
had the run of the terrace alongside the gargoyles.

Her early black and white lyrical photography had something akin
to a Humphrey Jennings documentary. Something grand and monumental too, in the manner of Toland or Tisse; a touch of Riefenstahl's
Triumph of the Will. Her photojournalism for *Fortune*, and *Life* were propaganda for the American way of life, industrial muscle. She was endors-
ing Maxwell Coffee on radio as sharecroppers in Georgia ate snakes
and cowdung.

Whatever stepped above the ordinary would hold her attention. She
developed American push, believed the axiom 'Go ahead . . . shoot off
your own cannon!' The patriotic theme-song of *Life* magazine assured
Americans that they had cause for pride in their country. In the mid-
1930s, the longsighted picture-editor Dan Longwell had recommended
that Time Inc found a picture magazine: 'A war, any sort of war, is going
to be a natural promotion for a picture magazine. The history of European illustrated magazines bears that out.' A 1950 survey indicated that

over half the population of America saw one or more issues of *Time* magazine in any three-month period, a total audience of 26,600,000.

Margaret Bourke-White wrote to her editor Wilson Hicks that she was 'homesick to get back to war': the double whammy! 'My life and my career was not an accident,' she said once. 'it was thoroughly thought out.' Long under analysis, though considered successful in the world's eye, she died of lingering Parkinson's Disease on 27 August 1971; had changed her surname (born Margaret White in the Bronx) to make it sound more impressive, had two broken marriages. She was perhaps lucky with an editor such as Henry Luce; photoeditors Billings, Longwell and Wilson Hicks.

Her work was of another time. Perhaps our freakish times requires a more freakish recorder: the squint askance of a Diane Arbus. The bio reads like Vicki Baum.

Hibernia, 25 January 1979

23

Hope Deferred

Flannery O'Connor, *Wise Blood* (Faber & Faber)
Flannery O'Conner, *The Violent Bear It Away* (Faber & Faber)
Flannery O'Conner, *Everything That Rises Must Converge* (Faber & Faber)

Special rules obtain for those creators who were snatched away young, or driven mad by inner vision rarely corresponding to the generally known world of the here and now—Keats, Rimbaud, the demented Richard Dadd. In 1951 Flannery O'Connor developed disseminated lupus erythemotosis (Red Wolf), an incurable disease of metabolic origin from which her father died when his daughter was fifteen. By 1955 she was on crutches—steroid treatment had caused bone disintegration—and in 1963, when the lupus was dormant, she developed anaemia from a fibroid tumour. The operation for its removal reactivated the lupus and she died in 1964 at the age of thirty-nine.

Like Eudora Welty and Faulkner, she spent most of her life in the Deep South, living with her mother on a dairy farm in Georgia, raising Muscovy ducks, Chinese geese and peacocks.

Her output, though not large, cut deep. Her themes: bigotry and backwardness, the lives of the freakish 'not insane enough for the asylum, not criminal enough for the jail, not stable enough for society.' Satan's fearful powers in forms various; in fine, the near-impossibility of following to the letter the Good Lord's stern injunction to love thy neighbour as thyself. Faulkner himself had said it over and over: The oppressed live permanently in a kind of daze.

These moral fictions abound with oddballs and freaks. The South's rejectamenta go in for abusing or 'buttering up the niggers.' Her White Trash shows up in a mighty bleak light, with here and there a touch of loathing. She is the implacable enemy of niceness, the self-complacency of the sanctimonious, the bogus-pious, all 'a heap of vanity.' She disliked intensely the work of Carson McCullers, who died three years after her, of alcoholism, aged fifty; and professed not to have read Faulkner, which is difficult to credit, given the amount of straight-faced pie-jawing in regional dialect, very Faulknerean in mood, with which her work abounds. Her Catholic vision, if it can be called that, is exceedingly bleak and Calvinistic; 'the entry into the world of guilt and sorrows where even the mercy of the Lord burns.' The young preacher Tarwarter in *The Violent Bear It Away* 'expects to see wheels of fire in the eyes of unearthly beasts.'

Semi-crazed preachers afire with the Lord, already encountered in Eudora Welty's *Delta Wedding*, go rampaging on through the wilderness, alive to the 'hard facts of serving the Lord' in a land of unbelievers O'Connor liked to quote Allen Tate's dictum: 'Technology without Christianity is, I think barbarism quite simply.' She sets a rural conservative Christian ethos against the encroachments of Northern homogenising industrialism; not taking her honesty quite as far as Faulkner, who boasted that he was prepared to arm his Blacks and fight the Civil War all over again, on the wrong side. One can swallow much far-fetched stuff from Mr. Faulkner, even gross improbabilities, because his novels were folk-tales made contemporary; Flannery O'Conner's vain attempts to follow him along that path end, as often as not, in Grand Guignol.

But then again it's no easy matter to render convincingly the inner turmoil of imbeciles; and a housebound invalid would have restricted contact with the Great Outside. The novels are less successful than the stories, all pervaded with the high rhetoric of Redemption, showing the same grim mendicant pride of the struggling poor. A profusion of animal and insect metaphors and similes attempts to force together inner and outer landscapes, and fail. Outcasts are introduced into decent homes with disastrous results. 'What he do is him,' says the Negro dairyman Randall of his friend Morgan. 'What I do is me.'

Her world is one of loss and fire, a world 'made for the dead.' The mother of the spoiled son has a

> heavy body on which sat a thin, mysteriously gaunt and incongruous head. . . . There was an observable tendency in all her actions. This was, with the best intentions in the world, to make a mockery of virtue, to pursue it with such a mindless intensity that everyone involved was made a fool of and virtue itself became ridiculous.

Fr. Ignatius Vogle S.J. is seen in a dream 'with a mysterious saturnine face in which there was a subtle blend of mysticism and corruption.'

Johnson, the crazed preacher, devours a page of the Holy Bible: 'I've eaten it like Ezekiel and I don't want none of your food after it not no more ever.' When Tarwater gets the call he:

> knows that he was called to be a prophet and that the ways of his prophecy would not be remarkable. His black pupils, glassy and still, reflected depth on depth of his own stricken image of himself. Trudging into the distance in the bleeding stinking mad shadow of Jesus, until at last he received his reward, a broken fish, a multiplied loaf.

Her stories lie in that peculiar terrain between Katherine Anne Porter (*Pale Horse, Pale Rider*) and Eudora Welty (*The Golden Apples*), more overwrought in manner than the former, less whimsical and poetic than the latter. Both novels are, I fear, failures, but failures of an exalted order; the elements striving consistently towards the horrific, the unspeakable, do not always cohere. Pushing for extreme effects, she slips into turbidities at times, when the stitching-together or cross-fertilising effect with metaphor and simile fail. The shrunken head pilfered from the museum, the drowning baptism, do not quite come off, in the way that Benjy's love for the cow, or even the notorious corncob, succeeded for Faulkner. A curious fact with these possessed Southern ladies: when they turn their hands to novels they all fail—Mrs. Porter's *Ship of Fools*, Eudora Welty's *Losing Battles*. Carson McCullers's *Member of the Wedding* was more an extended short story.

The three brief prefaces appended to each volume are fine in their way but tend to reveal too much of the plots, and should be read last, if at all. V. S. Pritchett, in his preface, is perspicacious, but not even he can agree on the correct spelling of Haze or Hazel Motes in *Wise Blood,* which is given both ways in the preface and both ways in the text, becoming 'Hazel' again for the blurbwriter. The jacket designs are wanting in distinction and the colophons (mosquitoes?) in *Wise Blood* more a distraction than a decoration. Still, it is good to have these three works in paperback at last.

Wise Blood (1952) was her first novel and *The Violent Bear It Away* (1960) her last. She published two collections of short stories, these here and *A Good Man is Hard to Find* (The Women's Press, Ltd.), two collections of non-fiction: *The Habit of Being* (letters) and *Mystery and Manners*, occasional prose. Her cast of mind was odd, but then she lived in an odd place all her life. Her work is set in the absolute standard of what American fiction aspires to be.

24

Doctored Letters

John Barth, *Letters* (Secker & Warburg)

T. S. Eliot defined the novel as a work of fiction in which characters are created and shown in significant relation to each other. But what is deemed significant changes from century to century: Cervantes would have had difficulty understanding what Borges was on about in modern Spanish. Irish readers are lost to Beckett's French fiction and are mostly bored by English translations of it. The past: 'a holding tank in which time's wastes recirculate,' Barth avers. The diligent researcher, Alumni Centennial Professor of English and Creative Writing at John Hopkins, has published a long pseudo-novel rich in association if poor in suspense. The story as such hardly matters. The characters are lifted from Barth's earlier novels and here allowed to talk themselves silly. Done with *avant garde* contraptions he is looking for a way back to 'aboriginal narrative, a route to the roots.' The aim is to evoke the origins of fiction in the oral narrative tradition. A novel-in-letters, six stories entwined to make a seventh or an 'old time epistolary novel by seven fictitious drolls and dreamers each of which imagined himself actual,' in the manner of Sterne and Smollett, or Bellow's addresses to the living and the dead in *Herzog*; a far cry from Goethe's high-fashioned old incitement to early suicide, in the better-lettered times gone by.

As postal rates rise and semi-illiteracy increases, few people would write such archly styled and gossipy epistles as these, not even professional writers. The horny gossip is as indiscreet as Byron's. Public affairs may intrude into these private matters (Lady Amherst) but the diction remains deliberately archaic.

Although I am in sympathy with the theory of the thing, it is difficult not to weary of the method, explaining itself in some detail on pages 40, 81, 151, 340-1, 531, 534, 654 and elsewhere for all I know. Few fellows are more prolific of explanation or more addicted to unwarranted confidences than your southern attorney-at-law—witness the longeurs of Faulkner's Gavin Stevens.

Marshyhope State College becomes a State University, but Harrison Mack's 'freeze-dried faeces' is never found; Niagara Falls is turned off by U.S. engineers for repairs and a waxworks destroyed by fire on the American side. A character who thinks himself to be George III's Madame de Staël rides by in a carriage; Washington city is burnt (in 1812) and the Indian wars fought all over again, as a film crew shoots footage of past history recreated on plywood sets.

The dangerous modern military presence is felt, some ancestors recalled, a past no less sanguinary invoked, Sharon Tate murdered anew; all this with wife-swapping, role-changing, incest, pseudo-characterisations, impostumes, doubts as to paternity, much fornicating. 'Have you learned in the evening of your lives what we never knew in the morn of ours?'

What with winds and following tides, good wine, excellent lunches aboard the skipjack *Osborn Jones*, remorse for what's past and cannot come again, the Roman feeling for the graces of life departing brings *The Unquiet Grave* to mind:

> Goodbye, Point No Point, fit title for the story of my life.
> Goodbye to all things south of Bloodworth; I shall not pass your way again.

American spelling throughout.

Hibernia, 11 September 1970

25

Peanuts

John Updike, *The Coup* (Deutsch)

The fiction of John Updike is as American as molasses or the Gross National Debt. He is a fussily aspiring writer, but unfortunately his couples have never grown up, still at the heavy petting and necking stage. Hence their engrossed interest in feminine underwear, tradename Lollipop or Spanky ('the cleft barely masked by the gauze of a thousand perfect circlets'). Moralising sits very uncomfortably upon him, and he goes in for a good deal of it.

Could this excessive load of verbiage be yet another form of conspicuous American wastefulness, of overload? Ham-fisted metaphors and silly similes fly, for he is nothing if not inconsistent; and this can lead to many patent absurdities. My high hopes for this novel were soon dashed. Above the 'hypothetical slice of desert' called Kush, the clouds are likened to wildebeest and giraffes compared to clouds. No desert can ever be 'hypothetical.' A girl's breasts are the shape of 'freshly started anthills' and there is an odder reference to an 'absent-minded penis' (ever encountered a rational phallus or a thinking penis?).

A question not answered, in Updikese, becomes: 'Ezana's rejoinder [vile noun] was aborted [vile verb].' 'She, sensing the eschatological drift of my call, had chosen to sustain her side of our exchange in elemental, traditional costume' becomes, when decoded: Perceiving that he was horny, she decided to receive him in the nude. A cup of chocolate is 'unimpeachable.' Do you get that? While an obese female is 'fat as a queen termite,' but soon 'pity leaped in her, as a frog disturbing a pond.' Where's the termite? Worse is in store: two pages on comes a reference to 'the sarcophagus of fat into which she had been lowered.'

A widow who is 'this tired-looking diarrheic angel' on p. 228 becomes 'the pallid American beauty' on p. 230 (diarrhea cured?), before ending as 'the freckled she-devil' of the page following. But surely, as Bloom could have told him, classical statuary and angels have no anus?

Slither here.

The narrator is variously 'I,' Ellolou (Freedom), Happy (Haps), Bini, Hakim Felix al-Bini, Flapjack, or just plain Nigger, in his days of American servitude. You are not forced or obliged to believe in him as Bellow would have you believe in Eugene Henderson or Moses Herzog; or as Marquez obliges you to believe in his Patriarch and a presidential palace full of vultures. One cannot believe in Kush, formerly Noir, nor in the dictator who is said to run it. In the first place, he is not a dictator: for if a true tyrant ordered innocent tourists to be machine-gunned, then machine-gunned they would be. But not here. A dummy is set up and we are bombarded not with his opinions but with the author's, for what they are worth.

I can neither believe nor recall any of the characters, nor their names, in the five or six Updike novels I have read and been exasperated by; nothing remains, only hazily 'liberal' states of mind and, of course, loving descriptions of frillies. There is an old Viennese proverb: 'If you want meat, you have to pay for the bones.'

His awkward compounds baffle me: 'the crunched leg of the unhome-town left tackle.' He must have the greatest trouble putting a plot together; for it has to be sustained by inner cohesiveness or else collapse. You just cannot accept *The Coup* as a genuine memoir written by this vague dictator fellow exiled in the South of France; and certainly not after page 13 when the *oratio obliqua* becomes a hypothetical present that will continue to the end. Some of his excesses recall the muscle-bound Styron, the straining for dramatic effects of Fitzgerald at his least plausible (Dick Diver). Africa is not his line of country. Nor is the 'spongy turf of psycho-historical specula-tion,' which Bellow (again) has commandeered (*Herzog, To Jerusalem and Back, Mosby's Memoirs*). But Bellow is tough-minded and has a mordant humour all his own; much of it directed against himself, as a Jew.

Updike is the chronicler of Middle American inertia, the gargantuan consumers of the abundant beverages from 7-UP to milk shakes, ever plagued by the continuum of women 'above him, around him, always.' The 'erotic turmoil of bedsheets' is his chosen terrain; and only there does the writing become—however feebly—alive.

After many vicissitudes, our mild-mannered hero retires with one of his four wives, the jogger, and some of their children (not his) to the South of France—for Kush was formerly the French possession Noir—where they are to be seen sitting at open-air cafés, drinking *citrön presse*. He is thought to be working on his memoirs.

The novel here is supposed to be the gas of that past, involving discussions with the Minister of the Interior. But Bellow has beaten him to it with *Henderson the Rain King*.

26

A Whispering Gush

John Updike, *Bech: A Book* (Deutsch)

In this his thirteenth title, sixth novel, John Updike strays a little from his chosen ground. Forays are made into Soviet Russia and Romania. He encounters a Bulgarian poetess:

> Dear Vera Glavanakova—It is a matter of earnest regret for me that you and I must live on opposite sides of the world.

Panty-sniffing.

Couples set out to expose the sensibility and lifestyle of the upper middleclass of the Eastern seaboard, 'Tarbox' being an old New England town turning exurb, where the principal pastime is adultery. In those split-level houses fixed in their formal gardens, what gives? Plenty, though it's almighty boring. Updike writes of that schmaltz-grub, the good life in the communal pigswill. The small town that Sherwood Anderson wrote of in *Winesburg, Ohio*, has spread itself until now it must be as extensive in area as the Virgin Plains. This is Updike's hunting ground—'the dark plains of American sexual experience where the buffalo still roam,' in Cheever's mocking formulation. The cosy American suburban life that Nabokov detested and dismissed so acidly in *Pnin* and *Lolita* is here designated 'Brewer.'

Updike employs a prose style as padded as a Green Bay Packer's protective stuffing, as difficult to move about in as an astronaut's space-suiting with the helmet on. There hangs over the whole enterprise a strong stench of the inconclusive, the wastefully inconclusive; his themes become will-o'-the-wisps that evaporate—those gardens, lawns, golf-courses, candy bars and drugstores, those endless catalogues of interior bric-a-brac are seen through swimming and adoring eyes ('she turned and was wearing bikini underpants with tiger stripes, beneath the saffron gauze of her

pantaloons'). His relentless pursuit of the ladies is a cover for his pursuit of
the *mot juste*, which can lead him, quite breathless, into some very tangled
syntax: 'Music approached from one direction and a coat check girl in
tights from the other':

> She pivoted towards a long-toothed gallant waiting grinning on
> her right, he exclaimed 'Darling!' and their heads fell together like
> bagged oranges.

Cokes, summer lawns, toilets and master bedrooms, some of the toi
lets occupied by women ('a whispering gush') and most all the Master
Bedrooms with couples practicing fellatio. The details are exhaustive;
Updike, as Stendhal, is obsessed with women, their moons and their
tides, their times and their changes.

At the Deutsch launch of *The Coup* in London, I told Updike that what
I missed in his work was the poor. He did not reply.

The more he tells (gives away), the more he loses; his a pale and bloodless talent that stops just short of the point, where life would roughly
begin. Like Robert Creeley, he has nothing much to write about, except
his own inner processes; possibly neither of them are novelists.

> The presence of the baby fills the apartment as a little casket of
> incense fills a chapel. Rebecca June lies in a bassinet of plaited
> rushes painted white and mounted on a trundle.

The sweetly reasonable American reality he offers us is a sort of casebound Hollywood (*The Man Who Came to Dinner*), or a Norman Rockwell
cover for *Saturday Evening Post*, a sticky verisimilitude:

> She rises to clear away the plates and stands there, thumb on
> chin, staring at the centre of the white table. She shakes her head
> heavily . . .

> Across from him her broad pelvis, snug in a nubbly brown skirt, is
> solid and symmetrical as the base of a powerful column. His heart
> rises through that strong column and enraptured his love for her
> is founded anew yet not daring to lift his eyes to the rest of her he
> says . . .

He eats three pieces of shoo-fly pie and a crumb in the corner of his mouth comes off when he kisses her breasts goodbye in the kitchen.

Strong scene in the Club Castanet, distressing interior monologue, and some sneers at his English publisher ('Bech hugged his publisher. Waxy old tux . . .'), who can no longer afford to have Mailer on his list, following his agent's demand for a very substantial advance for *An American Dream*. Bech is supposed to be Jewish. 'A genuine male intellectual Jew with hairy armpits': shades of Moses Herzog. *Commentary* let him use a desk. 'A certain *ecrivain jeuf* shat plenteously . . . hot gaseous stuff.'

Bellow, a writer who improves as he ages, once made a trip to Peoria in Illinois. He questioned the people as to what was worth writing about in that gaudy and boring city; the answer was that there was nothing worth writing about in their lives. Not all moments of life can be said to be interesting.

You know what Updike is getting at, in a general sort of way (since he is nothing if not thorough); but the great fault in his writing, and this is something that he has gone to great pains to master, is smoothness. Then, too, his conception of life is rather vulgar; indeed almost as vulgar as Salinger's. Updike is a fine critic, and has become a defender of the European *avant garde* (his *New Yorker* articles on Hamsun and 'Grove is My Press, Avant My Guard'). A collection of his critical thoughts might be as interesting as Graham Greene's, recently out in Penguin; both being non-stylists passionately interested in style.

Hibernia, 10 September 1971

27

In the Land of Glut

John Updike, *Problems & Other Stories* (Deutsch)

After two decades of marriage his couples are parting. What remains constant however is the broken-backed limp imagery full of neologism and digression, unmistakably Updikese, a whispering gush. Two examples:

> 1. Though in college a Soc. Sci. major and in adult life a do-gooder, she ceased to read a newspaper.

> 2. They became superb at being tired with one another. They competed in exhaustion. 'Oh, God, Princess, how long can this go on.' Their conversations were so boring.

There is no feeling of the past in his work, it is as modern as formica or plastic, which perhaps explains his popularity. Readers of *Newsweek, The New Yorker, Playboy* or the glowing prose of *The National Geographic Magazine* would feel quite at home there; you don't have to work very hard at it.

Perhaps he tried too hard to be affecting; but lechery (and his mind is more prurient than either Mailer's or Michaels's) and quackery are bedfellows. A weakness for waitresses and receptionists resurfaces; the girl in the 'seductive halter' is forever giving him the hot eye. John Bailey has remarked on the heavily manipulative adverbial and adjectival clauses in the work of Iris Murdoch. Among the more esteemed American prosers, Updike writes sloppily, as demonstrated here:

> 3. He turned. Who are you? His apprehension ricocheted confusedly, in the room's small space, off this other, who, standing in its centre, simultaneously rendered it larger and many-sided and yet more shallow, as if she were a column faced with little diamonds.

> 4. Yet, a summer ago, as canary-yellow bulldozers gaily churned a grassy, daisy-dotted knoll into a muddy plateau, and a crew of pig-tailed young men raked and tamped clay into a plain, this

transformation did not strike them as ominous, but festive in its impudence; their marriage could rend the earth for fun.

The feeble irony of the close cannot revitalise the rest nor pull it into focus. Updike has a weakness for cockeyed similes and metaphors: a smile is 'preserved as in amber'—which might just pass, but what about her tongue (here we go again) 'darting about like a rabbit in the head-lights' (given the fact that Rabbit is the hero of the series). 'Corinna was still conscious but leaning against him like a flying buttress.' Or a Corin-thian column? 'Rejoinders' are often on tongues; sarcasm 'brushed' aside; questions 'posed.' His masters are Cheever and Henry James, disastrous influences. All are travellers in the land of glut and guilt. The 'majestic removal of contingency' continues to exasperate and baffle him; it is unclear whether or not he finds these petroleum extractors and 'develop-ers' as dull as the reader might.

Faulkner, writing of a bolt of cloth in a Mississippi store, could tell you something about the store, its owner, something about cupidity and greed thrown in for good measure. Updike's metaphors and similes operate in the void. Atlantis is given a plural form in the last of only three stories that suc-ceed; elsewhere, psychological analysis becomes voyeuristic lingering, spasms of ruminating interludes, philosophical tripe, the ornately bogus. Only when he cannot find any suitable metaphor will the true images come unbidden; the archaeologist dying of lung cancer is free to speak un-Updikese:

> The Farnhams lived inland, in a state people confused with Ohio, the fertile flatness, the tall skies, the way trucks rolled day and night made them happy, because these things were theirs alone . . . He had got out just in time. Atlantis was now sunk beneath the sea.

The authentic breath of a real America blows through these few pages, the people speak for themselves in their true voices.

Thrice now it has been my unhappy lot to review a new Updike work. The school reunion is well done; Haysville's past comes alive; the old couple driving home. For the rest, it's the old mixture as before: the halter on the brown back, the whore, American middle-class wastefulness. This is his sixth collection of short stories. John Updike's fidgety fiction gives me the creeps.

Hibernia, 22 May 1980

28

Tales from the Killing Ground

Richard Brautigan, *A Confederate General from Big Sur* (Cape)
Richard Brautigan, *The Hawkline Monster: A Gothic Western* (Cape)
Richard Brautigan, *Trout Fishing in America* (Cape)

It is an axiom of an old date that the best comic works have a sad centre, from Aristophanes to Aragon, on to *Confessions of Zeno*; and Richard Brautigan is no exception:

> Half a block from Broadway and Columbus is Hotel Trout Fishing in America, a cheap hotel. It is very old and run by some Chinese. They are young and ambitious Chinese and the lobby is filled with the smell of Lysol.
>
> The Lysol sits like another guest on the stuffed furniture, reading a copy of the Chronicle, the Sports Section. It is the only furniture I have seen in my life that looks like baby food.
>
> And the Lysol sits asleep next to the old Italian pensioner who listens to the heavy ticking of the clock and dreams of eternity's golden pasta, sweet basil and Jesus Christ.

The Grove Press dust jacket featured Larry Rivers's *The Next-to-Last Confederate Soldier*, a faceless dummy under Old Glory. Some of the original headings and spelling are retained. Brautigan takes as his theme the American Civil War (rather as Flann O'Brien took Irish mythology, our heroic past) and foisted or grafted it onto a contemporary urban (San Francisco) scene. It would be difficult, if not impossible, for an Irish or Spanish writer to treat *their* Civil War as either myth or joke, certainly not 'the last good time this country ever had.' The Vietnam War had come and gone, the heyday of Haight-Ashbury and pot; and the ghosts of Union and Confederate dead impart a sad gloss to these engaging capers. Shades (if you want to be Irish about it) of Thomas Francis Meagher, the Fenian Volunteers, the Irish Brigade, Devoy's Postbag.

Brautigan, as Nathanael West before him, is free of what Pound called 'emotional slither'; in a way that Philip Roth, for instance, is not. Brautigan's work is very clean, despite the fornicating. It would be good to see all his short novels published in one volume. *Trout Fishing in America* is out in Delta paperback; with A *Confederate General from Big Sur* and *In Watermelon Sugar,* this would make an acceptable Christmas present for a broad-minded Aunt.

In *The Hawkline Monster* Brautigan rides again. Blank spaces must equal, or even exceed, the spaces filled by text; in the manner of a taciturn wit who speaks only when there is something worth saying. He is an eccentric, a magician of sorts; good at making the reader feel—as I think Gide said of Malroux—'the strangeness of natural things and the naturalness of strange things.' Odd to chance upon an American belonging to this more European category of strange fish.

Here he turns the Wild West on its head; as I read I thought, strangely, of Michaux's old *Mes Proprietes* (1930). A cruelty that first became apparent in *Watermelon Sugar,* life in a Hippie commune viewed ironically, is here given its head. It would be a pity to reveal any of the involved plot, which goes meandering off into the American past like a stagecoach. He has a narrative facility as deceptively easy as Runyan or Mark Twain; and like Twain, he is a poet of the great outside. Though the events described here are purported to take place in 1902, modern slang is let loose with 'shit' and 'motherfucking.' It makes a pleasant change from—well, you name them (Vonnegut Junior's 'glittering half-truths' and posings). With Brautigan, America again becomes the continent of possibility it was once; the energy of the language harks back to Gertrude Stein and early Hemingway (*In Our Time*).

The consumption of food and drink is notable; and the fornicating, innocent as a river. Strange. The Hip lingo is presumably a defense against the Giant Sloths. Here is a city slicker who has retired to the backwoods. He has a lovely silent mind.

Trout Fishing in America is closer to Jarry's *Supermale* than to the distraught rhetoric of Roth's *Portnoy's Complaint*. In English writing I can think of nothing to compare with it—Belloc's *Bad Child's Book of Beasts* (1896)? Edward Lear? *More Beasts for Worse Children* (1910)? English humour tends to square off with the social stratifications (Waugh and Wodehouse), always with a condescending eye levelled at the Lower Orders; fine with its ear for the mumblings that pass for conversation among the luckier ones (Wooster). 'All classes of this island converse in understatement and irony,' quoth the Arch-Tory Anthony Powell.

The higher up the social scale you go, the more reduced the vocabulary: 200 words at the top, much the same as the Inuit, who has good reason for keeping his trap shut. Though *down* the scale, your highly articulate Cockney with his rhyming slang has so far produced nothing better than *Fred Basin's Diary*.

Hibernia, 8 January 1971

29

The People of the Spirit

Saul Bellow, *Mr. Sammler's Planet* (Weidenfeld and Nicolson)

Actual dreaming began with the Jews, the people of the spirit. 'Our descendants will shudder,' Heine wrote,

> when they read of the ghastly life we lead. Our age—which commences with the Crucifixion—will be regarded, as the greatest age of diseased mankind . . . Our healthy descendants will hardly understand us. All about us the splendours of the world will vanish; we found them once more within our inmost souls. I die of the unnatural anxieties and the sweet horrors of our time.

Saul Bellow, Russian Jewish by blood, Canadian by birth, a native of Chicago, writes with much heart and always with great dignity of his own oppressed race; unlike other American Jewish writers, he goes back into his past to seek standards to justify or explain the present. For, like Mailer (though for different reasons) he finds the present none too rosy. Most of his work has been concerned with Jewish characters, manipulators or manipulated in a Goy society.

'In America,' he wrote ironically, 'the abuses of the Old World were righted. It was appointed to be the land of historical redress.' Well, yes and no: there are more Jews in the metropolitan area of New York than in the whole of European Russia; go ask them. But Dr. Samuel Braun, like Bellow himself, has 'no prospect for putting the world in rational order.' Bellow's labours from *Herzog* on are soul-searchings, beseechings to a greater Authority, prayers. Not a gloomy vision of mankind. Beckett's, being narrower, is far gloomier.

'Those who try to interpret mankind through its eyes are in for much strangeness—perplexity.' Perplexity is a strong word with Bellow. He is a celebrator of the City as Faulkner was of the Wilderness; and his Jews no more understand the Goys than Faulkner's Whites understood their Blacks. His attitude to progress, with good justification, remains sceptical, as Peacock (to paraphrase: The March of Mind has marched in through the back parlour windows, and out again with my spoons):

> The dreams of nineteenth century poets pollute the psychic atmo-sphere of the great boroughs and suburbs of New York. Add to this the dangerous lunging staggering crazy violence of the fanat-ics, and the trouble was very deep . . . You could see the suicidal impulses of civilisation pushing strongly

And behind this, the South-loving barbarians: Gaugin, Stevenson, Baudelaire, de Nerval. Like Leiris, Bellow holds a degree in anthropol-ogy. It shows. Adorno, Marcuse, Norman O. Brown are deemed 'worth-less fellows.' So what are we to make of Timothy Leary, William C. Schatz, Dr. Fritz Perls, and other fashionable witch-doctors? Not much; fair game for ridicule, they go unmentioned. Head shrinkers, practitio-ners of Gestalt Therapy, charlatans, nuts:

> The labour of Puritanism now was ending. The dark Satanic mills changing into light Satanic mills. The reprobates converted into children of joy, the sexual ways of the seraglio and the Congo bush adopted by the emaciated masses of New York, Amsterdam, London . . . Liberty, Fraternity, Adultery!

Dark romanticism now takes hold. Thus Bellow:

> Great cities are whores. Doesn't everyone know? Babylon was a whore . . . Penicillin keeps New York looking clean. No faces gnawed by syphillis, no gaping noseholes as in ancient times.

'The unrestrained obscenity of the People, bewilder and distract you,' wrote Haydon the painter, of Paris in 1814. 'Such is the power and effect of this diabolical place, that the neighbourhood, like the country around the poison tree of Java, is made mad by its vice and infected by its principles.'

In *The Victim, Seize the Day, Henderson the Rain King* (this is not one of his more Jewish novels but contains their traits: the narrator 'driven into the world. A man who had fled his own country, settled by his forefathers.

A fellow who played the violin in despair, seeking the voice of angels'), *Herzog, Mosby's Memoirs*, Bellow has examined the Jewish Predicament in its various forms; and in *Mr. Sammler's Planet* he considers the Jewish Curse, only thirty years back in time, less. His employment of American vernacular idioms, operating on more than one level, sets him apart from his colleagues. The break-up of the old family ties would concern a Jew. Sammler, a refugee from wartime Poland, is a ghost in America ('The external appearance of the Polish Jews is frightful,' noted Heine not long after the 1819 pogrom). For Mr. Sammler, the music of Wagner seems suitable for a pogrom:

> In Cracow before World War I he had had another vision of it—desperate darkness, the dreary liquid yellow mud to a depth of two inches above the cobble stones in the Jewish streets. People needed their candles, their lamps and their kettles, their slices of lemon in the image of the sun. Theirs was the conquest of grimness with the aids always of Mediterranean symbols. Dark environments overcome by imported religious signs and local domestic amenities. Without the power of the North, its mines, its industries, the world would never have reached its astonishing modern form.

Hibernia, 11 September 1970

30

Natchez Trace

The Collected Stories of Eudora Welty (Marion Boyars)

She writes as the Impressionists painted. I first read *The Golden Apples* thirty years ago on the leads of Kenelm's Tower, a wing of Howth Castle rented out by a painter friend, who had chanced upon a copy in the Reading Room of the American Information Service in Dame Street, Dublin, a service long discontinued. Few knew of her existence, though Ben Kiely praised her. The Yeatsian echo in the title had attracted my painter friend and thereafter he would refer to Yew-Dora with some awe; she was a discovery. The Deep South was a mighty strange place and she brought it closer, the degrading heat south of New Orleans in a hamlet called Venice at the southernmost tip of North America where a middle-aged couple danced at Baba's Place:

> Surely even those immune from the world, for the time being, need the touch of another, or all is lost?

Or the lift of smog in San Francisco, summer:

> There was a soft gleam. Above, blue slides of sky were cutting in on the fog. The sun, as with a spurt of motion, came out. The streetcars, taking on banana colours, drove up and down, the line of movie houses fluttered streamers and flags as if they were going to sea.

Wilderness and metropolis are seen with this curiously engaging eye; then the yearning for levity takes hold and the colours stream away. Something there of Marie Cassatt—female figures as mere touches of colour in a darkened loggia; a touch, too, of the dandy Degas, the figures have such dignity. 'No Place for You, My Love' must be one of the strangest love-stories ever written, not least because the word 'love' is never mentioned. It harks back to Sir Thomas Wyatt's 'Prove to Me that I Change, My Dear':

> You've seen grass blades go through bubbles and they still reflect
> the world, give it back unbroken.

The 'habitual hills' of San Francisco on a clear day undergo some transformation, when Eugene MacLain, an employee of Bertsinger's jewellery store, slaps his wife's face over breakfast, without a word, and lights out for a walk, in 'Music from Spain.'

'He struck her because she was a fat thing' is modified to 'He struck her because he wanted another love,' which in turn is modified to 'A face from nowhere floated straight into that helpless irony and contemplated the world of his inner gaze.' It is twin to a story about the other MacLain brother who works in a bank in Morgana, California.

Eudora Welty was first published in the *Southern Review* in the late 1930s. Encouraged by Katherine Anne Porter, rather as the young apprentice Faulkner was encouraged by Sherwood Anderson, both she and Faulkner went on to improve upon their respected mentors. Here is a life's work: 41 stories or 622 pages from four collections and some Uncollected Stories from the 1960s, one—*The Demonstrators*—dealing with a civil rights murder in her hometown, the other story 'Where is the Voice Coming From?' is written from the point of view of the murderer, a nameless white man on Deacon Street in Thermopylae:

> Always I see him fall. I was evermore the one.

Faulkner had written on such a theme; the lyncher gazing out a window, waiting for the law. The theme of the dead child returns elsewhere. Guinea pigs are running underfoot in the dark. Alligators come down the Pearl River. The 'stench of sensation,' she claims, is like 'anesthetic made visible.'

A great model for our Irish scribblers bogged down in the mundane, the humdrum.

Books Ireland, April 1982

31

In the American Grain

Nicholson Baker, *The Mezzanine* (Granta Books)

Now from Granta comes *The Mezzanine*. Anticipating another of those blustery broadsides beloved of editor *extraordinaire* Bill Buford (*Dirty Realism*, Salman Rushdie), going on the smart jacket and copious footnotes, the heart sank.

But hold your hearses, gentle browsers!

A new sort of excellence is here deployed, appealing to our gentler sensibilities not by what is included but by what is omitted.

For American fiction the matter and manner is very French in thought and style, precision not far removed from Queneau, Jarry or Pinget, or Jacques Tati for that matter, ridiculing the plastics factory, 'the mute folklore of behavioral inventions.'

Plot is as minimal as you could wish, and we are spared any embarrassing intimacies between narrator Howie and his girl, spared even her name; she is allergic to milk, for it gives her 'blood-flecked diarrhea.' As he perceived reality at the age of three while hallucinating in a measles fever, so today, not having changed much in twenty years, now gainfully employed in this nameless corporation where the flushing urinals in the men's room remind him of a passage in Hopkin's Journal:

> I held the chosen shirt in the air with my little finger hooked under the collar and shook it once. It made the sound of a flag at the consulate of a small, rich country. Now—was I ready to put it on?

The employees greet each other minimally, 'Take it easy' or 'Oop!' Les Guster the vice-president is brushing his teeth by the faucets of the corporate toilet *before* lunch. The plot, such as it is, involves the purchase of shoe-laces during the lunch break. 'Tunes sometimes lived all day in the men's room'—'Yankee Doodle Dandy' rendered with 'infectious cheerfulness.' Much strangeness here too: 'the beautiful chrome-plated urinal plumbing, a row of four identical states of severe gnarledness which gives you the impression of walking into a petrochemical plant, with names like Sloane Valve and Delany Flushboy inscribed on their six-sided half-decorative boltlike caps.'

He has observed the holy expression that women have only for themselves in mirrors: 'slightly raised eyebrows, opened throat, very slightly flared nostrils.' New-hires visit the men's room eight or nine times daily, 'seeking acclimatisation.' The organisation is seen as a sort of tropical forest full of exotic flora and fauna: Eldon trays, Braille in the elevators, Dave, Sue and Steve either departing or returning from the lunch-break. The visit to the CVS pharmacy, rendered with a poker face. 'The ice cube deserves a historical note.'

The originality of novels depends on the emergence of a distinctly new embryo, a never-seen-before chrysalis that opens out (even when appearing to close), affording the amazed reader a shock of pleasurable surprise. This can be said of *Fiesta, Malone Meurt, Katz und Maus, La Jalousie, The Last Tycoon, Bartleby the Scrivener*. And now *The Mezzanine*. Rhapsodies in the springtime and the sun shining on a place where you wouldn't expect it to shine. No better work, along those distinctly French lines, has come our way since James Salter's *A Sport and a Pastime*.

The Irish Times, 1 September 1989

32

Lynching in the Everglades

Peter Matthiessen, *Killing Mister Watson* (Collins Harvill)

Ten thousand American Negroes were lynched out of hand in the last two decades of the nineteenth century, almost all innocent of any crime. The Sunshine State of just eighty years ago seems today as remote as Tyre and Sidon. Justice was uncertain and expensive, white people were expected to settle their own quarrels: 'A gentleman don't strip his shirt when he works with niggers.' The Everglades were a refuge for runaway slaves, Confederate stragglers, and Half Way Creek (the scene of this judicial murder of October 1910) was one of the pioneer outposts on the swampy mainland, together with nearby Chokolosker Island; they were the last points of civilisation on the southwest coast.

In his six-year search for relevant data, Matthiessen has 'reimagined' the life and death of E. J. Watson, who lit out from South Carolina one bright moonlit night, settled eventually in Florida, hid in the Ten Thousand Islands, defied the Law. He was wanted in four states, being implicated in several murders; and was gunned down in the end by two score deputies appointed *after* the killing. The story is told mainly in the words of inarticulate neighbours—the Hamiltons, Bill House, Mamie Smallwood, Carrie Langford, Hoad Storter and Sheriff Frank B. Tippins.

The young John Cheever had used the device of old family documents exhumed and deployed this as part of the fictional progress of *Wapshot Chronicle*; as does Peter Matthiessen here, to refute the popularly accepted facts of the Watson legend. His version of those unruly times, those durn greasy redskins, that white trash, those far from uppity niggers (small case) may even read more convincingly than Faulkner's stylised notions of the Mississippi basin, the black and red man's destiny. 'Here in Florida, they aimed to pen up any Indian they hadn't killed, ship that redskin sonofabitch to Oklohomo':

Fear was already in the air, like the scent of haze from far off fires
in the glades . . . I was having nightmares. Mister Watson would
look up in the window, that big barrel chest and that broad hat, and
the moon glinting on his gun and whiskers.

In the process of reimagining that time and place, he has created
a monster dark as Ahab. In 1884 the Fort Myers (pop. 300) Debating
& Literary Society in their first meeting debated on the subject 'Are
Women Intelligent Enough to Vote?' The dry sizzle of the aroused rat-
tler could be heard on the 'fertile sod-broke ground' no longer farmed
by Seminoles, the earth-spirits removed and tamed by Catholic missions in far-off Oklahoma. Hemingway had of course written of the
Florida Keys, of Bimini, with all his latterday flatulence. Here Peter
Matthiessen's cooler head and steadier hand does a better job. Now that
the Wilderness has been tamed, the writer as hunter (the carpet-bag-
gers come after the pioneers) is superseded by the anthropologist and
naturalist, the crazy ecologist coming for the last pickings.

Matthiessen has already demonstrated what he can do in *The Snow
Leopard*, *Under the Mountain Wall* and other works of non-fiction; and elsewhere in his collected stories, *On the River Styx*.

While multiple murder goes on in the swamps, Halley's Comet
'showed up in the springtime of that year and set the sky ablaze night
after night,' a thing to wonder at. It was shown to Miss Eudora Welty,
then a child:

In a unholy light where the sun rays come piercing down through
the smoke's shadow, something was hanging in that hellish air and
whatever it was kept me from calling. I wouldn't go nowhere near
a man who looked like he had set himself afire.

The Irish Times, 14 June 1989

33

Fresh Horrors

Alexander Theroux, *An Adultery* (Hamish Hamilton)

What Proust was pleased to call the 'suffering and recrudescence of love' (a sore or wound reopened) is the subject-matter of Alexander Theroux's third novel, all 27 chapters or some 400-odd pages. It is written in the oleaginous manner of Messrs. Alfred Hayes, Stefan Viczency or John Updike, but with some fresh horrors of his own added; the urgencies stale upon the page. Faint traces of a briefer but perhaps more honest novel still adhere; it is a work that fairly cries out for the blue pencil.

The action revolves around St. Ives, New Hampshire; sorties are made into Boston to consult therapists. The leading lady is Farol ('Desperado') Colorado, about thirty, with green eyes, divorced Lloyd Dzundza of Syracuse.

She is into Movicol, Surbex, Filibon, Tryptophan, Placidyls, Hadol, Derifil, Doxiden, Pathilon, Vistrax, also group therapy, has joined a woman's exercise group, plus a course on wood carving at the Cambridge Center for Adult Education, puts in time on the squash courts, when not working at the framers, where one fine day in marches cruel fate in the shape of Christian (Kit) Ford, a prat of the very highest order ('I paint'). In no time at all they are hard at the game of the two-backed beast.

'After love the pharmacia,' said the cynic Cioran; but here it is before love, with love, after love, if one dare call it 'love,' a word brought horridly into play.

Here's Kit: 'I'd always wake up to find looking down at me a face making the noise of a toy rubber pig.'

'Sooner or later one must inevitably head down an unknown road that leads without assurance even beyond the range of the imagination,' babbles the infatuated one (Theroux?). What big brother Paul objected to in Faulkner—a rhetoric forced at the expense of sense, so that thoughts and words fly up off the page, become gibberish—is everywhere in evidence here, in a text pregnant with italics. The lines of dialogue quiver with a bogus sincerity; screamers everywhere, wise-cracks and zingers:

Adultery is the vice of equivocation.

A prudent archer always has a second bowstring.

Farol gives up smoking, takes to jogging, is soon into bread-making, brioches, potato doughnuts, drop scones, *crumpets* for Chrissake. Her lunch might consist of cheese combos in pita bread with sprouts, easy on the mayo. She makes 'irresistible' duck quacks, goes 'comically' cross-eyed in her imitation of Sylvester the Cat, calls him 'Bunky,' 'Cookie Puss.'

If Meryl Streep is ever called upon to play Farol (that pharmaceutical echo) in the movie version (music by Lal), she will have her work cut out. Try this for size, Meryl: 'She went visibly tense as she heard my question, glaring at me, one eye a drill, the other a slit, her lips compressed like a person tasting bitter seed.'

Now say this (your green eyes misting over): 'I was like you . . . But I realised I owe something to myself. I had to get in touch with my feelings and learn to plumb the depths of all I myself could be and do.'

Or this (glumly): 'I just want warm weather and birds.' (jest-wanna-woimwettah-an-boids.)

The Freudian-contaminated air is aswirl with these vain entelechies. The out-of-doors as such hardly exists (The Dexter Shoe Outlet, Al's Diner, The Sandy Neck Lounge and the cat food section of Galoupi's), so there is no relief from the lethal self-absorption of the doomed protagonists, digging away for portentous clues to the condition (very ill) of their all-American inner psyches.

'The only certainty is that the trip has to be made. I remember thinking if the same returns not, the difference could be prevented.'

H'mm.

'Tiny' Maxine at the Yawnwinders' party is barking at someone. 'Drink had given her the look of a flounder with migrating eyes.' Come now. Barking flounders? Do they migrate? Or fish fly?

Here they do.

Meanwhile, as Lal's music swells, 'the shushing trees held night in their branches and we were alone in the falling moon-light of the yard.' Streep and Redford.

Run for the exits.

The Irish Times, 4 February 1989

34

Narco

Richard Ford, *The Ultimate Good Luck* (Collins Harvill)

For ex-Marine Quinn the Centro at Oaxaca feels like Vietnam again: 'a crystallised stillness above the rooftops and a swarming, full-bore eeriness in the street.' This gives rise to feelings he never had before, even late in a war where American soldiers went drugged into battle: 'a conspicuous undisciplined fear of enormous injury'—a peacetime fear only too well founded. He is one of the drugged ex-combatants of Vietnam, making an honest buck as a 'seven-on, seven-off fitter' on an oil rig, and a dishonest buck stealing cars. He comes to Mexico to spring his woman's brother from jail, and fails to do so.

Danger arrives hotfoot with its bad smells and fractured syntax, criminal code words for beastly circumstance. 'I can't see how you rate this place nice,' the Negro said. 'I want you to tell your boy to start doing me right.' 'Asshole' is the mildest pejorative. 'Ugliness went on at all hours, but you saw it by accident or not at all.' Richard Ford has learnt something from Chandler. This is his third novel, following *The Sportswriter* and *A Piece of My Heart*, a volume of short stories, *Rock Springs*:

> Everyone in Vietnam had been sick and the war had finally been run on sick time. People depended on each other according to sick intervals, watched each other with the affection of diseased response. But in Mexico it was dangerous. It singled you out.

Two kilos of Colombian cocaine are missing, not recovered; some shooting and the hewing off of an ear ensue. Murder is part of business, protection of interest rates, an eye on mergers, the contract, the fix (Marlowe has begun to sound like a phoney dick). In Chicago the Negro junkie has the manic expression of someone about to go to war, the look of fighting off cowardice with insanity.' It reads like the scenario for a Buñuel movie; terrorist bombs going off, guilty characters in ravaged terrain; the flat, sinister Mexican light.

Echoes of *The Postman Always Rings Twice*, *The Friends of Eddie Coyle*, from those great practitioners of hardboiled prose, James M. Cain and George V. Higgins. The American criminal's chronic homelessness strangely echoes Camus's alienation, arbitrary killing as *acte gratuite*, knocks on the door of misfortune. Little is divulged of the *cose secrete* of the two protagonists, Quinn and girlfriend Rae (surname not supplied); possibly because there is so little to reveal in those two stoics. We do not know what they are thinking or if they are thinking; neither does Richard Ford. When surprises come they take you unaware; no symbols where none intended. The snowman in the centre of the eastbound track for Detroit is smiling perfectly into the face of its own hot doom.

The narrative is stamped out with the rapid sureness of a branding iron:

> It had been raining in the Centro. Above floors, the air in the government palacio sat still and dense. Electric lights were off for siesta, and a sweet fodderish rain fragrance hung in the deputy's office . . . In the street big monsoon drops had begun smacking the cobblestones.

> The office had scalloped flutings on the cornices, and on the wall in the shadows was a large imperial portrait of Juarez in a red ermine cape and a gold filigreed crown he couldn't have lifted. The portrait had once been painted for someone else and Juarez's little rodent face added, so that he looked like a sideshow freak staring out from a body that was too large for him and that had him worried.

Several things are going on simultaneously here. In the Portal de Flores the early evening the light turns chartreuse. Surrealism runs through the streets of Oaxaca. Adios, Dionisio Angel Perez (machetes). Adios, Forastero Deats, the spade. The stinking particulars are dead right.

The Irish Times, 21 June 1989

II

Recurring Refrain

An imperceptible smell
of sulphur in the air

35

Down the Line

Richard Carline, *Stanley Spencer at War* (Faber & Faber)

The pantheistic ecstasies of bird-watcher-naturalist Henry Williamson creeping through no-man's-land at night, close enough to the enemy lines to hear the Huns talking, was not quite Stanley Spencer's style.

Renoir *fils* may have been positively relieved when a Bavarian sniper put a bullet through his foot, for it sent him back to Blighty, while Leger in the artillery remained astounded by the precision tooling on the open breach, Klee was bored with route-marching and drill and Gaudier-Brzeska kept whittling away at a captured German rifle stock, to make it less threatening, less potent.

These were normal enough reactions; but for the holy mystic from Cookham, a 'rejoicing criminal' with hair clipped short, the enemy, hidden Bulgars—and he only saw dead ones on the Macedonian front—was a wonderful mystery. And the mountains of Macedonia in which that unseen enemy moved only filled Spencer with 'an eternal joy.'

Salonika was not landscape; it was a spiritual world. The English Socialist Orwell, digging trenches and seeing only Republican sewage, would have been bemused, while Auden played ping-pong in Madrid.

'Up the line again, the sap of life has returned,' he wrote on 3 March 1918. 'I would far rather be out in the infantry than be working as an orderly in a hospital in England. I think my period of service is not a denigration but of being in the refiner's fire . . . could you send me a sketch book (cartridge paper I like), some pencils also.' Shades of Goya.

One Muirhead Bone recommended to the Ministry of Information that Spencer be appointed War Artist. 'We were marching under the beeches; their shadows simply poured down the soldiers' backs.' Like Blake or Palmer he believed that all that lives is holy, was in his own art 'a walking altar of praise.'

Obsessed with gravestones, he loved the order of domestic things; scaled correctly, all compositions were reduced to 'one unifying lump,' that even included Bulgarians. His peers were Giotto, Fra Angelico, Masaccio, Masolino, Piero della Francesca, Giorgione, Claude:

> I begin my pictures by letting them grow out of the sky on to the roofs, then slide down the roofs on to the ground. Then I run out of the bottom of the picture as soon as I can, so as not to allow any 'Foreground' to appear. Giotto and Masaccio were marvellous at getting things to *happen* in the foreground, 'here' as I call it.

His father was perplexed when the son, aged sixteen, announced that he wished to be an artist. He became the Slade's most distinguished student. For marriage, broken off twice (as with Kafka) he was 'morally unfit,' believing in polygamy.

He liked to walk on Hampstead Heath at fair-time and watch the roundabouts. Who else but Bosch has painted the face of God, a face one cannot even think of:

> I was thinking of how to paint God's face . . . I am very vague about it, but I think, perhaps, it's a face that has the same unanalysable expression that a flower has. His face should be a new and never-before-seen thing like a new and never-before-seen flower that is more convincing of its flower-likeness than a rose and with more sweet associations than there is in the scent of a rose.

Paul Nash's religious paintings and design tapestry look very secular by comparison. *The Resurrection* was bought for a cool £1000 by the Tate.

Giles de la Mare of Messrs. Faber adjudged that Spencer's writing, despite being so expressive in itself, often lacked continuity. Well, I could have done with more of it. It is at least more modest than the pontifications of the high and mighty Henry Moore.

The selection was made by Spencer's brother-in-law. An exhibition of paintings by Spencer and his wife is on view at the Anthony d'Offay Gallery off New Bond Street. His nudes are as scarifying as Lucien Freud's. Marriage with its periods of rapture conflicted with Spencer's creative aspirations, which made it difficult for the woman.

He suffered from quinsy and was operated on for gallstones during work on the great Burghclere altar paintings, not frescos but oil on canvas. On a double-page spread these are too reduced for my failing eyesight, though the less interesting *Paradise* from Slade School days is well reproduced. One would have preferred *John Donne Arriving in Heaven* rather than *The Mayor of Maidenhead Visits the Technical School*.

I saw the marvellous Spencer Retrospective at the Royal Academy, all those brown boilersuited workers beavering away in tubes and cylinders; it was a knock-out and I felt sorry that the artist himself wasn't present to marvel at it:

> 'They don't look like war pictures,' he wrote; 'they look rather like Heaven, a place I am becoming very familiar with.'

As Malherbe used to say, 'I have lived like everyone else, I want to die like everyone else, I want to go where everyone else goes.'

Hibernia, 18 May 1978

36

Outlandish Places

Bruce Chatwin, *The Viceroy of Ouidah* (Cape)

To travel afar is to rediscover the self, an active form of daydreaming. The English, often thought to be a stolid and unimaginative people (particularly by the Irish), were much given to it and became adepts. Raleigh sailed *twice* around the world after booty for his Queen; Captain Chichester in our day sailed a lonely course, possibly to get away from his wife. Mary Kingsley had travelled into West Africa, Gertrude Bell and Esther Stanhope into Arabia, Freya Stark into Persia, Lady Caroline Lamb into exotic foreign parts; and all had returned to tell the tale.

Lady Betjeman had been carried around Andalucia on muleback; as before her Kingslake and the Jewish Jesuit Palgrove had all gone 'into the light and dusk and hawks and dark and nothing,' as Chatwin elegantly phrased it.

These following in the steps of the late Victorians, Duncan and Forbes, Burton and Doughty; onwards to Graham Greene and Paul Theroux, the American become Londoner by adoption. The English habit of wandering through out-of-the-way places had produced its characteristic travel literature, often fresher than its fiction.

Following up the success of *In Patagonia*, Bruce Chatwin has turned his thwarted travels into the mad kingdom of Dahomey to good account, as pseudofiction, a purposeful dream of a slaver past; with results as felicitous as his first foray:

> Beware and take care
> Of the Bight of Benin.
> Of the one that comes out
> There are forty go in . . .

So runs the old slaver's rhyme. In the nineteenth century the Kingdom of Dahomey was a Black Sparta squeezed between the Yoruba tribes of present-day Nigeria and the Ewe tribes of Togo. The people called their Kings 'Dada,' which means 'father' in Fon; and the only source of income was the sale of their weaker neighbours. In 1977 it became the People's Republic of Benin, and the fetish priests had a new fetish—pictures of Lenin. Chatwin had returned there to collect material for a life of the white Brazilian slave-trader Francisco Felix de Souza, who had come to the coast in the early 1800s for the slaves who were sold as manpower into the mines and plantations of Brazil.

The manner of the telling, the rapidity and repeated shock of the imagery, suggests both Babel and Borges, no mean mentors. Writing of such pristine clarity, afrolic with life and irony, seldom comes our way and cannot fail to delight. Unknown terrain and people speaking in strange tongues, using unfamiliar customs, challenge boredom and bring us back to a better sense of ourselves. This can be interesting even when the talent to express it fully is wanting, as with (say) Rosita Forbes; not everybody can be Marco Polo, nor Beagelhole, nor Captain Joshua Slocum. But here is a great invigorating talent comparable to Freya Stark. Soon the magic names crop up: Pernambuco, Bahia, Tapuitapera. It only occupies six short chapters or 155 pages but seems much longer, so rich is its texture:

> He drifted round the City of All the Saints in a suicide's jacket of black velveteen bought off a tailor's dummy. Flapping laundry brushed against his face. Urchins kissed him on the lips as their fingers felt for his pockets. His feet slipped on rinds of rotting fruit, and puffy white clouds went sailing past the bell-towers. His principal amusement was to follow funeral processions. One day it would be a black catafalque casket for a stillborn child, or a grey corpse wrapped in a shroud of banana leaves.

It makes a pleasant change from the inly luminations of the old aunts who remained at home.

Hibernia, 18 January 1980

37

Loot

Richard David (ed.), *Hakluyt's Voyages: A Selection* (Chatto & Windus)

Piracy on the high seas had always appealed to the English. The first Elizabeth invested in the privateering sorties of Drake, the Earl of Cumberland and others. It was known diplomatically as 'purchase,' the acquiring of prizes on the high seas when broadsides or boarding had won the prey; later recorded in nearly two score volumes with matchless *elan* by Patrick O'Brian, the peerless armchair navigator, in his Aubrey-Maturin saga of the Napoleonic period.

The Elizabethan preacher and divine Richard Hakluyt, given the soft life that Church and titled patronage could confer, spent over forty years transcribing the ramblings of sailors and navigators. All that touched upon England's maritime expansion, that old rapaciousness, was grist to his mill: ships' logs, bills of lading, diaries and histories, lies and justifications—the traffic and discovery for as far back as memory and scholarship could reach.

Taking this mess and ordering it into the *Principal Navigations* of 1589 and 1598-1600, the industrious Hakluyt collected, copied, translated, edited or rewrote some two hundred narratives compromising about a million and a half words. He wrote as a Renaissance scholar, leisurely and copiously, in emulation of Ramusio, whose *Navigationi e viaggi* had appeared between 1550 and 1559. He wrote for the honour of England; he was the man for the job.

There are accounts of business and trade, the Muscovy Company in Russia and the Middle East, feats of navigation, tales of slave-running, attempts at colonisation, adventures in piracy, diplomatic episodes, admissions of fortune-seeking and an ordinary expectation of suffering. Add to this the flotsam of adventure; men strewn away into terrible circumstances. Add to this: observations on geography, anthropology, geology and climate, religion and government, custom and language, trade and general flora and fauna; long careful narratives artfully composed.

Despite all this variety and effort, Hakluyt perceived and brought out a unique evidence of integrated sensibility; the words are the expression of the man, they extenuate nothing; here is action made manifest and imprinted immediately, enduring as gravure, accurate as good film. We are on our way into the heart of things. But perhaps the book's lasting greatness lies in the all-pervading savour of heroism, the more remarkable for being largely unnoticed. When fully revealed, it is overwhelming. Hayes on the drowning of Sir Humphrey Gilbert; Hortop reckoning up the twenty-three years of his captivity—'Master, you see the wonderful extremity of our estate.' The whole of Hakluyt is an extraordinary gloss on that characteristic Elizabethan text, the lost art of cutting a dash.

'For conversion of particular greatness,' quoth Raleigh, 'there is nothing more noble and glorious than to have felt the force of every fortune.' The butcher of Smerwick and stout citizen of Cork had seen it all, put many a foe to the sword.

Meanwhile, in the Vatican, His Holiness was in a terrible wax and throwing the plate about, for much Vatican gold (one million crowns) had gone down with the Armada. The elements had always conspired against European Catholicism, the wind always blew against the Duke of Parma. Storms had dispersed the Spanish fleet onto the rough Irish coast and Master-Butcher Bingham dispatched 700 unfortunate Spaniards who had the misfortune to be marooned in Ulster.

In the drenched September of 1589 the Castilian Captain Cuellar cast adrift, had found himself wandering near Sligo and gave a harsh account of the 'savage Irish' at their pillaging and looting. For those luckless Spaniards washed up on Sligo beaches fared no better than their brothers slaughtered out of hand in Ulster.

To Captain Cuellar's eye, the girls were ravishing but unwashed and in rags. It had been a foul August; crows and wolves were devouring corpses around Sligo Bay in those hard times so ably chronicled here. The pages of Hakluyt are the most truthful and variable records in English of a time and a people long gone.

Review refused

38

By the Damascus Stream

Caroline Moorehead (ed.), *Over the Rim of the World: Selected Letters of Freya Stark*
(John Murray/Michael Russell)

Armed with compass and clinometer, aneroid, rangefinder and her own indomitable spirit, Freya Stark sets off into exotic lands. 'I wanted space, distance, history and danger; and I was interested in the living world'; she was keen as a needle:

> I do wish I could jump off from here into the middle of Arabia.
> It is good to be on the very edge: the desert has its extraordinary
> fascination, quite inexplicable—the emptiness and the buoyant air.

In Bagdad in 1932 when she started work on the *Bagdad Times* at the remuneration of £20 a month, the High Commissioner's wife pressed her hand, murmured 'So glad we are rescuing you from going native'; but Freya Stark had been going native all her life.

The spring of the Eastern enchantment was the acceptance of insecurity. Again the shocking roads, ancient paving slabs, a funeral tower on a hill, pine-scented air and Central Asia 'round the corner.' A lonely life and much ill-health, suffered stoically, had further sharpened perceptions already sharp; she was quick to detect humbug, had little sympathy with the seedy world of Graham Greene, the vanity of Dr. Axel Munthe. The past is alive and vivid to her always: the Graeco-Roman lost city of Side overgrown by bushes, bits of mosaic and marble showing, the harbour silted up, 'even the ruins are alive.' She seems permanently young in spirit.

> I sometimes feel that time is non-existent, that everything is now:
> such a strange feeling, climbing up the gorge with the rocks, the
> landscape, the difficulties, all there the same.

She explains to a Turkish taxi-driver the tactical moves of the battle of Sagalassos. She hits off a character in a swift line, a place in a rolling paragraph, the desert seen for the first time, the 'gigantic corridor of death' between Tobruk and Benghazi in April 1950 with the tanks and guns rotting away. There is about her own character more than a touch of Eastern fatalism, the acceptance of all things that live; she holds nothing back. What a novelist she would have made!

But the seventeen volumes of travel and the four great autobiographies are there, together with the eight-volume edition of letters published by Michael Russell.

'Sprung from an earlier generation, Dame Freya Stark has escaped the decay of literacy which has smitten the rest of us,' wrote Patrick Leigh Fermor in his suave Foreword. Well said, for there is something unusual in the lucidity of her uncluttered style, its smooth balance and even flow. 'In writing as in speech her sentences always fall on their feet with a light, spontaneous and unfaltering aptness.'

Appropriately enough she and Byron shared the same publisher, Jock Murray; a publisher not in the least miffed when asked to explain the slowness of his sliding scale.

She made marvellous capital out of a harassed time, like Theroux after her, showed a feminine weakness for hats and the old cod Bernard Bereson, worried about her appearance and weight, was the first woman outsider into Persia, went rafting up the Euphrates when already into her eighties.

There are extraordinary descriptions of London as a dead city on 2 September 1939, of Queen Mary at Houghton Hall, of Algiers in August 1943:

> But it was thrilling to fly over that long desert route of the Eighth Army, and look down and see the criss-cross patterns of the tanks for miles and miles, and the pitted bomb-holes thick as moon-craters, and see the long coastline and the black road with little slits for dugouts, and Benghazi a white blur of ruins against the sea. Then a great expanse of chessboard squares so beautifully planted, with their little rectangle of houses and court in the centre of each, where the colonies of Tripoli began. We looked down on the swamps of Ageila, oyster-coloured and puckered like the inside of a pearl shell; and then the huge salt swamps that close the Mareth line, like white veils drawn over the sands, and the ridge of Tunisia stepping up

behind; they seemed like the spikes of a huge fan held in the hands of death, so vast and bare.

Scene upon scene springs to life, the past is still vivid and alive for her; she sees Alexander the Great with white wings on his helmet crossing the stream before the battle of Issus, Darius and his army put to flight into the mountain passes. 'What a fine way to learn history!' And again:

> The sharp horizon of the sea, dark with the Aegean darkness where one *feels* the invisible light. It is the most exciting of all horizons, as if the whole intensity of life were there hidden; it makes one feel as if a Siren sang.

Opulence made her uneasy: she scribbled on the exalted notepaper at Petworth, 'Why the feeling of fundamental discomfort?' She rode a camel for nine hours a day over a six-day trek, loved the nomadic Bedouin, the wild folk of the barbarous fringe, read the *Iliad* in Turkish ('not a very useful language for every day, except in times of massacre'), accepted the whips and scorns as they came her way. In later life her appearance in a room caused a flutter.

No wonder. The little plain-faced girl lying on her stomach under a table, reading a book at Dronero, would grow up to be a marvel. At the age of ten she was reading Spenser and teaching herself Latin. The letters to her mother are most affecting; those to her publisher models of friendship and of censure, when required.

No moaning, no boasting; the Lourish women refused to believe that she was a woman. The creepy Elinor Glyn ('seventy-four, without a wrinkle, red hair, green velvet and pearls, lovely eyes heavily kohled) saw not a middle-aged woman but a young man pure and enthusiastic caged in a woman's body, using it gracefully but aloof inside it.

Male, female or sibyl, the teeming life of strange places gripped and held the imagination of Freya Stark, and this is one of the secrets of her power as a correspondent. She saw herself divided, as a man might perceive himself if he were Chateaubriand or Stendhal. Tourists are content to see places, the traveller wants *to be*; the world is divided into those who wish to be and those who wish to do:

> I think if one remains truthful in oneself, the truth in others comes

out, whether in society or desert; there is no particular adapted locality for it apart from one's own heart.

And not even God Almighty Himself would she ever let loose with a pair of scissors at one of her books; the only acceptable alternative being her old friend Sir Sydney Cockerell, at a pinch.

London Magazine, February/March 1989

39

Dark Rites

Ted Hughes, *Gaudete* (Faber & Faber)

The Reverend Nicholas Lumb walked hurriedly over the cobbles through the oppressive twilight of an empty town, in the North of England.

So it begins. Soon the streets are turned into mass-graves. Human figures are seen in a bright, shining and clear light; only their motives are dark and hidden. After Reverend Lumb's gross attentions, the women are in distress indoors.

A lynching posse armed with pitchforks and a twelve-bore rifle surrounds a lake in private parkland, a bull-farm in the north of England near an unnamed village eight miles from an unnamed city. It is the last week of May; under a red-plumed sky Major Hagen draws a bead of the head of the Reverend Lumb swimming away for dear life. By the time the .318 Mannlicher hunchbacked bullet has sunk among the lily-roots, two women have committed suicide for love of Reverend Lumb, one is pregnant by him, and at least two others in the family way; in the course of the day he has fornicated with nine in all, some unwed.

It's as weird as Faulkner's *Light in August*—the Percy Grimm, Rev. Hightower, Joe Christmas sequel, the automatic's magazine emptied into the shielding table, the castration with the butcher's knife. Somehow it holds together, although I do not claim to understand all of it.

An Anglican clergyman is abducted by evil spirits into the nether world; the spirits create a duplicate of him to take his place in this world, and to carry on his work. This changeling interprets the role of minister in his own way. The narrator recounts the final day and the events which led to his cancellation by the powers of both worlds. The original man reappears in this world, but changed.

Epigraphs from Heraclitus and Parsifal Book XV adumbrate the

Twin, the Other; the new Christianity, designed exclusively for women, goes up in the smoke of Lumb's pyre.

The description of bountiful nature, swarming around human vice and corruption, are extraordinary; the view of women no less so. The wren in *Macbeth* is mentioned *en passant*. It was once a projected movie scenario; some of the stills might have been rejected Bacon paintings—the Alsation dog in mid-air, the beating-up of Mrs. Evans, the felled poacher Garten.

The bald-headed and lecherous changeling does much in a day, aided and abetted by armed and desperate men. A white Ford Cortina carries Mrs. Westlake to her assignation; Dr. Westlake's grey Daimler arrives too late, as does Dunworth's white Jaguar. Betty the bar-girl arrives by bike at the quarry. All the females of the parish are corrupted.

> A new presence, like a press of wind, fills up the air, a thickening vibration. An echoing yawn of roar through all the mass of leaves. It pours down the sunken road. . . .

The original Reverend Lumb appears in the West of Ireland in an Epilogue, to summon an otter out of the sea and frighten three children, leaving behind a sodden notebook of densely corrected verse; the priest, trembling, transcribes this seemingly pantheistic poetry addressed to God. For Pauline Hagen:

> Rooms retreat.
> A march of right angles.
>   Barren perspectives
> Cluttered with artifacts, in
>   a cold shine.
> The rooms circle her slowly,
>   like a malevolence,
> She feels weirdly oppressed.
>   She remembers
> A shadow-cleft redstone
>   desert
> At evening.

Iceburgs of taste, spacing and repose.

Hibernia, 10 June 1977

40

Yangtze Bends

J. G. Ballard, *Empire of the Sun* (Gollancz)

Perhaps grown tired of the strictly ontological basis of SF urFiction with its dubious dicta that outer space can be equated to our inner world—your head it simply swirls—J. G. Ballard the ex-Leys man, has, in this his fifteenth title, turned resolutely back to nature, *human* nature that is, with a longish account of some most unsettling proceedings in and around Shanghai circa 1942-46 and young Jim's (presumably Ballard himself) internment in the Japanese internment camp at Lunghua; all seen through the eyes of our adolescent hero.

It reads grim as a fairy tale: innocence lost in the forest, the substitute home as trap and torture-chamber, lost parents become huntsmen and cruel stepmothers, the witch somewhere ahead, waiting: *Hansel und Grethel*. Or: Huck Finn and another Jim lost in a China fallen to the Japanese, the Mississippi become the Yangtze, with its funeral pyres on the Bund, the flower-laden coffins floating out to the estuary, where in due time the Japanese submarines will turn into American submarines, Pearl Harbour become Nagasaki, and the whole sorry business begin all over again—*Les Jeux Interdits*.

It makes for a most extraordinary read, the images tumbling over each other in an effort to say it all, tell the impossible. Peacetime in old Shanghai seems hardly less peaceful than Occupation, with public stranglings, the Graf Zeppelin Club thugs searching for Jews, bloody heads of communists (small c here) on pikes along the Bund, the threatening smell given off by all Japanese soldiers, and the impersonal way the bodies of the freshly slaughtered are viewed and accepted by our hero, who is after all only eleven years old.

One could carp and say that this stoicism is authentic, but not some adult sarcasms; the hand of the grown Ballard has waited forty-odd years to release upon us this Hound of Hell. Nor has his long apprenticeship in SF been entirely wasted; witness the slow apparition of a company of Japanese infantry in trenchworks outside the city, 'their heads barely visible among the nettles and wild sugar-cane,' reading letters and smoking, awaiting Pearl Harbour, already a day later in Shanghai as a result of time differences across the Pacific Date Line.

Ballard's father owned a cotton mill on the Poonung shore, worked by underpaid female coolies who ignored the son; the grand mansion on Amherest Avenue is run by nine servants, a White Russian governess, chauffeur and gardener. This empty mansion is the dark forest he re-enters: 'the air was stale with the smell of strange sweat,' intimations of rape, his mother's bare feet in spilled talc on the bedroom floor, goat-feet dancing with her.

The olfactory sense is very strong, the sense of threat and loss; as behoves a lad not only lost but closer to the ground than you or I. The English, whether as property-owners or prisoners, do not come out of it too well, now that the Latin primer is cast aside.

The 'threadbare ceremonies' accorded the 'pilots of the dusk'—young Kamikazes on suicide missions against American carriers in the East China Sea—have a special appeal for him, as most things to do with flying. The Mustang attack on the air-base, the Super-fortresses flying three miles above the Yangtze valley, the 'potent atmosphere' that hovered over the cockpit of the Japanese fighter sunk in weeks (adult version of Jim's model glider), the B-29s' blue and scarlet parachutes dropping K-rations, tins of Spam and *Reader's Digest* from the open bomb-doors—all this is rare.

The flash from Nagasaki is seen 400 miles away in Nantau Stadium, 'for a whole minute a white light covered Shanghai, and soon Kuomintang units are killing grounded airmen and ground-crews 'in batches.'

It has the remorseless nightmare quality of Joseph Roth's *Die Flucht ohne Ende,* the same harsh ethereal lighting; or, nearer home, Alan Burns's *Europe After the Rain,* which I take to be among the best war-novels to come from these shores. Grass has done it in German and Primo Levi in Italian. It runs straight on out of sight like an autobahn, as undeviating, as alarming.

To be born in a foreign place gives you a divided mind. Disgust with life is just as good a leaping-off place as any. Don't drink the waters off the funeral piers at Nantoe. (But it may be already too late.)

41

Dinner at Lipp's

David Gascoyne, *Paris Journal: 1937-1939* (Enitharmon)

It is not good for man to keep reminding himself that he is man, Cioran wrote in a fine cautionary prescript. 'To brood over oneself is bad enough; to brood over the species, with all the zeal of a fanatic, is worse still—it offers an objective basis, a philosophical alibi for the arbitrary woes of introspection.'

> 'The Chinese towns are blazing,' writes Gascoyne. 'Shanghai is being devastated; women wail among the Spanish ruins.'

This 'lost' diary of the English surreal poet David Gascoyne is an eerie enough compendium covering the period June 1937-October 1939 or from Gascoyne's twenty-first to twenty-third birthday. He had written no poetry since 'Elegiac Stanzas in Memory of Alban Berg' in the summer of 1936 and would write nothing again until 'Holderlin's Madness' in September 1937, while ambitious plans for two novels (*Son of Evening* and *The Anointed*) are considered and then—wisely—discarded. A precis of the latter, and title, reads alarmingly like one of Herr Stuart's early *Blut und Boden* redemption-through-suffering effusions; the arsy-varsy ecstatic reverie.

Paris, the lamp lit for lovers in the wood of the world, was never such an unsubstantial faery place. Melancholy sensitive chaps tend to get very tied up in themselves and dark introspective brooding laden with dire prognosis and hellish foreboding has ever been young men's staple ever since *The Sufferings of Young Werther* produced a veritable epidemic of suicides in the last quarter of the eighteenth century.

Czechoslovakia has just got it in the neck and soon it will be Poland's turn to suffer while the Führer looks triumphantly grim and Goebbels is grinning fit to burst; while Chamberlain and Daladier merely contrive to look sheepish.

In Gay Paree an extraordinary assembly of chinless wonders are on display, many of them reduced to initials. 'Roland much the same, *au fond*, but rather *adouci*.' Igor Stravinsky conducting is likened to a cross between the sinister dwarf headmaster in *Zero de Conduite* and a rat; Valéry is an old white horse. The predatory eye is ever on the alert, now admiring the awful paintings of Georges de la Tour, now the statuesque dead nudes of Ingres ('tortured, neurotic, exposed'); later he receives a curt letter from his publishers Cobden-Sanderson, announcing that *nothing* can be done about the financial situation and threatening legal proceedings if he changes publishers. I am only too familiar with that gritty tone.

He continues to dine and wine—dinner at the Select after tea at the Fiore followed by all-night carouses in Monmartre. The tone teeters between that of diarists Harold Nicolson and Denton Welsh. Many references to meals alternate with moaning and soul-searching. War-austerity sharpens the appetite of the English *haute bourgeois*; the whetted appetite an obscure form of profiteering.

In a 'wireless address' to the nation, Chamberlain speaks slowly in a sad and exhausted voice and the diarist's Jansenist inertia gives way to 'periodic spasms of furious lubricity.' Under analysis with Mme. Jouve, some curious facts come to light. A 'ridiculous *puder*' used to make the infant Gascoyne suppress his urine, and Harrow did nothing to improve matters, nor did Salisbury, where he is got up in an Eton suit and white frills.

But soon restraints are flung aside, amour is very much in the air as *pneus* fly, but Danish lover Bent departs in a huff for Copenhagen, Lee rebuffs him kindly and Desmond Ryan invites him for a dirty week in Monte Carlo.

For the happier time in these fairly miserable two years there is no record, as is the way with happy times, with Denham and Edward in the Alps. Back in the Rue de Bac, Gertrude Stein holds the floor, by spouting on about the human race, intimidating the Spenders. Auden sits with his back to a café window, silent for a change. In Laurence Vail's place at Megeve, Djuna Barnes is being bitchy about Jane Austen; Anne Goossens gets Gascoyne into trouble with some likely lad.

The *italicising* is copious. He keeps encountering Tristan Tzara in Montparnasse, arguing that Christianity owes its success thanks to its conception of justice, before handing out leaflets announcing his new poems.

The diary is less successful in invoking France than Connolly's *The Unquiet Grave*, or the same author's *England Not My England*, written in 1927-28 when Connolly was slightly older than Gascoyne; certainly there is a lack of humour. *Au fond,* one has need of a little more *sang-froid*. And what of the German girl whom Gascoyne was supposed to marry, and who wrote to him so decently?

Here and there the poet whom Coleridge would perhaps have understood emerges in descriptions of mood and place:

> There seems to have been certain evenings in those days, in Spring, when I was prey to a particular kind of excitement that I would give much to recapture now . . . The sky was the colour of warm lead, yet the atmosphere was full of a latent silver-greenish light; it was as though it were about to snow. The shadows in doorways, the empty spaces of open windows, took on their greatest power of suggestiveness. An imperceptible smell of sulphur [hung] in the air.
>
> April 1938

Hibernia, August 1978

42

Soldiers' Pay

Alan Burns, *The Day Daddy Died* (Allison & Busby)

His work does not fall neatly into any known English category, and co-experimentalists lag far behind. The late B. S. Johnson and the late Ann Quin from the Calder stables, the still active Ballard and Moorcock, Ian McEwan, an admirer of Burns. Greene's earlier entertainment *It's a Battlefield*, Orwell's *1984* and Berger's *Pig Earth* have some of the qualities of tough surface tension that mark Alan Burns's work.

'It was called the system: each one's terror gave the system weight.' The American writer John Hawkes wrote in this vein. 'A huge weight of rain drove like iron across the park.' Brother Bryan Graveson is one of the walking wounded from the British Army of malarial India. Narrator Officer Graveson (Dan) is cashiered for incitement to mutiny, unwisely offering Marxist arguments at gunnery practice.

This is Alan Burns's seventh novel, resuming where *Celebrations* (1967) left off; for *Babel*, as *Dreamamerika* and *The Angry Brigade* must be counted as duds when compared to what had preceded them: the novella *Buster* (1961) and the novel *Europe After the Rain* (1965). His is an aphoristic style of writing, following in the footsteps of Lettau, Mallea, de Lautreamont; a style which is sometimes inclined to run away with him. What is going on in our minds has always been and always will be a product of society, wrote Marx. Hence, presumably, brothels.

Buster was an unconventional novella about an Army family, a narrator fallen into much reduced circumstances. *Europe After the Rain* dealt with a totalitarian regime and its harshness and the difficulty of any kind of normal life under such a system.

Celebrations was about the factory belt, seen from the point of view of the owner Williams. I have myself worked in factories around Ealing and this one is the cream of them all:

An idiot child was born with too many toes. The new factory measured seven miles from east to west, three from north to south. . . . Six hundred workers killed each year represents a statistical average of nought point four.

Towards the end Williams and his son Philip are dead, the personnel in bad shape. 'Machines cannot be developed in a year. All you need is common sense, in triplicate.'

This short novel is about the shifts widow Norah Welch must make to live, strangely attracted to army sergeants; with three kids in care, one in clink:

> When she had the baby, the nurse asked, what will you call him?
> Norah did not know, she had not thought about it.
> The nurse said, 'Call him Eugene Andrew.'
> Norah said, 'All right.'
> 'And now let me show you your baby.'
> The gruesome plump thick pink boy was pushed across the bed.
> In a white room crowded with babies the young woman concealed her child, she was trying not to be noticed. She kept turning, she had burned its lower lip, you could smell the flesh.

A parcel of grotesques infest these hundred or so pages: Mr. Adams the Probation Officer, the sinister Dr. Peck, the scarcely female Major Brocklebank of the Salvation Army, charge-hand Jordan of Gateshead. Here lies the true England of high-rise apartments in the sky, the disgruntled young running wild, ECT and phenobarbs, EXIT, the desperate roisterers Rita, Lil, Shirley, Peter and Betty, Gino and Anne, a motley crew. 'It starts as self-love, not self-hate. It turns to hate because you can't bear what you're doing.' Where have I heard this acerbic tone before? Dostoevesky's notebooks?

> Arthur did not speak for a month. He would work for a time and then stop, his face go rigid, and his hands. Two minutes later he'd be working again. When he started speaking again he said he was a friend of Henry Ford.

This brief book, brilliant and disturbing, a very accurate commentary on the England of today, is his best to date, linking back to *Buster* of 1961. The collages are a mistake.

At the end the Welch family have grown up, own an old house 'with character' in South Norwood. It's already in need of repairs, but they are all off for a holiday in Corfu.

The Irish Times

43

The Vapours

Val Warner (ed.), introduction to *Charlotte Mew: Collected Poems and Prose*
(Carcanet & Virago Press)

Charlotte Mew (1869-1928) was the third child of Frederick Mew, son of an Isle of Wight farmer. Insanity ran in the family like the streak through Brighton Rock candy. A brother and sister both became insane in later life; the recurring curse of madness was 'the incarnate wages of man's sin.' Her temper was naturally keyed very low; denial and renunciation featured predominantly in her work, passionate encounters produced yearnings, always negated, often quite arbitrarily. She and her sister would never marry, for fear of passing on the terrible taint.

She admired Mr. Browning. Her first work was published in *The Yellow Book* in 1894; a year later the Wilde case closed the magazine. In London the family fortunes declined. She took her own life (with lysol) in 1928, aged fifty-one. Her friend Alida Monroe knew of stacks of MSS salted away in trunks; but after her death very little was found. Pound is credited with liking her poetry, but this I find hard to believe:

> Oh! Christ who never
> knew
> The poisonous fangs that
> bite us through
> And make us do the things
> we do . . .

She was no Emily Dickinson. She admired Emily Brontë and Christina Rossetti: the love-songs of women who have never loved or been loved. Her nature was solitary. Her fiction does not please by astonishing, as does the work of, say, Sylvia Townsend Warner, some of Dorothy Richardson, parts of Virginia Woolf.

In the introduction, Val Warner refers to that craving for religion which so often went hand-in-hand with inversion. 'The half-clad girl of the wretched picture-shop came into view with waxen hands and senseless symbolism.' The thoroughly run-down Victorian woman suffers from the vapours, the fashionable curse of 'nerves,' is disturbed and upset . . . '*unstrung*.' Servants are much taken for granted. Carnations that bloom in the garden of the Sisters of Our Lady of Compassion are, *par excellence*, the flowers of seduction and desire. Diffident gentlemen speak haltingly to ladies, others made their address with 'retarded' speech, gloves removed.

The plotting, such as it is, smacks more of P.C. Wren (*Beau Geste*) than Henry James. Titled ladies figure. Mildred Playfair 'crossed the room and threw herself upon him.' ('I . . . cannot and I will not let you go.') Monsieur Vidal is after Mademoiselle Anita, but in the nicest possible way. French expressions fly freely. *Véritablement? L'amour est la passion cruelle qui désole et qui trahit—Voyons!*

Siegfried Sassoon came to tea. But in a later lodging the two Mew sisters would not invite guests; no one could possibly be asked to visit.

Hardy liked her stuff, as did Walpole and Bridges. May Sinclair helped to bring it to the attention of Edward Garnett. She carried on a friendship and correspondence with Sidney Cockerell. The sub-Jamesean parenthesis pile up: 'I too believe, I hoped he might have something to tell me, be able to throw some light upon the edges of the cloud by which, in thought, we were both still, for me, overwhelmed.'

Sunday Tribune, 28 February 1982

44

Dry Thoughts in a Dry Season

Gerald Brenan, *Thoughts in a Dry Season: A Miscellany*
(Cambridge University Press)

Gerald Brenan is older than the century upon which he sits. He lives in a house that Borrow would have liked, closed in on three sides, with a bamboo plantation, in Churriana, which is situated in the hills behind Malaga, where he is sometimes to be seen, carrying a shopping-bag by the bus-terminus. He wrote *South from Granada*, had the rare honour of being elected mayor of his village, speaks a Spanish as polished as silverware; and contrived to offend the touchy Arland Ussher, *twice*, inadvertently. The insult was duly recorded in the latter's *Spanish Mercy*.

It is not easy to make generalisations about the Spanish; Unamuno could only manage it by imagining he was studying Cervantes. Like Brenan writing about love, which is mostly about jealousy. Ussher in *his* travel book was merely travelling through a Spanish part of his own brain. The equally touchy Brenan declined to be considered an Irishman.

The Miscellany before us is considerably reduced, and, to judge from the date on the foreword, has come very slowly off the presses. Nevertheless it was well worth waiting for, if you like well-bred Commonplace books, with here a *soupçon* of acid, there a drop of vinegar. The sprightly octogenarian, photographed on the cover in the company of a dove, has given us a book that his dead friend Cyril Connolly would have been proud of; its style is not too dissimilar:

> One winter evening Sir Leo Chiozza Money, a public figure of the twenties, was discovered by the police in a compromising situation with a prostitute in Hyde Park. He was arrested and charged with indecency in public. Winston Churchill's comment was: '*Five* degrees of frost! *Seventy* years of age! It makes me proud to be an Englishman.'

He has learnt to love England by living out of it; which is perhaps the only possible way to even like it. Contemporary Britain would distress him greatly. The fourteen sections of the book—People, Nature, Introspection—do, as anticipated, vary in interest. On Nature he reminds me of Kilvert, who on principle always expected the miraculous and was generally not disappointed, in a rustic land of hot mince pies and frozen skies. He is very good on the big freeze-up of January 1940; cycling over from Aldbourne to Maiden Court for tea and supper with V. S. and Dorothy Pritchett:

> The snow flew out, carried by a violent wind. It was a pretty sight as the little village with its railway station, canal and church, like one of those model villages from which one learns German in a school reading book, was suddenly covered by a slanting fall of snow.

Nature and life are better models than the library and the card-index system; without straining for profundities, he is all the time making revelations:

> The charm of the English countryside with its fields and hedges lies in the rediscovery of things known long ago and familiar since childhood. That of foreign countries lies in their unfamiliarity.

What comes across most of all is the curiosity of the Englishman. On marriage and insects he is equally sound. The motorways are exterminating the hedgerows and the songbirds:

> Great Pan is dead. The nymphs of the woods and the streams have departed and the electric generators have taken their place. But some of our psychic roots, which attached us to life, have gone with them and so we say, as none of our ancestors would have said, that life is pointless and absurd.

The shabbily dressed fugitive in the jacket photograph seems in a hurry; but how sound he is on the bee-eater, the snail, the cuckoo, the whale, the wonders of evolution, our lost heritage; sound as a bell. He likens the Australian bulldog ant (which seems to have fighting and killing its genes; if one of these species be cut in half, a battle ensues between head and tail, the head seizing the tail with its teeth and the tail defending itself by stinging the head, and the battle continuing until they both die or are dragged apart by other ants) to Ulster.

He is alive to deficiencies in the poet Spenser, no friend to Ireland, who wrote *The Faerie Queen* but couldn't think; alert to hash-taking (one cannot think straight when under the influence), or the beauty of Brunelleschi's vast dome in Florence; and if he is dull on religion, one must concede that it is difficult to be amusing on the subject, unless one is Michaux and the religion Eastern.

Francis Wyndham discovered Jean Rhys some years ago; now Senor Brenan puts in a claim for Dorothy Edwards, a Welsh schoolmistress who could speak a number of languages and published a collection of short stories and a novel in the late 1920s before committing suicide in 1931. Edward Garnett wrote of her in the third volume of his autobiography.

Delighted to meet at last with someone who considers that Henry James had shot his bolt around 1899 and that *The Ambassadors*, *The Wings of the Dove* and *The Golden Bowl* show a loosening of grip. But it is surely wrong to suggest that Virginia Woolf's manner of writing leads inevitably 'to a loss of that expectation as to what is going to happen next that is the backbone of all fiction and gives it its tension'? The shawl that shifts a fraction of an inch in the empty room in *The Waves* is more dramatic than the spectacle of Anna Karenina ascending a long flight of stairs at Count Tolstoy's behest.

Pick a page at random: 'I dreamed that I was a hare leaping through a dark forest. Following a narrow path I came to the edge of the trees and saw the stars showing through a rift in the clouds. I saw one particular constellation, then raced back under the trees.' His totem animal is the hare ('I too lived by flight and escape'). In the foreword he writes:

> The general cast of my mind inclines me to a moderate scepticism, hostile to cant and dogmatism, and to believing that whatever opinions we have should be held with humility. For this reason I make no claim to truth or justice for any of these little pieces, however dogmatic their tone may appear to be. Let the reader take them as he wishes.

Hibernia, 17 January 1980

45

Twilight in the *Saal*

Dorothy M. Richardson, *Pilgrimage*, 4 vols. (Virago Modern Classics)
vol. 1: *Pointed Roofs, Backwater, Honeycomb*
vol. 2: *The Tunnel, Interim*
vol. 3: *Deadlock, Revolving Lights, The Trap*
vol. 4: *Oberland, Dawn's Left Hand, Clear Horizon, Dimple Hill, March Moonlight*

How is it that women writers can describe light so well, from Djuna Barnes's sinister *Berlinerzimmers,* and *Allees* that are seen as not end-less but already doomed; to the Kenyan uplands in Baroness Blixen's *Out of Africa*; the Italian Alps in Freya Stark's *Traveller's Prelude*, or the eerie diurnal and nocturnal atmospherics encountered in the works of Sylvia Townsend Warner—all ring true (even if one has never been there: I mean inside a woman's head) and of their time, all troubled and mysterious?

To those must now be added one who was perhaps the oddest of them all: Mrs. R.M. Odle who wrote under her maiden name of Dorothy M. Richardson, first practitioner of the stream-of-consciousness in English.

Her interiors (the stuffy train carriage approaching the Swiss Border in *Oberland*; the *saal* where Emma Bergmann plays a Chopin Nocturne in *Pointed Roofs*, the ski-slopes and Max Ernst moons) are as fixed and mysterious as those of Vermeer, the painter *par excellence* of Time arrested, the flux controlled, duration tamed.

Trapped like fish in a now brightly illuminated and then obscured aquarium tank, as the light dies, the dead ones move, speak again, must suffer still.

Confronted with this formidable expressive power, backed by obser-vation that is, to say the least of it, unflinching, Sybil Bedford seems to weaken and Kay Boyle becomes specious, coyly bogus. There is no self-pity on display or the High Rancour (or Higher Silliness) displayed by Radclyffe Hall, and the waspish humour stings.

What was not intended as high farce but became so (*The Well of Loneliness*), or *petit-point*, became penitential as oakum-picking in the unremitting labours of Ivy Compton-Burnett, becomes in these 2,000 odd, and odd they certainly are, onward-flowing pages, a rich tapestry of authentic fancy-work

The first volume is slow to catch fire, which it does without any warning twenty-five pages in, during the *Vorspielen* in the Waldstrasse *saal*, presided over by Fraulein Pfaff. A girl pianist has

> high square shoulders and high square hips—her brow was low and her face thin, broad and flat. Her eyes were like the eyes of a dog and her thin-lipped mouth long and straight until it went steadily down at the corners.

The affection displayed for Germany and all things German (Schumann) cannot have gone down too well with English critics when the first volume of thirteen appeared in 1915 with a description of a girls' finishing school for the daughters of gentlemen in Hanover in 1890.

To dive into it, as one is compelled to do, gives a wonderful liberating lift to the spirit, a sense of going forward and forward through space and time.

Her father despised the grocery trade which had given him his money, went bankrupt, wanted to be a late Victorian gent, bought a house in Barnes, another in Finsbury Park, made unwise speculations, lost all his money again.

His wife committed suicide with a carving knife while on holiday with daughter Dorothy at Hastings; hardly surprisingly, Dorothy is dead against refinement, Dad is called Pater, the air she can hardly breathe is thickly late Victorian, gassy and close, stuffy.

Pater dislikes newfangled music (Grieg) and the politics of Mr. Gladstone. Unspeakable family friends watch the talented daughter suffer at the piano, the Pooles and the Radnors politely applaud—'poor cold English things.' No wonder she has a passion for fresh air. 'Nice,' correctly spoken, is a convulsion of the lower face, like a dog snapping at a gnat.

She is in the tradition of the Brontës, compulsive chroniclers of an English disease not yet diagnosed. Too removed from the hurly-burly of life and its rough passages-of-arms, Virginia Woolf's inner illuminations seem, in comparison, to be merely states of neurosis, weak wattage, approaching the unhinged; while the unremitting labours of Henry James, the Londoner by proxy, with overtones of camphor balls and port, became an interminable parenthesis with little joy—'the ultimate male destiny backed by means and position'—in short, the hard unreality of things deliberately arranged.

Few novels seem to be written with all five senses engaged, as these; the search is for 'being in an eternal way of living.' The skaters on the tree-lined rink 'cooped upon their sunken enclosure,' go gliding 'as if for ever,' recalling, in its mood of celebration and pure snow-filled joy, Mr. Pickwick on the ice, or Lemuel Sears ('an old man not yet infirm') skating on Beasley's Pond in John Cheever's *Oh What a Paradise It Seems*.

The scene that 'clamoured now to be communicated in its first freshness' (*Oberland*) takes off where Edith Wharton's *Ethan Frome* hardly began. Vereker is twice referred to as the 'hostess.' Who was Lycurgus? 'The one who would make others aware of worlds outside their own.'

She was educated at Southborough House, studied French and German, logic and psychology under a headmistress who was a disciple of Ruskin; and was a friend of H.G. Wells. What did Wells say to Dorothy Richardson on the subject of golf? (His father had once played a game of fives with Nabokov's father.) And what did he think of her novels, supposing he read them?

The movement is into strangeness, the being off the chain of accustomed things, the misery of social occasions. The impulse is towards 'all things whose being was complete, towards that reality of life that withdraws at the sounding of a human voice.'

The red-hot mass of fire and the bottle of green Chartreuse warming by the fireside on the blue and cream tiles points towards Proust.

Hibernia, 10 January 1980

46

Sappho & Co.

Radclyffe Hall, *The Well of Loneliness* (Barrie & Jenkins)

The plot might have been lifted from Freudian case-histories or a bad biography of the Gordons of Gight. The English abroad, egad; the Annals of the Odd!

Here again the appalled reader encounters the 'manly ease' of boyish women beloved of Colette; perverted fussing, the bright flush of satiety. With its high devotion to gallant gestures, this old shocker—first published by Cape in 1928—rivals *Beau Geste* in unintended foolishness; drama recycled as bathos.

It has been reprinted ever since, rolling in like a dense Scottish mist, and is now numbered among modern feminist classics with the Virago imprint. My mother, a voracious reader, would refer to it with a certain awe, for it was said to be *shockingly* frank.

Dedicated to OUR THREE SELVES, the narrative winds its way as convoluted as the wayward female heart itself. At Morton Hall, country seat of the Gordons of Bramley, to Lady Anna and Sir Philip ('a tall man and exceedingly well-favoured') is born 'a narrow-hipped, wide-shouldered little tadpole of a baby, that yelled and yelled for three hours without ceasing.' Enter our heroine, on Christmas Eve, christened Mary Olivia Gertrude but answering to Stephen.

At seventeen Stephen is as tall as her own father, which causes flutters of doubt in her bosom: 'Am I queer looking or not?' Sandowing exercises follow with ex-Sergeant Smylie, in order to fight duels for wives in distress. This tall social misfit rides *astride* and soon the spring meets are heavy with tacit disapproval. What *can* one do?

A deuced odd account of a fox-hunt followed by conversation with 'Raftery,' her thoroughbred Irish racer, in the stable. Sir Philip is soon dispatched by a providentially falling branch in a February snowstorm. On meeting Angela Crosby of The Grange (American, reputed to be low

Music Hall and fearfully pushy), the wife of a Birmingham magnate, Stephen orders *three* suits at Malvern, with grey matching neckties, and the local yokels are agog. 'Hats would be lifted with obvious respect, while a humble finger might fly to the forelock.'

Lesbian love is associated with the odour of slightly damp logs mixed with dry ashes and a caged bullfinch warbling 'O Tannenbaum,' 'Dangerous yet bloodless' loving ensues and a precious pearl purchased in Bond Street; between the love-lorn pair no vestige of shyness ('I feel as though I've known you for ages'). Gardeners and grooms ('men smelling of soil') wait in the wings to convey messages (''e be trusty, that's what 'e be'), with intimations of love and oneness with the earth, cementing the twain.

And quite soon they are kissing like mad in a big limousine parked in the Malvern Hills and absent husband Ralph (the rich Birmingham magnate) dismissed as 'a nagging mean-minded cur.'

Be it said that males throughout the 447-page romp are likened to our canine friends and the dogs themselves given apt male names, Tony and David, the former a trusted go-between. All the men are dogs in disguise, dumbly serving their tempestuous mistresses. Stark naked confessions are wrung from lips that 'grew white while they confessed.'

Another buying spree in the West End follows and the purchase of a 'goodly assortment' of Crepe de Chine pyjamas and heavy silk masculine underwear. Comes the Great War, with inverts born in increasing numbers, and our heroine is beautifully scarred on the face. But before you can whisper Pierre Louys, Book Four is upon us: Paris, London, Comptessa de Mirac, love for Mary Llewellyn and a villa in Ortava, tinted lemon yellow, where ragged fellows play deftly on their guitars. In the distance a rugged line of mountains, er, loom.

Radclyffe Hall was as snobbish as Maugham or Vicki Baum, greedy for the good things of life, full of the bigotry that comes with acquired wealth and the pleasures of bossing inferiors about, with its attendant cruelty, the abrupt sacking of the long-serving, aptly named Puddle.

Horse-imagery is prevalent throughout, as in the early stories of Djuna Barnes. The style gallops, to accommodate all that must be said, all that cannot be said, the heroics and the female gallantry. Rockets of pain; *burning* rockets. No bond more binding than that of affliction. The bally thing beggars description, blundering along.

Hibernia, 24 January 1980

47

That Swine Hardcastle

Sapper, *Bulldog Drummond* (Everyman Classics Thrillers)
Sapper, *The Black Gang* (Everyman Classics Thrillers)
Sapper, *The Third Round* (Everyman Classics Thrillers)
Sapper, *The Final Count* (Everyman Classics Thrillers)
Sapper, *The Female of the Species* (Everyman Classics Thrillers)
Sapper, *The Return of Bulldog Drummond* (Everyman Classics Thrillers)

The xenophobe is there certainly; with more than a hint of the anti-semite. Mosley and his Blue Shirts have joined the SAS. All foreigners are suspect, potential bounders.

In Germany, Hitler is about to get his leg over; and of course, Chamberlain soon at a loss, for he is *not* dealing with a gentleman.

Was Captain Drummond himself a true blue squire? A rereading of these schoolboy yarns suggests the contrary. Beefiness turns abject before fragility and the gallant manner ('Sweet maiden, bring us mugs of port, I pray thee!' Try this approach down at The Pig and Whistle) is only a cover for masculine embarrassment, for hearties are always uncomfortable in the presence of the fair sex. Bulldog starts jibbering when vamped by Comtessa Bartelozzi ('beetling up' on the Plymouth train to be confronted by Irma Peterson herself, waiting in a chauffeured limousine at Paddington), who has already ruined poor young Bob Marton, the solicitor. Bulldog admits to belonging to various London Clubs, and indeed 'has consumed innumerable kippers' in select nightspots about the West End, and will soon be dining (caviar and Clicquot, three foxtrots, God knows how many fags) with this man-eater in the Custard Pot in seedy Wardour Street. The backless black evening dress did it:

'My dear Comtessa,' he murmured, bending over her hand, 'forgive my British bluntness, but you are superb.'
'British bluntness, *mon ami*,' she answered with a dazzling smile, 'is often preferred to Continental diplomacy.'

The Bulldog Breed always believed in straight dealing from the shoulder, preferably, with 'gloves off,' as Drummond put it. The tracking down, unmasking and ritual humiliation of creepy foreigners is a variant or extension of good old British blood sports; the cruel, gentlemanly code. Remember too that capital punishment is still in operation and felons topped early in the morning behind high English prison walls. Legal quibbles will be 'thrashed out' in court; some shivering Semitics thrashed to within an inch of their lives. Captain Drummond's unflappable sporty types are racists to a man.

A strain of misogyny persists through all five volumes and was continued by his friend Gerald Fairlie in seven follow-on volumes after the early demise of the Master.

Sapper was obsessed with secret underground passages. The walls grind together, drippingly propelled by remote hydraulic machinery, and Drummond flees for his life, in a way that would have alerted Dr. Freud.

The underlying assumption is that untrustworthiness is common to Dago, Wog and Frog, who are more or less described in these terms. Faced with ingrained shiftiness, and the females worse than the males, Drummond and his gang go into action, as arch-fiend Carl Peterson plans to poison London by dropping a semen-like substance from a dirigible, egged on by Irma.

Were the famous playing-fields, the straight bat, the stiff upper lip, the mud of the Eton wallgame, the ritual fagging and flogging in public schools so repugnant to Shelley, but a steadying preparation for the Officers' Training Corps, the elite regiment, campaign medals, a closing of ranks (the thin red line)? British class prejudice in all its forms, 'good' form, is rampant.

'A set of good clean fellows, playing the game' might just answer, so thought Townsend Warner, the master of Harrow. Playing *their* game with the stiffest of upper lips at OTC training, in *esprit de corps,* true Blues for every social occasion. 'A faint smile twitched round Drummond's lips, but his face was in the shadow.'

'Middle stump gone west,' Drummond murmurs, quite forgetting that foreign *canaille* were ignorant of the national game. The foreigner in evening clothes who raises aloft a soft black hat to Drummond in South Audley Street ('A thousand apologies, Sir!'), asking the way, turns out to be Benito Gardini the two-faced Italian secretary to the renowned financier Sir Edward Greatorex—'there flashed over his face a look of such diabolical hatred as only a Southerner can give.' And soon Peruvian Eagles are plummeting. Yankees fare no better, Hardcastle the movie mogul is dismissed as 'a swine.'

Born Herman Cyril McNeill in 1888 at the navy prison at Bodmin, Cornwall, where his father was Governor, 'Sapper' was educated at Cheltenham College and the Royal Military Academy at Woolwich. He served in the Royal Engineers (the 'sappers') 1907-19, saw active service, finishing as Lt. Col. H. C. McNeile, MC. His Bulldog Drummond books must have struck a chord, for they enjoyed enormous success in their day.

As ignorant lads growing up in the Irish countryside, my younger brother and I read them voraciously; for they offered us a most exciting and exotic England. In *The Return of Bulldog Drummond* (1932) the action begins on Dartmoor in a thick fog. Phyllis Drummond ('white clean through'), the Captain's better half, is absent in America. The staff had barricaded itself in the pantry and turned on the gramophone. Drummond owns cook, butler, chauffeur, presumably a gardener, and runs a Bentley. We surprise him enjoying a postprandial nap, snoring his head off ('something majestic about the mighty cadence'), when a shot rings out. Hands thrust deep in trouser pockets, Drummond strolls to the window (Hammond at slip, changing ends):

> Suddenly his eyes narrowed: the figure of a man running at top speed came looming out of the fog. He raced towards the house, and on his face was a look of abject terror.

Haughty male voices giving orders resound through these pages ('Get Mr. Darrell's kit out of the car, Jennings, and tell Parker to put her away') and the effortless superiority of the English gentleman was never so evident; the inbred decency of the Anglo-Saxon brute, the bully in John Bull. But what (in heaven's name) is a Bronx, the cocktail ordered up by Drummond from barman Charlie at the Ritz Carlton?*

Servants at the end of every bell-pull and below them again the 'men of low mentality'—the criminal classes. A vast public mourned his death in 1937 at the early age of forty-eight.

London Magazine, October/November 1989

---

*A Bronx: 2 parts dry gin to one part of French and Italian vermouth. Squeeze in orange juice, shake a cocktail shaker, and strain into glasses. Delicious. Recipe from *London Magazine* reader John Whitehead.

48

Down There in Bohemia

Jean Rhys, *Tigers Are Better-Looking* (Deutsch)
Christina Stead, *The Puzzleheaded Girl* (Secker & Warburg)

The melancholy emanating from these seventeen stories by the author of *Wide Sargasso Sea* is pervasive; a melancholy distilled by time. The mood pervading throughout is one of feminine low spirits, a depression unsustained by too much verbal energy.

The earlier stories appeared in a collection entitled *The Left Bank*, under the aegis of Ford Madox Ford, who supplied a long and adulatory preface. It was published in 1927 by Cape, the year they brought out Hemingway's first and best novel, *Fiesta*.

The later stories were highly praised by the critic Francis Wyndham, who had rediscovered her, appearing in *London Magazine* and *Art & Literature* between 1960 and 1966. The period jargon is evocative as an old familiar tune; 'ruddy,' 'you mutt,' 'old cock' as terms of endearment. The longest and best story is 'Vienne.' 'Ugly humanity, I've always thought.' Some of the stories seem ill-conceived in plot and slipshod in their exposition—'The Lotus,' 'La Grosse Fifi,' 'Again the Antilles.' Some ('Till September Petronella') verge on bathos; others ('From a French Prison,' 'Tea With the Artist') plunge resolutely into it.

Milieu: Paris and London in the 1920s.

Subject-matter: Female misery.

Genteel poverty has perhaps induced the melancholy *ennui* in the metropolitan bed-sitters around Paris and London. In Gay Paree Djuna Barnes and Janet Flanner reign as Queens of the American colony; Mary Reynolds is in love with Laurence Vail and the scaffolding is already going up on *Finnegans Wake*.

The Left Bank (subtitled 'Sketches and Studies of Present-Day Bohemian Paris') preceded Beckett's *More Pricks than Kicks* of 1934 by a decade. The writing, so sure and serene in *Wide Sargasso Sea*, here hardly rises to the level of a good Graham Greene 'entertainment' (*It's a Battlefield*), devoid of the latter's clandestine stealth and epigrammatic bitterness, although it does contrive to sound an authentic note here and there: Euston Road and Camden Town like a grey nightmare in the sun.

Championed by Wyndham, two of the earlier novels have been reprinted by Deutsch: *Voyage in the Dark* (1934) and *Good Morning, Midnight* (1939). When *Postures* (1928) and *After Leaving Mr. McKenzie* (1937) reappear, her *oeuvre* will be complete.

Rhys's publishing history calls to mind that of Djuna Barnes whose first stories appeared about the same time, also under the aegis of the tireless Ford. The best moment to strike a note nearer home—the Caribbean, 'the deepest, the loveliest in the world,' hinting to the powers ahead. The war has ended, the melody lingers on: *La Paloma, La Reve Passe*.

Christina Stead is Australian. *Cotter's England* and *The Man Who Loved Children* and seven other novels are unknown to me.

The setting of these quartet of novellas is New York, Paris and Delaware; the depth and width of the lode not at first apparent. Much bile is in evidence, even for a woman. A disastrous weekend in Chartres and the demise of the Imber brother, vain of his strength, poisoned by ivy, produces memorable moments in *The Right-Angled Creek*. The torrential talker George Paul is not easily forgotten; the Delaware incident is as dense and farcical as Faulkner's story of artists rusticating.

The shrew Lydia, with her back-rash and ludicrous mother, comes from the women's glossies and retreats back into them. It's Paris in the fidgety 50s, UNESCO and the GI Bill of Rights; American girls with slippery smiles sit around in the Dome:

> The spirit languishes in a dress of rags.
> The wayward heart of woman that doesn't want to be caught
> and hasn't been caught.
> Love, I spit it out . . . I spit it out.

Hibernia, 6 September 1975

49

Non-Lives

Beryl Bainbridge, *A Quiet Life* (Duckworth)
Elizabeth Taylor, *Blaming* (Chatto & Windus)
R. C. Hutchinson, *Rising* (Michael Joseph)

'A blithering Jerry down on the shore,' barbed wire across the wet sand, Nissen huts, unexploded Luftwaffe bombs, valved wireless sets, night carts, rifle range, sodium lights above the roundabout, all are authentic parts of the shabbiness of England just after the war, in the new Beryl Bainbridge.

How pleasant to read, for a change, authentic dialogue; how pleasant not to be preached at. The action occurs just after the war; sited between the Wirrel and Lytham St. Anne's, that coast and those towns are sharply evoked—the disused lighthouse on the estuary, the damaged statues 'tilting on cracked and monumental pedestals in the square,' Queen Victoria on a chair of stone; the Mersey estuary and the 'demolished city.'

A marriage between an unsuited couple goes steadily wrong; 'the wounded beast in the dark scullery' (husband and father) likes to bandage his estranged family, give kaolin poultices, listen to the Third Programme. The stench of tom-cats issues from the mouth of the air-raid shelter. The prescriptions here are all cautious, admonitory—'Don't talk soft, woman.' 'Behave yourself!' 'Pull yourself together.'

'A flash of electric blue came, from the railway crossing as the Southport train sparked on the frozen rails.' The ending comes too pat and precipitate for my taste: the cutting down of the sycamore tree, the father's fatal stroke, the abandoned sister weeping for her lost POW; too predictable in a way the rest is singularly not; as though the author, now thrice in the running for the Booker Prize, wished to hasten to a close. The ear for the period is uncanny; the eye too. I thought of the Surrealist N.F. Simpson, Alan Burns's early novel *Buster*. 'Silly little sausage.' Bleak utilitarian, demobbed, rationed Britain.

Don't read the blurb; it's most misleading. The title is ironic, like most of the contents. Funny as Hell.

The characters in *Blaming*, this novel, or throttled romance, are in a continuous tizzy about trivia. Much eating goes on, as compensation; much sighing, more weeping. Characters think 'nervously,' are inclined to 'dawdle' over breakfast, and then make 'mad dashes' for the door. The plethoric reflexive pronoun is put to its shifts. From naught come to naught gone. Now read on.

Life at Laurel House, Laurel Walk, is not all a bed of roses. Nick and Amy go on vacation to Istanbul, where Nick, a successful painter we are told, dies of a heart-attack. Martha, an American writer, befriends Amy, but comes to a sticky end herself. There is a butler-person called Ernie Pounce. The house is 'faded but pretty' ('All so neat and tidy . . . with the lawn-mowers going in the evenings.') Amy occupies most of the book. Her son James works at Sotheby's. There are two obnoxious brats, whose witticisms are recorded. Dora attends the *Lycee Francais*. The Rev. Patrick Padstowe, Vicar, puts his foot in it. The widow casts aside her weeds on the last page and decides to hell with it all, she'll marry the family doctor, Gareth Lloyd, a frequent visitor. The brat Isobel 'firmly snuggled down,' and soon, 'most relievedly.' It concludes itself. Isn't it bad enough that such pseudo-lives must be lived, call it living, paper-thin; intolerable that we must read of them too:

> The old magnolia grandiflora was dropping leaves with quite a clatter.

Elizabeth Taylor's work was admired by Messrs. Wiggin-Spurling-King. 'Just wanted to finish James's bed.' 'Do take your coat off.' 'There were sunny showers and outbreaks of rain at lunch.' Stacking up plates, putting forks into a jug of water, heavens will it ever end?

The seventeenth novel by R. C. Hutchinson, which he was working on when he died, is a foray into the byways of South American history, based on some dark doings at Cubiquite.

'Loudening' knocks on doors, fatigued horsemen, faithful half-wit retainers, condors, llamas, dreams of 'transient fragrance,' feature in a book which seems longer than its size admits, as one goes route-marching on heroics that would not have come amiss from the pen of P.C. Wren himself. *And* communings with nature in the frequently absurd manner of Malcolm Lowry. The adjectives are very odd. 'The pulpous soil still closed like greedy lips on his every footstep.' The blurb reveals the plot; it would be a pity to give it away. Servants 'skedaddle' when bandits come, the body of Señora de Juanos is almost buried in the wrong grave, in the rain; Colonel Sabino falls off walls, walks in the jungle, hearkens to Pater Ambrosius; jaws are taut and trembling, calamitous news comes hard upon calamitous news, similes and metaphors are darkly jumbled, the thinking one maze of non-sequiturs. Humble peons, Atun Papac, Villa Carpa vino, *kachasa*, unseen bandits, shaddocks (?), long-windedness, gusty palaver, the whole dimly illuminated by the 'light of introspection' as curtains perform a 'curious saraband,' and pensive glances are thrown, looks of dawning surprise exchanged. 'Father Diego, poker-faced like a tourist in an art museum, knelt and put an ear to his chest.'

The nature-rambles are priceless. 'When the voice of a hermit finch broke out like a practiced soloist's from the muted hubbub of the under-growth he surmised that dawn could not be far away.'

Rising has the length but not the force of Marquez's *Cien Años de Soledad* (surrealism runs through the streets of Mexico City) and lacks the hard details, and the brevity, of a Borges. The plot meanders about like the Amazon ('great lips parted in a mournful smile') encumbered with a diction that sinks it in bathos:

> The mist has been enfeebled by the maturing sun, it hung its flam-
> ing curtains which a fresh gust of wind abruptly pushed aside.

The 'circumjacence' of a manageable world is absurdly depicted, making the going arduous. How they talk and suffer, these intolerable bores! Mestizos are 'preposterously mustached,' Indios and 'local indi-genes' given to gnomic utterance. One reads on, eyes starting from the head in blank amaze at such misplaced energy. One misses the wily stratagems of a Borges; *atributos y adjetivos*. Fresh gusts. The author died before this long novel could be completed. 'Objectless, he turns and wan-ders back towards where a home of sorts, a wife, a family, had once been constantly awaiting him . . .'

And there it miserably ends.

Hibernia, 19 November 1976

50

How Utterly Maddening!

Jeremy Lewis, *Playing for Time* (Collins)

In the damp kingdom of the unfunny line, presided over by Morecombe and Wise and cuddly Coren of *Punch*, a lame English wit reigns supreme.

From whence does it derive? So cosy, so costive, so middle-class, so damned allusively complacent: *1066 and All That? Winnie the Pooh? Cold Comfort Farm?* The effortful straining for effects suggests the extended afterdinner anecdote, the purposeful drone of the club bore: Wodehouse or Beerbohm.

Sapper and *The Beano* were in accord with *The Pink Un* that Wogs began at Calais and all foreigners (or genuinely non-English persons) were, *ipso facto*, rum coves.

To this august company of bores now must be appended the name of Jeremy Lewis, late of Seaford, Cambridge and Trinity College Dublin, with his maiden publication *Playing for Time*. What with madcap pranks in Byzantium, in 'apprehensive vein' in America; then TCD and Dublin again, where this gangling minor public school misfit struggles through his version of the 1960s' *nostalgie de la boue*, 'life was as it should be once again':

> I felt that one day I would grapple with the all-important question
> of the existence of God, but kept—and have continued to keep—the
> old gentleman waiting in the wings like some luckless tenant farmer
> ringing [*sic*] his hands in expectation of a possible reduction in his
> rent. This terrible passivity afflicts me still.

In the bleaker reaches of genuinely unfunny books, a species of complacency resides and refuses to budge, as gangrene in a wound; while a desperate affability (see extract) is directed against the unfamiliar: the foreign and the tasteless; are not the wretched pair synonymous?

Perhaps it is necessary to work from deprivation viz. the early Chaplin, Buster Keaton with the cannibals, not to seek a safer alternative version of it: *The Ginger Man, Mercier and Camier,* Vladimir and Estragon, Hamm and Clov, the heroes hardly house-trained.

Those comforting lies began with Chesterton and A.A. Milne, Jerome K. Jerome's *Three Men in a Boat*; but this stuff is no longer amusing, the humour has all run out of it, Merrie England was yet another damned lie; every time an Englishman opens his mouth he puts his foot in it.

The comic gets its impetus by the multiplication of the obvious, the possible, and then stretch it to infinity: Jack and the Beanstalk. The multiplication of the possible, mark you, not the impossible. If you can't get the diction right, the story won't follow:

> My mother shot out of the tent in her nightie and spoke sternly to the bear, who slank away looking sheepish . . .

Robert the Old Chigwellian has

> a shock of straw-coloured hair that shot up from the side of his head like an inverted ice cream cone . . .

and four pages on is taking off a matador at the office Christmas party with

> a narrow-eyed tossing of the head, causing his curious cone of hair to bob up and down like the windsock at Northolt Aerodrome.

Whether 'travelling frenziedly' about the United States in a Greyhound coach or encountering 'disagreeable-looking iguanas' in Meridan (presumably Merida in the Yucatan) or a 'rather bad-tempered woman looking surprised and cross,' the phrase follows the stock response, since all deviations from the acceptable norm (Eastbourne?) are outlandish. A terrible passivity afflicts Jeremy still. The metaphors are not so much mixed as scrambled—Humpty Dumpty fallen off the wall.

Spectator 1987

51

Connubial Bliss

Giles Gordon, *100 Scenes from Married Life* (Hutchinson)

Dear Giles, just read your novel. The historical interpolations worried me a bit. Fair enough, Henry VIII and Catherine Parr, but what have great Italian lovers got to do with this limp London pair, this Edward and Ann Parkes, the ex-Eton, Oxford, Sandhurst Guardsman Socialist (?) with £5000 per annum executive job in a London advertising agency, who neither talks nor thinks in advertising cant?

I can't follow the under-plot, man. I'm glad you spared us closer contact with their unspeakable relatives and all that tiresome Scots Presbyterian background. The chapter entitled 'Edward and Ann Discuss Religion' induced the hot blush; possibly that was your intention.

Let me try and unravel my reservations, dear boy. Having embarked upon a theme in itself essentially tedious, and as it were walked alongside those thin lives, neither cutting through into their helplessness and boredom nor rising above them to curse them (as well you might), blast them from the page, or perhaps most difficult of all, endeavour to live with them as they are, *be* them, you must be defeated in your purpose by the limp diction used, that is only too exact—i.e., 'opt out,' 'cope with,' 'ego being involved,' 'grinned a little sheepishly'—that sets you, and the reader, apart from them. How can you mock the airline advertising jargon when the text itself is riddled with a jargon as lamentable?

Now the plot (a difficult one to illuminate): a ten-year marriage—three children, holidays in Sussex and the Yorkshire coast—*wobbles* (a mistress, a week in Venice) but rights itself after much guff on the last page. The Parkes, it must be said, are as dull as ditchwater or the dire pair in Eliot's *The Cocktail Party*.

The ambulance chapter worked best for me; it belongs to a better novel. The shifts from first-to-third-person narration and from past to

138

present tense gave the jolt intended but (by then) could do little to interrupt the calmly blameless progress of the plot.

It began to appear possible that we were about to be made privy to the secrets of their inner lives. An awful thought. Perhaps more piling-up of detail *à la* Butor (a dull fellow) was needed, *in extremis*. Your problem I'm afraid. The sensualist in you was not released in this. The interlude in Venice might have made a better novel, if I may be so indiscreet. The similes were widely imprecise. Best of luck (you'll need it).

Hibernia, 25 May 1978

52

Glowing Cinders

V. S. Pritchett, *Selected Stories* (Chatto & Windus)

Affection for womankind—a nature at odds with itself—characterises the fiction of England's premier literary critic. The putting on and taking off of clothes is a donning and doffing of masks; moments of self-laceration (the scarred divorcée in *Blind Love*) or their moments of stupefying glory (the poorer sister humiliated in *The Cage Birds*).

Dealing out or taking punishment, his characters, male and female, young and old, are infused with life, gorged with it to an almost Dickensian degree. Drunk with themselves, they are drunk on life—Pickwick skating, the dwarf Quilp hanging upside-down to peer into the speeding carriage.

Only the expatriate Irishman William Trevor has an ear as keen for English idioms, the racist jibe—'a common lascar off a ship.'—This is Mr. Singh, who speaks a glittering and palatial English; whereas old Mrs. Draper speaks from the bowels of history: 'Constance had principles; we have the confusion of our passions.' The parentheses are wicked; few have rendered better the *feel* of London.

Pritchett has famously declared: 'Knock on the doors of half the houses in London and you will find people with relations all over the world.' It's a long way from our parochial miasma, Plunkett's 'sickly sweat of desire,' McGahern's old sock.

Questions of money, too much of it or the lack, divide the class chasm and the sprightly diction veers this way and that to follow after: George Clark, eighty-two, inactive queer, dreams of social life at Staff HQ, Haigh, Ronnie Blackwater and others would turn up, a bit of gunfire added an interest—the octogenarian clubman dreams that he has kissed the teeth of George V. 'With the servants it isn't fair to leave a drink about'—the voices of the rich are a grave chorus of male self-approval. An actress in a London restaurant has 'soft hunting eyes,' the blind solicitor smells tennis balls and grass off his divorced secretary.

Mr. 'Wolverhampton' Smith, faith-healer and swindler, marches off the page; a heavy throws a scene on the Geneva train. The plots are very odd; on the right bank of the Seine, on either bank of the Thames, 'the sad, dirty dividing water.' The dust thereabouts is the dust of families that have gone.

Many of these fourteen stories are love-stories; one of them taking place in the dark, one of the protagonists blind. People know themselves as unreal in the sodium glare of the streets:

> For the light of the chandeliers quivered again, dimmed to a red cindery glow and then went out . . . The audience dropped *en masse* into the blackness, the hall sank gurgling to the bottom of the sea and was swamped. Then outside a door banged, a telephone rang, feet shuffled and a slow animal grunting and chattering started everywhere and broke into irreverent squeals of laughter . . . There was the sudden heat of breath, wool, fur, and flesh as if the audience had become one body.

Hibernia, 18 May 1978

53

Malignant Crabs

Robin Maugham, *Conversations with Willie: Recollections of W. Somerset Maugham*
(W. H. Allen)

These *ersatz* conversations, *quasi* verbatim, were extracted from folio note-books kept by Lord Maugham, covering the period 1945-65, by which time the equally *ersatz* Great Man had passed away.

As a transcript of real conversations they are wanting and read rather like the stilted dialogue of Maugham's fiction, bolstered up with many lame interjections perhaps intended to lend veracity to the whole, now published thirteen years on.

The author who thought to abridge *Temps Perdu,* who wept as he wrote cruelly of his dead wife in *Looking Back,* speaks throughout like the hero of a bad play; possibly one of his own, for he wrote twenty-six in all—five of them were running simultaneously in the West End in 1905.

Oratio recti switches from nephew Robin to Barbara Back. The soured uncle said her memory was inaccurate, giving improbably verbatim accounts of incidents which she may or may not have witnessed. Unlike-ly matter is cellotaped together by Robin Maugham's winsome diction, showing a fondness for adjectival manipulation (the triple-backed beast): Beverly Nichols is 'smart, small and witty in a kind way,' Osbert Sitwell 'majestic, venerable and witty,' Peter Stern 'happily effusive and loqua-cious,' Gerald Haxton 'wayward, feckless and brave,' Sir Harold Nicolson 'twinkling and benign and extremely friendly towards me.'

A deal of gruesome dinner parties follow lunches at the Savoy and Dorchester, menus are given in full; the dogs of the Villa Mauresque, Maugham's Xanadu, are devoured by his hungry servants. When the war ends the consumption of food continues unabated and meals are devoured 'at express speed' by the rapacious and taciturn nonagenarian.

Dodo Benson, Chips Channon, Emerald Cunard, Noël Coward ('sprightly as ever') and other worthies make short set speeches and vanish off-stage to applause. Hugh Walpole was none too pleased when ridiculed as 'Alroy Kear' in *Cakes and Ale*. Devastating points are made with dry martini in hand, cigarette in holder stabbing the air. 'I'm told that now the English have been hoofed out of India, they quite like us.'

The Anglocentric view of the world (where Wogs certainly began at Calais) is all-pervasive, the eating of four-course meals continues with unabated gusto; the massacres at Cawnpore, Mysore, Travencore, Hydrabad, Burma, Penang and Singapore do not invite comment nor any further wit. Brother Freddie, fiercely monocled, becomes Lord Chancellor. The queer nephew and the twinkling and benign (the mannered manner becomes catching) Harold Nicolson were causing scandal by associating in a yacht moored at Nice and Maugham offered to buy off the Viscount for £50,000, should he go into politics and become Governor of 'some island,' to boss the natives about.

The lofty manner had always been more in accord with 'Sapper' and Warwick Deeping. *Encounter* didn't like Maugham. He was not generally liked, seemed able to forget friends when they were no longer useful to him. The last gasps of British colonial power and pride are its chroniclers, Kipling and Maugham. He can dine off silver plate, eleven servants wait on him, eight million copies of his books are sold, Penguin bring out 100,000 copies of ten titles, his plays are performed around the world.

But he is not a happy man; cataracts are forming in his eyes, 'a black fog seemed intermittently to have enveloped his mind,' he suspects his French servants of stealing money, of eating his dogs.

He believed that he had witnessed the death of Sir John Moore at Coruna in 1809; sought comfort in the past; was burdened by the present and feared the future. It is not a pretty picture; fits of rage and misery attempt to combat the oncoming darkness. As in the final volume of Proust's incomparable work, pederasts are discovered in and under every bed—the French King Henry III, King Saul, Jonathan and David in the Old Testament—'the whole thing was a completely queer affair.'

Lady Bateman ('a tremendous snob'), who had hired a train to pass through India, is tolerated though stone deaf. Of another old friend (G.B. Stern) Maugham said: 'She was a vulgar Jewess. She's broke now, and I have to help her.' Barbara Back was 'thoroughly common.' The contempt for the lower orders, the retinues below stairs, Kipling's 'lesser breeds,' is striking. There is a paucity of wit; it filters through as baleful ire, caustic asides.

'You know, dying is a very dull affair, and my advice to you is to have nothing to do with it' is the best he can manage in the way of wit after a good meal. But A Greater Crab was to claw him down in the end. The tortured old man in the darkened room lived on to be ninety-one, a year older than Djuna Barnes dying alone in Greenwich Village.

Some of Maugham's Westmoreland forebears had inherited land in Ireland, property belonging to the O'Neill clan, whom they slaughtered at a banquet. Property is murder; the possessing classes can be ruthless, as was Somerset Maugham himself. Did anyone ever dare familiarly address him as Willie to his face?

Hibernia, 4 May 1978

54

Cyril & Co.

They must have been arguing about Cyrano again for someone fatuously remarked that of course large noses were a sure sign of large members and male virility:

> Some women were remarking how the virility is in relation to the size of their noses and Lys Lubbuck jumped out of her chair and said: 'It is quite untrue, Cyril has a *very* small nose.'

So wrote the catty Nancy Mitford to Evelyn Waugh.

Now wishing to change the subject, moody Palinurus shrewdly observed that what prevented Noël Coward from being another Congreve was the fact that he couldn't think. Cyril and Barbara were lovers and had seen *Waiting for Godot* twice, the second time with Peter Watson, the angel who had financed *Horizon;* and all three had dined afterwards at the Café Royal Grill. It must have been soon after this when Connolly and Barbara lunched with Maugham, Alan Searle and Angus Wilson; teasy Barbara in her fitch-lined overcoat (for it was winter) slipping out unobserved for an assignation with George Weidenfeld (who certainly *had* a big one) in a pub just around the corner.

Cyril had ordered an especially succulent piece of beef but everyone complained about a loss of appetite; Searle protesting that he was suffering from liver trouble and could not eat meat. The Malignant Crab (Maugham) said that at his age one could look back on the most promising writers of one's youth, and deary me they might just as well have never *written a word*. He praised the *coeur de filet de boeuf* that was so delicious and tender and said he had enjoyed *Godot* because the second and more difficult act had been up to standard and that was damned difficult to pull off. Wilson protested that *he* couldn't like any play with tramps in it and furthermore he didn't much like the idea of people being wanderers who didn't settle down in life. His own play, *The Mulberry Bush*, on the other hand, was very good. At this stage he was mightily flushed in the face from the vintage port. Maugham advised him to attend rehearsals as often as he could, tactfully omitting to mention that in 1908 *he* had five plays running simultaneously in the West End.

Alan confessed that he, for his part, had hated *Waiting for Godot* and could see no sense in it at all. The tramps' dirty feet had worried him and he couldn't see the point of the small boy. They said they could all see *his* point and all frankly admitted to having some trouble with the plot.

Afterwards in the quiet of the country (where Barbara shared a cottage with Cyril, who was prone to fart and addicted to hot baths) Palinurus admitted, 'I always like seeing Maugham and Alan Searle. I find them restful, modest and well-mannered.'

Restful, *modest* and well-mannered! Why, it could be a prescription for success on the West End stage in the post-war era. Viz: T. S. Eliot: *The Cocktail Party*. Christopher Fry: *The Lady's Not for Burning*. Noël Coward; *Nude with Violin*. Such modest ambitions!

Cyril Connolly (1903-74), 'Palinurus' of *The Unquiet Grave*, founder of *Horizon,* author of *The Condemned Playground, Enemies of Promise*. Liked to let his wind go free.

Somerset Maugham (1874-1965), author of twenty-six plays and many novels. *Of Human Bondage* was praised by Connolly. Lived to a ripe old age.

> I still possess a telegram summoning me to the Euston Hotel in 1929 and signed 'Joyce' which I took to be the Christian name of a girl I knew; a misunderstanding which was never cleared up satisfactorily with either of them.
>
> Cyril Connolly

> Poverty crippled the first half of Joyce's life, illness the second, and he died almost as poor as he had begun. He died suddenly of a duo-denal ulcer, a poor man, and Miss Weaver paid for his funeral.
>
> C. C.

James Joyce (1882-1941), born under the sign of Aries (2 February). His nature, according to himself, was 'Sluggish, slimy, skithy, sliddery, stick-in-the-mud.'

One of Paul Theroux's characters (Paul himself?) with a degree in English worked as a longshoreman in Singapore harbour; his job entailed

ferrying hookers out to a moored ship. He confesses to his work-mate:
'I'm mad about Joyce.'

'Is that the skinny one in the yellow dress?'

'You guessed it.'

> During the afternoon he lay on the beach, as he loved to do, finger-
> ing the pebbles for texture and weight. Occasionally he had a burst
> of energy, and during one of these vaulted over a wall and fell, for
> his sight was poor, on the other side, hurting his arm.

> In the evenings he visited local pubs, sipping a little cider (which he
> did not care for), but mainly listening to several conversations and
> able to follow them all. In his hotel room he read a series of strange
> papers and magazines: *The Baker and Confectioner, Boy's Cinema, Jus-*
> *tice of the Peace, The Hairdresser's Weekly, The Furniture Record, Poppy's*
> *Paper, The Schoolgirl's Own, Woman.*

> He stayed in the Torquay hotel in July 1929 with his wife for three
> weeks before proceeding to Copenhagen, where he was not expect-
> ed in the offices of *Politiken.*
>
> > Richard Ellmann, *James Joyce*

James Joyce certainly was a rum cove. He could be difficult, met George
Moore seven years after the publication of *Ulysses* and said it would please
him if Moore would accept a copy of the French translation.

Moore, being diplomatic, a genuine gent, replied: 'I shall be delighted
to accept any book you choose to send me, but I hope you don't mind me
reminding you that I can read English.'

Joyce smiled a . . . *hesitant* smile, but sent the book anyway, in French.
Moore wrote back in French to thank him—'I look forward to reading it
all winter.'

After having read a few pages he commented to Janet Flanner: 'It
cannot be a novel, for there isn't a tree in it.'

Joyce and Moore maintained exaggeratedly courteous relations until
Moore's death, when Joyce sent a wreath inscribed: 'To George Moore
from James Joyce.'

I told this story about no trees in *Ulysses* to a mumbling old poet in
The Plough, the Irish pub near the British Museum. 'Nothing but family
trees,' he said wittily. As a young man in despair he (the old poet) had

stood on the edge of the platform in the Paris Metro, intending to throw himself under the wheels; but an express shot through, pressing him back against the Metro wall.

J.J. (1922 in Paris)
Sitting in the café of the Deux Magots, which faces the little church of St. Germain des Pres, I saw approaching out of the fog and damp, a tall man with head slightly lifted and slightly turned . . . to sit down opposite me. He asked for a glass of white wine.

For a moment there was silence. His hands, peculiarly limp in the introductory shake, and peculiarly pulpy—running into a thickness that the base gave no hint of—lay, one on the stem of the glass, the other, forgotten, palm out, on the most delightful waistcoat it has ever been my happiness to see. Purple with alternative doe and dog heads. The does, tiny . . .

There follows a description of J. J.'s extraordinary waistcoat, the doe and dogs' heads with tiny lolling tongues, allegedly sewn by his granny, but never described by any other in the wide circle of admirers; unless of course he only wore it once, and for Djuna Barnes, herself no mean dresser.

Was Jim having her on? Was she having us on? The dialogue is pure apocrypha; a come-on, a leg-pull. Both insisted on formality of address: *Mr.* Joyce, *Miss* Barnes.

Unpublished

55

On Storm King Mountain

This was of course total invention; the notion of Joyce on horseback was as ludicrous as that of Joyce big-game hunting with Hemingway; in any event the Joyce family had been so impoverished all their lives they had to keep moving house, burning the bannisters, keeping one step ahead of the bailiff. For the last forty years of her life she had lived alone at No. 5 Patchin Place in Greenwich Village, or twice as long as Melville's long demise as a customs inspector. She called it her Trappist period, and was to die there in 1982 in pain, a week after her ninetieth birthday.

When I paid a courtesy call in October 1995 Patchin Place was deserted. As was her birth-place, Cornwall-on-Hudson which I visited on a lovely blue day. An elderly lady local historian downstairs in the library was disinclined to talk of Djuna Barnes, her family or her work; the Barnes family were 'outsiders,' and they hadn't stayed long. Her birth there was never recorded.

'But she wanted to come back,' I said. 'Wasn't she buried here?' The lady historian was not prepared to discuss Djuna Barnes.

A few copies of *Nightwood* and *Ryder* were in the library's fiction list. Her ashes had been scattered in a dogwood grove on the slopes of Storm King Mountain. Of her work Kathleen Raine had written: 'Only in America was a tone at once so macabre and aristocratic still possible.' The expatriate American lesbians of the period had all ended up looking like Navaho squaws; all had put on weight and become monumental. Of course Gertrude Stein had always been Big Chief Sitting Bull.

Unpublished

56

The Faceless Creator

Paper read at Glucksman Ireland House, New York University,
11 October 1994

When I was living quite poorly in Dublin, I developed the ability to travel free on public transport. I willed myself to be invisible and no bus conductor dare approach me for a fare. I could travel all over Dublin for free—it was as good as being an Old Age Pensioner. I mentioned this ability to my wife and she suggested we put it to the test. We sat in the back seat on the lower deck of a No. 12, empty but for the two of us, the conductor and the driver, travelling from Palmerstown Park into what we call *An Lár* in the melodious Gaelic—meaning the Centre, in O'Connell Street. The conductor saw us, or seemed to see us, straightened out his leather satchel, approached halfway down the bus, seemed to remember something or see something or somebody else vaguely familiar passing by, somebody or something that reminded him of something else, that made him stop in his tracks; then he drifted away.

Speaking of invisibility, I first met Beckett during the run of the original English version of *Waiting for Godot* at the Arts Theatre, London, or when it had just moved to the Criterion; Peter Woodthorpe was playing what the critics called the senior tramp, and he was accompanying Beckett from Golalming in Surrey to Belsize Park in London where John and Vera Beckett had arranged a meal in their flat, for me to meet him. I had read *More Pricks than Kicks* and *Murphy* and had been knocked sideways by these two effusions of bile. Beckett himself, whom I had never seen, was coming from Golalming with a lady he had known in Trinity. Golalming and Ulm and Sing-Sing penitentiary seemed appropriate Beckett associations; I wondered whom I should meet—Democritus or Heraclitus? The man of flux and hollow laughter or the man of undispellable misery? A penitential association anyway. In the event I met neither; I met a courteous Protestant gent with a piercing blue eye, short cropped hair standing on end like the crest of a cockatoo, who dressed in the fashion of a Teddy Boy, with no discernible trace of a French accent.

Then out of the press of free-loaders, publishers' narks, nervous agents, bright publicity poppets, blurb writers and such riffraff, who materialized before me but . . . V. S. Naipaul!

'V. S. Naipaul!' I cried, both hands up as if beholding a vision.

But V. S. was having none of this malarkey. He caused himself to vaporize before me. One minute he was there, a darkly grimacing presence, and the next he was gone, vanished into thin air—which I take to be the natural element of such thin-skinned people. A correspondent of *The New Yorker* wittily called him a 'fastidious sourpuss.' A dark presence menacing as Lord Vishnu himself had been casting no little chill upon the jolly proceedings.

I am old enough to remember a time when famous citizens were not even recognised in the streets of Dublin and were free as you and I to go about their own business unmolested by the great common herd whose collective breath is noxious and whose collective heart is shallow and commonplace as a bedpan. I am talking of a time before television, that rough beast, had entered all our homes (but not mine) to do great mischief. 'The greatest single disaster in the history of mankind,' in the opinion of the late-lamented movie-man, Lindsay Anderson.

I appeared on an early RTE black-and-white one-off arts programme—an excuse to bring together Ben Keily, Anthony Cronin, the deathly pale publisher Figgis, your humble, and the legendary Flann O'Brien, author of *At Swim-Two-Birds*, whom I was most anxious to meet in the flesh . . . such as it was. Kiely, himself a cross between Mad Sweeney and Finn MacCool, a compulsive anecdotalist, and a great man for the genealogies and Irish family trees, like the Pope O'Mahony before him, had just discovered that he and Flann O'Brien were kinsmen. They were 25th (or was it 42nd?) cousins, twice removed. They strolled into the Donnybrook studio—I was about to say arena—together, already well-oiled as soon became apparent.

The plan had been to get your man into the studio sober and to ensure that he stayed that way by plying him with glasses of water. He seated himself opposite me and a ball of malt appeared as if by magic out of one cuff. He had pudgy hands and a shifty eye and kept moistening his lips, the tongue shooting in and out like a lizard after prey. As the programme developed it became clear that a good few balls of malt had preceded this one, as his manner became acerbic then belligerent, I might say hector- ing. He was chain-smoking and seemed to be attempting to remove his dentures, the better to spit venom at 'them'—unidentified parties in Gov- ernment posts or gurriers in high places who were out to get him and who presently would be named. This now horrendously public crusty manner caused a furore in the control room I can tell you. A note on yellow paper was swiftly conveyed to the flustered anchorman and the programme ter- minated before worse befell and libel writs flew—for it was going out live and unrehearsed. It was instantly replaced without a by-your-leave by The Dubliners, native sons in raucous session, with Ronnie Drew belting out a rebel song in his own inimitable way. Television sets were few and far between in the Ireland of those days and my mother was upstairs in the flat of a kindly neighbour, both of them glued to the edge of their sets, as you can imagine, when Ronnie Drew appeared, bearded to the eyes, armed with trusty guitar—the voice, rusty as a corncrake, going on about the rattle of the Thompson gun, may God forgive him.

'Oh look!' cried my doting mother. 'There's our Aidan! . . . I never knew he could play the guitar.'

Meanwhile in the studio Flann O'Brien turned to me and inquired civilly 'How had it gone?' under the impression that I was one of the studio technicians. I had not uttered a single word (good, bad or indif- ferent) on camera. We repaired to McDaid's for alcoholic refreshment. I stood the great man a double Scotch and identified myself as another admirer of *At Swim-Two-Birds*, which had been out of print since 1940 when the entire first print-run went up in flames in a London warehouse during the Blitz, in the company of *Murphy*, Beckett's first novel. What I didn't know at the time was that O'Nolan abhorred his first novel, hated its success, I should say, and was galled by anyone praising it. He refused to accept praise for such 'prentice work, dismissing it as 'a thoroughly bad book.' 'You should know better,' said he to me, the lizard tongue shooting out again, with the dehydration, 'and you a Christian Brothers' boy.'

Brian Ó Nualláin or O'Nolan wrote novels under the name of Flann O'Brien and a column in the *Irish Times*, called 'Cruiskeen Lawn' (the full jug or brimming measure) under the pseudonym of Myles na gCopaleen (Myles of the Ponies), which ran in episodic bursts for twenty-nine years, with gaps while libel actions were settled out of court. The column came out also in Gaelic from time to time, so that neither the editor nor 95%

of the readership could understand a word. A further alarming feature were fingers pointing out like little cannons at adjoining pieces in the paper; damning judgements were freely dispensed. No by-line picture identified him, and Brian O'Nolan could walk around Dublin and not be recognised by *The Irish Times* readers as the acerb fifth columnist of Cruiskeen Lawn. Interviewed by *Time* magazine he gave it out that the columnist was the illegitimate offspring of a Cologne basket weaver, and this whopper was swallowed. Brendan Behan said that you had to look twice at Brian O'Nolan to make sure he was there at all. No one knew what Flann O'Brien looked like; the more public persona, Myles, the watchful listener, creator of offspring of the quasi-illusory type, had left instructions with his publisher Timothy O'Keefe that no photograph and absolutely no biographical details were to be released. A photograph purporting to be that of the author which appeared in one of the reviews of *At Swim-Two-Birds* second time round in 1960 was not him, O'Brien said. The head seemed unfamiliar.

When *Editions de Minuit*, the underground resistance publisher in Paris, brought out the first volume of Beckett's Trilogy, no photographs were available. He had served in the Resistance and lived in hiding in Roussillon and no photographs were taken.

I used to play golf in County Wicklow with a friend of mine over the course at Greystones where the young Beckett had played with Dr. Gerry Beckett whom he nicknamed 'The Plantigrade Shuffler.' My friend Rowe had attended the same school as Jonathan Swift. The boys of Kilkenny School were offered a free day if any boy could find the signature of the famous old boy hidden away somewhere, scratched on a stone, possibly in the latrines.

Jonathan Swift had graduated in 1680 and gone on to trinity in Dublin, as had Wilde after him, as Beckett after him, as Derek Mahon after him. A boy claimed to have found the signature and went running to the headmaster to show him where the famous name had been scratched with a penknife so many years before,

Dean Swift
1675-80

in a crabby hand. *Dean Swift* indeed! The boy was immediately flogged for lying. But why couldn't the young Jonathan have seen himself fit for the Deanery of St. Patrick's one day in the not too distant future, and soon sitting down to write *A Modest Proposal* and *Gulliver's Travels*?

My mother, long gone to her reward, used to say that James Joyce had a bad face. Certainly it is not an appealing face, but closed up like a tightened fist. The goggly eyes seem to swim behind the thick lenses and will not focus on us; the severe mouth is unfriendly. He overdressed, wore too many rings, went with a cane, wore peculiar hats, struck stiff poses for the camera, looked like a magician. What I suspect my mother didn't like about Joyce was that he lived in sin with Nora Barnacle in sinful Paris and was the author of a notoriously dirty book called *Ulysses*; so he *had* to have had a bad face. I would go further: Joyce had no face at all. The death-mask tells you more than the living tissue. None of the great creators have faces. Not Virgil, I dare say not Plato,

nor Homer,

nor Shakespeare,

nor Dante,

nor Bosch,

nor the Brueghels father and son,

nor Magritte nor Michaux, two eccentric Belgians, nor your Faulkner of Jackson, Mississippi. Faulkner had his grandfather's face, a soldier's face that belonged to Major de Spain or Sartoris or General Compson or McCaslin or whoever it was, down there in the South, affirming his belief that suffering and grieving are better than nothing.

A friend of mine, a painter now dead, whose ashes were scattered in the Garavogue, compared the face of Kafka to an animal (a fox) caught by the flashbulb at night—the face of a furtive nocturnal animal one is not supposed to see. Céline (real name Dr. Louis-Ferdinand Destouches) has a face worn away by suffering. Beckett's face was a mask, and Baudelaire's before him; as was Antonin Artaud's in Rodez Asylum. John Cheever, the man from Quincey who died in Ossining, had his own reasons for having two faces. Bonnard's is an unformed face, semi-oriental, a self-portrait merely blocked in; the real Bonnard had gone out for a breath of fresh air, or a smoke.

Another face springs to mind, one who supped deep with horror all his life—I mean Jean Genet. Genet had two faces, and neither belonged to him; the Anima and Animus ever in contention. The author of *Stiller*, the Swiss writer Max Frisch who knew Montauk and lived for years in a Greenwich Village attic, had no face. With war imminent, Paul Klee's last agonized self-portraits converted his round Swiss face into a blood-red full moon under Saturn. Was it Brueghel or Hieronymous Bosch who painted his own face hanging as if decapitated in Hell? Who was it painted God in the garden like a ghost in a tall hat? Vaguely apprehended, a will-o'-the-wisp about to be wiped out, a footstep going out of shape in a puddle. You see what I mean?

An unknown man, with a round face hidden in a narrow-brim brown homburg hat bought in a Talbot Street hatters, walks in Dublin with the unmistakable shacked progress or *locomotor ataxy* of a chronic alcoholic, makes his way into McDaid's dingy bar in Harry Street and asks for the usual painkiller. The hat was bought for two quid and seems to be a fixture of his head. You could almost tell the time of day in Dublin by studying the various slants and tilts of the hat, angled at a more belligerent angle as the day wore on. Sometimes (when a storm was brewing) it pressed down over his ears like the lid of a pot on a stove. His most endearing 'invisible' character is a collective presence, faceless and nameless, the voice of the Plain People of Ireland, who are sort of distant Irish cousins of Faulkner's Snopeses. It is the collective conscience of the race of whom the nameless Dublin jackeen at the No. 52 bus-stop is one, the man who venerates his unnamed clever brother and speaks to a well-spoken gentleman, also faceless and nameless. The jackeen lives in Drimnagh, a nondescript area well suited to a nameless one. These nameless, faceless, 'invisible' ones speak to us most directly.

57

The Bombing Analyst

James Stern, *The Hidden Damage* (Chelsea)

To every race its own wrestling. Nations of course differ in degrees of rudeness. In the defeated Germans James Stern found a 'Cabal-like clannishness, a Bundishness,' through which ran, he sensed, a sinister streak: 'Anti everything and everyone not of German *Blut,* German *Boden,* and therefore highly dangerous.'

Stern, the translator of Kafka into English, finds himself interviewing blind and deaf German bombing victims from May to August in 1945 for USBUS (United States Strategic Bombing Survey) in thoroughly Kafka country—Frankfurt *total beschadigt,* the panorama of moonlit horror seen from the hotel balcony in Stüttgart; Nuremberg's *Alstadt* where the statue of Dürer sits in his stone robes above the rubble mountain of what had been Julius Streicher's bailiwick.

Auden (with Isherwood in tow) having fled from the Blitz and English bread-and-dripping is encountered in Moriarty's pub on Third Avenue, and puts Stern in touch with a man in the Pentagon.

Seven weeks later he had touched down on the Azores, en route to liberated Paris. *Mon Dieu!* Cognac is produced, Camels distributed; an uncanny silence prevails along the boulevards; all the café chairs under the plane trees are occupied by GIs sitting in rows, drinking watery beer at fifty cents a glass, staring in silence at the passing bicycles, the buggies and barouches. Weary-looking, shabbily dressed Parisians have sad stories to tell. 'You will never know what life under the Occupation was like.' Coffee is seven times its pre-war price and tastes like charcoal, but the Germans have gone. Monsieur Beckett and Suzanne Deschevaux-Dumensil have left the Vaucluse for the small apartment in Rue des Favorites, in the 16th arrondissement.

Germany itself, in anno zero, leaves even Auden (in his swanky American Army Major's uniform) speechless. The survivors of 'precision' bombing survive rodent-like under the Frankfurt rubble mountains. Munich and Berlin have taken an almighty hammering from the air. 'Destruction on such a scale takes the mind a long time to absorb.'

Furst Fugger von Glott has come out of it alive. With his dark spectacles, small grey-black moustache, bow tie, the sparse hair brushed back from the forehead, he is a dead ringer for James Joyce. The beaten *Wehrmacht* soldiers walking on the *Autobahn* have come out of Russia and will never forget it, nor will the veteran of three years service in Poland forget the massacre of Jews in Lemberg. Of ninety suspects rounded up after the 20 July plot against Hitler, eighteen arrive alive in Bayreuth from the Berlin jail in a journey that lasted over a week in a cattle-truck, seventy-two having been clubbed to death by SS guards.

Defeated Germany seems a long way from Aunt Flora out shopping in Shelbourne, Major and Mrs. Stern (Pater and Mater) down to two-course meals. Spencer the butler brushes and presses the young Master's uniform, polishes his shoes, lays out shaving kit. Union jacks flutter from the gate posts. 'You haven't altered a scrap.'

The Hidden Damage was first published in 1947 by Harcourt Brace, and this is the first English edition from a new London outfit. James Stern, who had written of Djuna Barnes, now lives with his wife in Wiltshire. To his grandmother's Knightsbridge house had come Robert Browning on foot from Wimpole Street on Sundays. Butler Hutton in tails opening the door to the enormous diningroom, the Canaletto on the wall, the Dresden china on the table, the egg and anchovy sandwiches.

Bally difficult to keep the grass decent with one man.

The Irish Times, 14 April 1990

58

Copping Out

William Boyd, *Brazzaville Beach* (Sinclair-Stevenson)

The blunt and beguiling honesty mentioned in the blurb is not too evident in the text; author and publisher are in cahoots. 'Audacious and fascinating' burbles the blurb; then, warming to the task, 'blunt and beguiling.'

But the drama seems contrived, bogus as the forest and its chimps. Most of the struggle (to make the plot sit up) occupies the murky never-never ground between perceived (the improbably named, symbolically of import, Dr. Hope Clearwater, ecologist) and the thing perceived; 'circulating speculations' in the 'huge cargo of analysis.' A plug of Socrates serves as epigraph: 'The unexamined life is not worth living.'

The plot, all pleats and tucks, concerns the wooing of Miss Hope Dunbar by a researcher and mathematician called, well, Clearwater, their marriage and his suicide. A sub-plot introduces a MiG pilot and some troublesome chimpanzees.

Dr. Hope has a sister called Faith who prefers to be called Faye, married to Bob Gow ('Super you could come!') by whom she has three children: Timmy, Carol and Diana.

Mother Eleanor has large tits and may have been having it off with the theatrical agent and old family friend, Gerald Paul. We encounter them at Ralph Dunbar's seventieth birthday celebrations in a marquee pitched on a 'capacious' lawn in Oxfordshire. Daddy, a former West End matinee idol, gives off an aroma of woodsmoke and a faint musty perfume. The Dunbars are clean.

Presently the marquee is occupied by eighty guests even duller than the wild chimps studied by the daughter in a place purporting to be Africa. The whole shaky artifice of plot quivers with moral certitude, launched into orbit by the plug from Socrates, to lend it authority and authenticity.

Dr. Hope is studying the behaviour of groups of bellicose chimps against a backcloth of jungle, allegedly jungle, allegedly chimps; and having trouble with Mallabar, her cheating boss, wouldn't you know.

> Mallabar pre-empted all criticism of the egotistical decor by classifying it as his fund-raising room.

The stuff in italics should be ignored, since it is even more lamentable than the main text. Here's Hope searching her co-researcher's room:

> The desk was clear. She went round it and opened two drawers. A chain of paper chips. An olive-green paper puncher. Three boiled sweets. She searched the other drawer. Empty. A tension and baffled excitement was beginning to quicken inside her. What was she doing in this man's room? What was she playing at?

Dr. Hope is chased by Dr. Amilcar's henchmen, eats pickled mackerel from Poland, whereupon the northern chimps invade the territory of the southern chimps and Dr. Hope is obliged to dispatch three of them: Pulul, Darius and Conrad. Rita-Mae also comes to a sticky end but not before baby Bobo is devoured by another chimp.

Dr. Hope's finding discomfits Mallabar, the MiG pilot does not return from a mission, the epilogue is all dying fall, drenched in bathos—remember *Marjorie Morningstar*?

> Out at sea the sky is filled with soft baggy furniture of clouds—the dented bean-bags and winded sofas, the exploding kapok cushions. The wind hurries them away, and leaves the beach to everyone and me, washed and smooth.

This ur-novel surges to a close with nine blank pages mercifully devoid of any further fatuities; pathetic fallacies abound.

The Irish Times, 8 September 1990

59

Lengthening Shadows

Michael Meyer (ed.), *Summer Days: Writers on Cricket* (Eyre Methuen)

It's an odd old game, more difficult than appearances might suggest, appealing to the English nature, its seasonal histories exhaustively detailed blow by blow, score-books printed into *Wisden* with graphs of scoring strokes in records broken—at the Oval in August 1938 Len Hutton (opener) scored 365 runs against Australia in thirteen hours, seventeen minutes.

Not all who write of it can do cricket justice; *Beyond a Boundary* is as much a history of the West Indies as a record of the game. Of the three-score odd who take the field here, not all are of equal merit: Alex Waugh recalls Surrey against Sussex at the Oval in the summer of 1914:

> It seemed appropriate that the last Saturday of peace should end like this, with grey skies, a light rain falling and stumps drawn early.

At Lord's in 1945, editor Meyer had to catch a train to Tonbridge and missed Miller batting with Constantine, Titans at play; but P. J. Kavanagh was there and saw it all. Philosopher Ayer is sound on Middlesex between the wars, Hearne and Patsy Hendren, the gay cavalier Compton. Poet Fuller watched Hendren take a blinder close in, recalls pork pies ('oval, deep, fresh, peppery') being very good before beer and ale became chilled at Lord's and the Oval.

Beryl Bainbridge's maternal grandfather saw Prince Ranji bowling at Hove, his shirt ballooning out like a sail; Ted Wainright was of the opinion that Ranji had never made a Christian stroke in his life, executing leg glides with diabolical finesse.

Freddy Ayer had watched Hearne making his last (119th) century at Lord's; while on 'The Hill' at Sydney another poet, Laurie Lee, was laid low by a bottle thrown by some irate Ozzi supporter. The poetry here subtended is lame enough, David Wright apart:

> The foot less prompt to meet the morning dew,
> The heart less bounding at emotions new . . .

Wright, deaf, who once played near Northampton Lunatic Asylum, may have been watched by Lucia Joyce. John Clare had died there.

Sir Bernard Lovell is coy on the subject of owls in ye olde English oaks. As England itself changes and changes, after the wars, so too does the nature of the great national game. Gentlemen and professionals are on an equal footing at last, a mass of paternalistic Edwardian rules and regulations swept away at Lord's, where now even West Indian supporters can feel at home. 'Here comes de King!' one cries as Lloyd slouches round-shouldered to the crease. 'Show dem de cane!'

The sloggers of the Sunday League and the one-day matches are making a circus of it, gum-chewing Butcher hammering drives into dispersed fields ringed by advertising hoardings and television cameras recording the Mexican Wave.

Wittgenstein thought to study Anglo-Saxon neurosis by observing behaviour during soccer matches, though perhaps for that troubled Kraut the appeal lay in the boyishly undressed nature of the play.

Playwright Pinter, a cricket buff himself, is in fine form, writing on the Middlesex all-rounder Arthur Wellard, who gave Pinter his England cap and the stump he knocked over when dismissing Badcock of Australia. Goddard of Gloucestershire bowls like a snake; Learie Constantine strolls negligently to the crease.

A fine parade of the past, famous names, the immortal dead, Louis MacNeice is again lowering a pint of tepid ale at the Tavern. Sometime in the late twenties Laurie Lee cycled from Stroud to see his home-county play the visiting Australians, and the fierceness of their game set him to wondering.

Hibernia, 6 June 1981

60

Pinter's Proust

Harold Pinter, *The Proust Screenplay: Poems and Prose 1949-1977* (Eyre Methuen)

Pinter's 'solid year's endeavour,' the reduced screenplay of Scott Moncrieff's translation of Proust's vasty *A la Recherche du Temps Perdu*, is now available to the *cognoscenti* in a single sumptuous volume.

It's a compression job to beat the band, a dozen volumes or half a million words compressed into 166 pages or 455 shots beginning and ending on Vermeer's *View of Delft*.

'The subject was Time.' Marcel in his forties hears the gate bell at Cambray, 'resilient, ferruginous, interminable, fresh and shrill'—the bell of his childhood. The film opens and closes on disparate aurals and visuals and throughout its progress the bell shudders.

Nicole Stephane (the ingenue of the Cocteau/Melville *Les Enfants Terribles*), owner of the film rights, approached Joseph Losey, who had worked with Pinter on *The Servant, Accident* and *The Go-Between*, and Losey brought in Barbara Bray as technical adviser.

The resulting *melange* is something to behold, an expensive scenario for a film as yet unmade. Those who put up money for motion pictures are hard practical men scarcely likely to have read Proust or, having studied this screenplay, understood what either he or Pinter is up to.

Pinter understands him alright. Dropped are Elstir, Bergotte, Bloch, Aime the waiter, the famous *Madeleine*, Marcel in striped bathing-drawers receiving a devastating snub from Baron de Charlus. But all else is replete here, even if in the wrong language and employing constructions never heard before in the darkness of the cinema: the Proustean Past Habitual (Swann's 'Because by next spring I shall have been dead for some time').

Pinter-made speech rhythms match the original: Albertine's 'I could see you wanted to know us. I could see you were interested in us.' Limpnesses elsewhere, not the screen-writer's fault, are less happy: Saint-Loup's

'How's the writing?' Marcel's 'Not a bad day, is it?' Exultant cries of 'Sublime!' at a soirée.

Many scenes of great beauty; some of great cruelty, always that grit in the Pinter pearl, the glint in the Jewish eye. La Raspeliere cliff-top by night, guests departing in the moonlight, the Baron suffering gladly in Jupien's brothel.

Is Andrée's 'to keep you away from her [Albertine], so that you [Marcel] wouldn't smell me on her' an addition, lifted from Beckett (*Play*)?

Pinter's own work has latterly shown a fascination with accumulated wealth and its appurtenances, as his own plays empty themselves of content (*Old Times*, *No Man's Land*); a fascination connected in some way with cruelty (*The Servant*) which is here given its head.

The first sighting of Princess de Guermantes, seated on a coral sofa in a box at the opera, wearing on her head a net of shells and pearls matching the necklace, a headdress of bird-of-paradise, would take some setting up.

A dinner party at Le Raspeliere, questions of protocol, hats of titled guests clutter the carpet at the Duchesse de Guermantes's grand receptions, as bare bosoms heave, a discountenanced footman on recognising another pederast announces 'His Royal Highness, the Duc de Chatellerault!' The Queen of Sweden is present, being gracious; what else can Queens do? The Queen of Naples defends her cousin, the fearsome Baron de Charlus, Duc de Brabant, Damoiseau de Montatgis, Prince d'Oleron, de Carency, de Viareggio, des Dunes, and not to be crossed on any account.

Beauvois tapestry in Mme. de Villeparisis's drawing room, a Nesselrode pudding for Norpois. And remember to keep your hat on when the King comes visiting, speak only when you're addressed, be proper.

As a picture of the period, the death of carriage-and-footmen society, it could turn out to be what *The Leopard* was not and what *Death in Venice* (the movie even more embarrassing than the book) aspired to be. Vermeer's mysterious interiors are here, the shadowy illicit activity; something too of Bonnard—the wrinkled sheets and highlights on bare flesh repeat sunlight on sea shaded by clouds.

The train in the clearing, the riderless horse galloping away, these are eerie metaphors. Who was it said that the character of Mme. Verdurin was created from a long memory (Proust's) for love and revenge? It's all here—the Rivebelle restaurant, Saint-Loup at his balancing act, the road to

Hudimesnil, the moving trees, the grandmother's stroke, Balbec casino, the frieze of girls, the road to Raspeliere, the Baron guarding 'Charlie' Morel, Marcel protecting Albertine. Albertine on the subject of eating sounds, the street-cry of the oyster-seller, eating monuments and temples (an old-fashioned ice-cream from Rebuttets or the Ritz). The lavatory woman in the Champs-Elysees, jealousy of course, sinister cruelties, the horror of non-entity read in a passing chambermaid's eyes. Losey will have his work cut out for him.

It's a film full of eyes: Gilberte, Charlus, Marcel, the camera itself: a great post-mortem on St. Germaine. Pinter's best work to date, for the movies.

An earlier *persona* is revealed in the companion volume, a lowly mummer in rep in an Irish Midlands Town twenty years back in time, before the success of *The Caretaker* and *The Homecoming*, long before he had to turn himself into a limited company for tax evasion purposes, presumably H. Pinter Ltd., to fox the Inland Revenue.

The prose is better than the poetry. His amusing account of touring Ireland just after the war with McMaster is very fine. Pinter missed little. 'Hutton and the Past' is marvellous: 'The handle of his bat seemed electric . . . every stroke he made surprises me.'

I could say the same of screenwriter Harold Pinter.

Hibernia, 25 May 1978

61

Gnarled Oak

Richard Little Purdy and Michael Millgate (eds.),
The Collected Letters of Thomas Hardy, 1840-1892, vol. 1 (Oxford University Press)

It must be conceded that Hardy was a fairly dull stick. Was he a snob? He liked to consort with dull titled folk and be invited to Lord Mayors's dinners, himself a member of the Savile Club.

If you harboured some suspicion that bantering correspondence with such dead-hands as Edgecumbe, Moulton, Gorst, Dobson, Clodd, Lane-Poole, Bunting and Udal, Squire Sprigge and Lady Wallop, might be a trifle on the heavy side, you would be perfectly right in assuming so. Letters to some Unidentified Correspondent do little to lift the tone.

Even those who appreciate his fiction could hardly be captivated by this rain of humdrum facts from a bygone period. And pained exchanges between authors and publishers change little over the years.

Accused of denigrating womankind in his fiction, Hardy's letters to the ladies convey a heavy gallantry. His second wife consigned many more to the fire.

This first volume of the definitive edition covers the years of his employment with the London architect Bloomfield up to the publication of *Tess* and the death of Hardy's father. The first thirty years were possibly the worst. Certainly they were hard for Hardy. A heavy preponderance of the letters are to editors and publishers, his agent Golding-Bright—what a lovely name for an agent!

Hardy was stiff about payments due, strict in the mailing off of receipts; otherwise he gives little away. Nothing much is revealed here. The lost letters could hardly have revealed much more. Bad reviews troubled him. Much of the correspondence is sour. He was given to melancholy.

Byron's letters to his publisher Murray are much livelier, fifty years before: More brisk and vigorous. His Lordship's English punch in the guts against a too pushful Venetian gent or the brilliantly mounted attack against craven Southey of *Blackwood's Magazine*, do reveal at least a stout English heart. He sparred with Jackson. Hardy would have been moping in Dorchester. The thick Piccadilly fog seen from the windows of the Savile Club follows him to Max Gate. Invitations to high teas or 'ordinary dinner' were no cause for rejoicing. Lamb's extended breakfasts would have been more convivial affairs. He once sat next to Henry James at a dinner-party, but seemed to prefer the company of Gissing and Gosse, or high tea with poet William Barnes. Clearly he relished the company of divines. He corrected publisher Kegan Paul when accused of being 'sprung from a race of labouring men.' No, by God, the Hardys had been master-masons.

By 1888 he was getting £550 for serial rights in the United Kingdom; in America £250 for advance sheets, exclusive of book rights. But there again good sales would never quite compensate for hostile reviews. He suffered smart raps from ill-disposed critics, such as George Saintsbury (not mentioned in index), who accused him of being a pessimist and a pagan; certainly the critic did not err on the first account. Hardy saw much sadness in this world and was reluctant to add to it in his fiction. He conceded a little to the conventions of the libraries. Possibly he did not like people. At all events he seemed happier with non-human life and growth, noted the disappearance of pink chrysanthemums in Dorset.

Ich woll and *er woll* were still used in northwest Dorset and Somerset in 1888. 'I heard *Ich* only last Sunday; but it is dying rapidly. I know nobody under seventy who speaks it—and those above it use the form only in impulsive moments when they forget themselves,' he wrote to Gosse, urging him not to spoil his digestion or lose sleep over *bad reviews*. He himself never forgot an editor's offer, held onto what he had.

Aubrey de Vere estimated that Sir Walter Scott's income of £10,000 in 1886 would be £100,000 per annum in fifty years' time. In July 1968 the Right Rev. Joseph Edward Fison, Bishop of Salisbury, while preaching in Dorchester at the opening of the Hardy Festival there, startled his congregation by putting forward the theory that all the Master's work had been done as an act of atonement for a sexual sin in his youth.

Review refused

62

Eighty Years On

Rebecca West, *1900* (Weidenfeld & Nicolson)

To argue brilliantly, by induction, from the particular to the general and vice versa, via applied psychology and a knowledge of history, is rare. Chateaubriand could do it, as could Emerson; so can Dame Rebecca, consummate mistress of the double- and triple-backed metaphor, the sagacious aside. Her elliptical construction 'Not by . . . so much as' operates like nutcrackers:

> More and more is the universe disclosing itself to human observers not by making revelations so much as by setting new problems. As for the subatomic world, it seems to exist as a crossword puzzle for physicists.

1900 was the period of the paterfamilias, large families, buhl-inlaid fire-screens in drawingrooms, maids carrying coal scuttles, hard cravats about flushed male necks, costiveness, dyspepsia, 'nerves' and water-cures, spas, the Boer War. The acetylene lamp had been invented, also the Browning revolver.

At a luncheon given in his honour at Claridge's, the rigid imperialist Lord Milner spoke of 'panoplied hate, ambitious, inimitable ignorance'; referring not to matters local but to that pernicious thorn in English flesh, the Boer General Botha. One can observe the blood pressure rising.

The Princess of Wales, not yet twenty-seven years, was suffering from a form of deafness brought on by excessive childbearing. It was the last year of Queen Victoria's long reign:

> I have very early memories of her as nothing more than a squat bundle of black clothes, mourning clothes (she went on and on mourning Prince Albert like a dog that will not give up on a bone),

propped up in a state coach or an open carriage with a Hanoverian pout of white gelatinous flesh showing in the shadows of her hieratical head dress which made reference to both widows' weeds and royal occasions.

In April of that year the Queen had visited Dublin on a recruiting campaign and been watched by a young and hostile James Joyce, who described her in terms as unflattering—Her Majesty was 'wearing horn-rimmed spectacles on a livid and empty face.'

Today Mrs. Thatcher is nominated as the first British female King, in a numinous aside. The photographs from archives and private sources are eyeopeners. Interiors held in medium-shot with a depth and shadow in the prints that recall the movies of Griffith and the cradle endlessly rocking; the office of *Success Magazine* in New York, the outstretched boots of the plutocrat.

Other images as remarkable match the text: Boer dead in a ditch at Spion Kop, old Renoir staring out at you, Elgar taking his ease on two chairs, the New York Plaza in high summer with a few trams passing and the place otherwise deserted. The thin faces of poor London kids stare back at one, almost a century on; Paul Kruger, implacable foe of England, is seated in a shabby patio hard by a large, comatose, ghostly stone lion.

Mafeking has been relieved after a seven-month siege, a cruelly, extended constipation. The richly left Cecil Rhodes is preparing a will to ensure that the De Beers fortune should finance the ultimate recovery of the United States of America as 'an integral part of the British Empire.' Whores were thought to be somehow comic; as indeed was the United States, in its own way.

Elsewhere in the world, Sarah Bernhardt, cruelly corseted, plays in *L'Aiglon*, while a plump and vivacious (not to say lubricious) Colette prepares to mime 'An Egyptian Dream' to music with Willy Villars—'a deplorable art form known as miming to music.' The vixen's eyes study you. 'Her physique was incoherent.'

A sweet souvenir snapshot shows the young Cicily Isabel Fairfield aged six being fed blackberries at Richmond Park by her sisters, Letitia and Winifred, with two cousins.

Nothing incoherent about *her*.

Hibernia, 25 February 1982

63

Zones of Insecurity

Donat Gallagher (ed.), *A Little Order: A Selection of Evelyn Waugh's Journalism*
(Eyre Methuen)

Suicides, in the old course of death, would lie at the crossroads, impaled.
Waugh, the melancholic, the Lancing snob and Tory-to-be, angry long
before the fashion started, liked best his worst book, *Brideshead Revisited,*
preferring it to *Vile Bodies*, his first success (1930). Though an ardent
Catholic of the rare upper-class purple-sprouting variety, he attempted
suicide, had a nervous breakdown, as shown in *The Ordeal of Gilbert Pin-
fold*. His last years, though productive, were not serene. 'A smell of cigar-
smoke in the night,' recorded one uncomfortable guest at his Somerset
mansion, 'and little whirlpools of anger.'

He was, granted, as great a snob as Sir Harold Nicolson ('It is impu-
dent and exorbitant to demand truth from the lower classes'), did not
believe in democracy ('Men are not naturally equal and can only seem
so when enslaved'), held a low opinion of the Irish.

This collection of his ephemera, covering the period 1924-65, is in
the main disappointing—with the exception of 'Half in love with Easeful
Death,' on Californian burial customs, the background for *The Loved One*.

He began a sour journal in 1960 and stopped it five years later, a
year before his death. The world's disorder and wickedness has increased
a hundredfold since his demise. Sceptical, much given to malice, he
deplored the coming Classless Society, the increasing uniformity of life:

> Suppose, as seems now likely [the motorcar] is rendered mobile by
> making the whole country into a speedway and a carpark, there
> will be no inducement to go anywhere because all buildings will
> look the same, all shops sell the same products, all people say the
> same things in the same voices.
>
> 'I See Nothing But Boredom . . . Everywhere' (1975)

In a few years' time the world will be divided into zones of insecurity which one can penetrate only at the risk of murder and tourist
routes along which one will fly to chain hotels, hygienic, costly and
second-rate.

He admired the work of Mandarins such as Sir Osbert Sitwell ('calm
leisurely pages'), Aldous Huxley, Max (*The Happy Hypocrite*) Beerbohm
above Saki or Graham Greene—another troubled Catholic convert. He
thought James Joyce exorbitant, corrected Cyril Connolly's defective
grammar.

'Elegance is the quality in a work of art which imparts direct pleasure; again not universal pleasure. There is a huge, envious world
to whom elegance is positively offensive,' wrote the Tory for whom
The Times was too Red.

'It is a common feature of all but the most recent fiction that a
character is falsely suspected of a misdemeanour and is able to
recognise his true friends from the false by their irrational beliefs in
his innocence. How many of my friends should I believe innocent
of what crimes?' he confides to his Journal.

A profoundly immoral principle, 'It will all be the same in a hundred years' time.' All morality depends on causality to the nth
degree. Every act of free will, good or bad, attenuates its conse-
quences to the end of time.

Timothy Evans, a lapsed Catholic, wrongly executed for murder, was
'Hellbent'; but as a result of his conviction 'returned to the Church and
died shriven.'

Waugh greatly admired Firbank. Praised Angus Wilson's *Hemlock and
After*, Henry Green's *Living*, Huxley's *Antic Hay* (because of the 'perfumed'
pavements of Bow Street, this was 1923, and no character used the telephone). He liked Anthony Powell's work, deplored Nancy Spain 'suck-
ing up to the cook' (Waugh's). Dr. Eaton of Forest Lawn ('Whispering
Glades' in *The Loved One*) was the first man to offer eternal salvation at an
inclusive charge as part of his undertaking service.

Waugh arrives at some curious conclusions about the American Irish
Catholics, the chain of clasped hands:

They alone of the newcomers are never for a moment taken in by the multifarious frauds of modernity. They have learned some of the superficial habits of 'good citizenship,' but at heart they remain the same adroit and joyless race that broke the hearts of all who ever tried to help them. ('The American Epoch in the Catholic Church,' 1949)

The sentiments of a true-blue English Conservative.

The Incarnation had restored order on earth; but he looked forward to the Last Trump. 'Had Ireland remained in the United Kingdom, Dublin would today be one of the great religious capitals of the world':

Before the Year of Grace man lived in the mists, haunted by ancestral memories of a lost Eden, taught enigmatically by hints and portents, punished by awful dooms.

Hibernia, 20 January 1978

64

Grocer's Wine

Henry Green, *Concluding* (Hogarth)
Henry Green, *Caught* (Hogarth)

In London some years ago an acquaintance of mine met, by arrangement, the recluse whose ashen face had never been seen on dust-jacket, press release or promotion-photos; but the reticent sad gin-drinker declined to speak of his work and passed away soon after.

Concluding is now reissued in a new edition by his publishers, this being the third, less handsome than the old editions. The story is set in a summer's day around the year 2000; but the unimaginable future comes over as much an anodyne as, say, *Howards End,* that most English idyll. Fifty-two years ago the end of the century must have seemed remote.

In a state school for girls the peace of the fifteen hours from sunup to sunset is mildly disrupted when Merode spends the night in her pyjamas in a fallen beech tree. Deaf old Mr. Rock, the famous pensioner, collects the swill; Mrs. Manley calls; the Principals, Miss Hermione Baker and Miss Mabel Edge, receive a curt State directive to go in for pig-breeding. Some of the girls comb the woods; Merode's friend Mary is also missing. Mr. Rock's grand-daughter is in love with Sebastian Birt; a police sergeant calls; the Misses Winstanley and Marchbanks have little to say for themselves, nor have Swathling, Ingelthwaite and Inglefield; Dakers is subdued; Dr. Bodle offers smelling-salts.

The main speaking-parts are taken by two Babylonian harlots; then the buzzer goes for tea. The Foundation Dance is deemed a great success; Adam the gardener is rustically rude. Also featured: Alice the white Persian cat, Daisy the pig, Ted the goose, who takes flight near the end. One could hardly blame the goose; for a silliness prevails throughout which is perhaps common to all girls' boarding schools—blame the pent-up libido. The general fatigue and 'nerves,' the incessant tea-drinking, and the jargon, date it in the drab wartime forties; as do some anachronisms—'bereft,' 'shewn.' The light of a hand-torch is alternatively 'a small megaphone of light,' 'a long cone of daylight' and 'a dunce's cap of moonlight,' all within a dozen lines. The plot is hard to follow, lacking the prescience of Monique Wittig's *Oponax* or the cruelty of Orwell's *1984,* the grim institutionalised future. The end of this century will be a good deal worse than this pessimist supposed.

An earlier novel, *Caught* (1943), was reprinted six times and is now into a new Hogarth Press edition. It is a better read, although the plot is equally unhelpful. This novel, a considerable 'fit of remembering back,' concerns the Auxiliary Fire Service which saved London in 'her night of blitzes' in 1940.

Another parcel of contentious bores takes over; but real anguish intervenes, though the characters still remain oddly stilted as Lowry's elongated workers. Auxiliary fireman Roe, the hero, is a bore. So is the heroine Hilly, unless the palm go to Dy, Dick Roe's sister. Boredom was possibly an infirmity with which Green himself was afflicted. Old Piper is described as 'the prize bore.'

The matter bracketed throughout the text reads as though written by another hand; or perhaps it is real emotion escaping—the child's 'astounding screech of hate and fright,' and on to the magnificent oratorio of London burning: 'the mile high pandemonium of flame reflected in the quaking sky.' The AFS men in the taxi on the bridge moving towards the great fire, are no longer Lowry figures, more Doré.

The red glow had begun far back: Roe aged sixteen in Tewkesbury Abbey, afflicted with vertigo on a ledge forty feet above the ground, sees the floor below hemmed with pews, the stone flags over which the sunlight has 'cast the colour in each window, the colour it seemed his blood had turned.'

Pye, Piper, Shiner, Chopper, Trant feature. Also a couple of Scandinavian broads, Ilse and Prudence, the latter 'tolerably miserable about another man, a pilot, who had gone away in August, who was now said to be marrying someone else.' The argot is consistent: 'Hi, cock!' Towards the end the huge fires rage. It was written in the period June 1940 to Christmas 1942.

Hibernia, 27 January 1978

65

Vinegar Dressing

Anthony Burgess, *The Devil's Mode* (Hutchinson)

'The horns brayed. The warriors shook their spears.'

Hark to the bray of the bucina! Hear the thunder of distant hooves! Enter the gooney Gipedes, the angry Akatzirs, the vile Visigoths.

The remote past is unreachable (as Golding demonstrated in *The Inheritors*) and the speech (grunts) of those long-dead ones long silenced, though Burgess doesn't seem to think so. This is the first collection of stories from the Monacoan polymath. The wild man from Borneo can no more resist word-play than Viv Richards can resist long-hops. Language *barriers* foresooth; fiddlesticks!

A streak of vulgarity mars his work, as woodworm an ancient oak, and there is such a lot of it. Mind you, notions of vulgarity vary from vulgarian to vulgarian and who is to say when showing off ends and *kitsch* commences? Nor does he wear his learning lightly, though the learned pedagogy sometimes comes across as a laboured bad joke, at which our elated author is the first to guffaw.

The collection compromises eight stories of varying merit and the novella entitled 'Hun,' which purports to deal with the rise and fall of an Attila 'Hunnishly drunk.' This exceedingly long shaggy dog story is told poker-faced in *pseudo oratio obliqua*:

> 'Any report from the Eastern flank?'
> 'Visigoths, my lord.'

Elsewhere (perchance in 'the thick Danubian forest') 'a firelit orgy, frank copulation varied with a little light torture.' And 'Dust, dust and dust, the flaring eyeballs of horses.' Pope Leo ('snowy of beard, vague of eye') is borne aloft on a litter, eager to hear Attila's first confession;

wild men go hunting wild boar on the plains of Hortobagy, steely-ringing:

> 'Let those men go, eh?' the general officer Ophonius said when they had, having been let go, gone. 'The Huns will not like that.'

> He swaggered about the muddy streets of the nascent town of Buda [waiting for Pest to arrive?], his crapula exacerbated by the noise of the hammer . . .

> Both envoys ensoured their faces in prolepsis at the thought of greasy stews of horsemeat and mare's milk warm from the udder.
> 'This,' Epigene gasped, 'is,' gasping, 'monstrous.'

Closer to home and to our time the cadences of 'low English Irish' are caught in the title story, when Mallarmé and a Parisian disciple visit the Dublin stews in 1889 and find Mrs. Mack already installed in No. 90 Mecklenburg Street and the whore Gabrielle ('parasol opened and variously inclined against sunshafts or leers') is balancing with grace on her lean haunches, 'admired, once whistled at by delivering draymen.'

Shakespeare argues not too convincingly with cranky old Cervantes in 'A Meeting at Valladolid,' and Watson unwittingly solves a tricky case for Holmes in 'Murder to Music,' after a performance of *The Gondoliers* at the Savoy Theatre with Shaw in the audience. Holmes tells Dr. Watson, or Burgess whispers to us, that he (Holmes) was taught Greek at Stonyhurst by Gerald Manley Hopkins and received punishment.

I once heard Burgess dumbfound an invited BBC Radio 3 audience when he delivered a paper on the musical qualities of *Finnegans Wake* and 'The Wreck of the Deutschland,' a witty defense of obscurity; delivered, claimed he, without notes.

He chivvies and bullies his readers as truculently as Wyndham Lewis was wont to do. A sort of cheerful male bounce and *braggadocio* prevails, well calculated to raise the hackles of any feminists bridling in the vicinity.

The Irish Times, 2 December 1989

66

Frothy Apophthegm

Anthony Burgess, *Earthly Powers* (Hutchinson)

Rejoycing [*sic*] in rude energy, a veritable stevedore of letters, Anthony Burgess is much given to frothy apophthegm, as this mighty tome testifies, all 649 strenuously onward-streaming pages of it. It was completed in 1980 in Monaco, where the artful tax-dodger lives in exile with his Italian Contessa wife to whom this present accretion is dedicated.

He writes best when in an ill-humour with his subject-matter; otherwise he preaches like Aldous Huxley, whose *Ape and Essence* these ruffled pages recall ('the howling of demons about whipping-posts'). The publisher's blurb should be taken with a grain of *salo*. He has thrown together a novel, or a consortium of plots, by sheer brute force. It does not make for easy reading, but those avid for plot may enjoy it. For a fellow fussy about *le mot juste,* Burgess writes sloppily at times:

'I said stop it Geoffrey,' I ground out.

'Bastard,' I choked.

Val threw his long limbs into the shabby armchair.

This with 'pre-empted' (as in 'pre-emptive strike,' or 'pre-empted in the breast department'—a most vile compound), 'sighted' children; not in the sense of 'we sighted land,' but in the sense of the children being able to see. Having a musical ear, like Joyce, he is good on dissonance: the handcranked gramophone winding down, 'Notherlildrink notherlildrink notherlildrink wondousanyharm' becoming long-drawn-out as 'Noa la drooonk.' Or again: 'If yoooo war the ownly garl in the waaaarld.' A technique lifted from the Circe section of *Ulysses* with some sour notes of his own added. 'Lat the grite big warld keep tarning . . .' 'For I ownly knew that I lav yew sao.'

Elsewhere the abuse flies thick and fast:

> A nolipped matelot with milky eyes had been watching me for some
> time round the bend of the bar. He now came up and spoke in my
> ear with bitter sincerity. 'You look to me like,' he said, 'a bastard
> that's fair crying out to be done, you fucker.'

The rich old disenchanted sodomite with his retinue of male compan-
ion-secretaries, the endless bitchery, recalling Coward & Co., Isherwood
and his Californian coterie of cuties, Auden-Kallmann and opera in the
afternoon, Calder mobiles turning sluggishly in darkened rooms. All is
excess; never use one adjective when three will serve better: 'Her cold
dry but generous lips.' Or again: 'I lighted up her Chesterfield with a
plain worn Rocher.' No, pardon, a '*gold* Rocher,' but who gives a damn.
A plain Player fag is lighted up with a 'plain worn Zippo'; now read on.
Only when the characters get drunk does a fitter sense emerge; a sense
of rage.

It is not the proper business of the novelist to discover solvents for
the world's ills. Pick a page at random and you will not discover a distinguished line, only grand thoughts that were perhaps best omitted; the
melody of mock patrician speech recalling Maugham, on whom our hero
may well be loosely based. A number of Noël Coward's discarded silken
dressing gowns make their appearance, as the tireless search for Spasm
resumes. Such knowingness in a novel can be distracting (the conjurer
rolling up his sleeves); the mannered manner is brutally sentimental,
though much puking and sodomy goes on. The narrator is as unpleasant a character as de Montherlant's Pierre Costals in *Pitié pour la Femme*.
Women have rarely been seen in an unkinder light; degraded by their
nature, by suffering, by female ailments, they are reduced to almost a
subspecies here.

The misogyny turns sourer still when a month of 'beneficent' torture in a cellar is described with some relish. Then a visit to the death-
camp—'We saw the forty gibbets and their forty hooks.' Goebbels has a
walk-on part, Himmler given some lines, the Duce struts and postures;
but the plot itself begins to seem as apocryphal as these wicked spectres.
Humpbacked Dahlke, firer of gas ovens, is 'an image of man as very
small and humped and ugly, whispering little songs to himself as he
rooted in nameless filth.' Pound in his Pisan cage, Maynard Keynes with

a briefcase under one arm, 'bodyshagging' Norman Douglas, all come in for some stick. The mock-derisory tone is sustained throughout.

Question: Could cynicism, deliberately foul, so far beguile itself as to cynically conceive of a large *bad* book? Could filth be filthier were it named? All the onrushing Gaderene swine here are caught in *The Clockwork Orange* lens—a slipstream of solipsism.

Sunday Tribune, First Issue

67

Infernal City

Anthony Burgess, *Beard's Roman Women*, with photographs by David Robinson
(Hutchinson)

Some fast work through the summer of 1975 at Montalbuccio, Monte Carlo, Eze and Callian, produced this glossy assembly of illustrated splenetics, the fireworks of a gifted linguist. The ornate gate-like chapter-headings are irritating, as are the needless photographs that detract from rather than embellish the text, well-leaded, buffed out and bitter. Credits roll for *Hexendoktor* Burgess ('acknowledged as a literary genius'), screen-writer, teacher and lecturer, with sixteen novels in the last sixteen years to his credit, plus eight works of non-fiction.

The plot is deliberately rank. Narrator Beard's wife Leonora dies of cirrhosis, after twenty-six years of marriage ('a signalling system of grunt and touch'), in an English March. The scene shifts to Rome, the cruel venal city of robbers. The phone rings at night. Burbank on the line; Warner Brothers want him. Now Beard is boozing with Ed Schaumwein (foaming wine to you, apathetic reader) at the Brown Bear, the Bistro, Chasen's; laid, before you can catch your breath, by photographer Paula Lucrezia Belli at the Beverly Wiltshire, while it rains in Rome:

> The noonday gun thudded from the Gianicolo and the Angelus started clanging from several campaniles.

Whereupon the undepilated sorceress flies off to cover the Israeli-Arab mess at Sinai, to the despair of unshaven Beard. 'Knocking hell out of each other, fratricidal bastards, shouldn't wonder. You know they are the same race really, yids and wogs? No foreskin, no pork.'

As war rages, La Belli's maddened ex-husband's coloured *amore* is spotted at Trastevere in the company of a fat man. The West Indian dirty novelist P.R. Pathan, author of *Hell is a City*, is on the warpath. Memories of an old love intrude (Sergeant Miriam Bloomfield of the ATS), the telephone rings again; it's Gregory Gregson.

Double gins at the Grand Bar with Gregson, who tells of seeing the dead wife Leonora coming out of Barclays near the Dorchester. P.R. Pathan and pederastic Roman henchmen strip flat. Wettish mornings follow. The dead wife phones. Fracas with scoundrely Vespa riders, and peculiar revenge exacted by their sinister girlfriends, practicing a 'Madrid speciality' known only to the Tamils. 'Up your coalhole, greasy wog.'

Miriam Bloomfield, *sans* left breast and with cancer of the rectum, reappears, drinking negroni at the Fiumicino Bar, I think it was, and Gregson 'skyjacked,' later phones from Bethlehem, where the elusive dead wife is seen dining at the hotel, now speaking fluent Hebrew. Lunch at Rugantino. Paula returns to denuded flat, abjures 'Holofernes,' another perversity (cf. Partridge's *Slang Dictionary*). Palestinian refugee children, all epileptic, are to be billeted in the flat.

Last chapter. Beard now married to Leonora's sister, Ceridwen. The late Leonora, or Mrs. Gweneth Hanson, is into her third death, having in the interval accomplished two resurrections, phones Beard ('Come and shag me, I want to be shagged before I die'), as the ghosts of Mary Shelley, Lord Byron and Percy Bysshe gibber offstage. Dr. Bloomfield gives Beard six months to live and later attempts to kill himself by ascending several flights of stairs. He then sets off with Gregson for a monumental booze-up.

Hope you got all that right. The specifics are hard to track and the pace throughout hectic, like film racing backward through a projector, in the manner of *The Day of the Locust*. It might make a good *film noir*, as was perhaps the author's intent.

Hibernia, 11 May 1978

68

Anthony Burgess at the London Savoy

In the dimly expiring late October afternoon light a family of imbeciles huddle by a traffic jam, viewing a poster for the *Ken Dodd Laughter Show*. Idiot smiles fixed and upstanding hair stiff as yardbrushes, they cry *'Tatty-by! Tatty-by!'* in high freak voices.

My taxi-man can speak four languages. Rain begins to fall as your correspondent enters the rich precincts of the Savoy Hotel, where famed soft-porn authoress Erica Jong has *not* booked in, following a murder on the top floor. Air-conditioning keeps the flowers fresh in the vestibule where floorwalkers and house detectives in dark suiting move sombre as undertaker's mutes. A great coal fire burns in the grate. The PA machine is tirelessly extruding news of world-wide calamities and the latest war news: ISRAELI JETS ATTACK tactatatackata LEBANON COAST *tickeytoc* DUPONT'S £4 MILLION LOSSES *ticketyboom*. Mr. Burgess, whom I have already met at the Hutchinson launch, arrives with entourage exactly seven minutes late. Effusive apologies.

We ascend slowly to a high suite overlooking the Thames and a vision of never-ceasing traffic headlights moving through the murk. A broad bridge seen through an open window. A leg-brace supports itself against one wall. Mr. Burgess orders strong coffee, offers Scotch; the entourage retires to another room.

Anticipating a blustery manner and possible truculence, judge of our surprise to encounter a handsome man in liturgical shirt set off by red tie, hair a sable silver, manicured nails, no discernible accent, the slitty eyes of a fellow inured to a hot climate (Malta, Malaya, Borneo); a *reserved* affability. Most happy to be interviewed for the new *Sunday Tribune*.

The dollar millionaire has just published his twenty-sixth work of fiction, *Earthly Powers*, for which Messrs. Hutchinson stumped up a rumoured £75,000 advance. Already 9,000 copies have been subscribed from an initial print-run of 15,000. Michael Korda, editor-in-chief of Simon and Schuster, paid a rumoured $400,000 (say £170,000).

The Booker Prize went to the sage of Bowerchalke, who came up to
Stationer's Hall from rural Wilts. Agent Deborah Rogers is said to have
sold the movie rights of *Clockwork Orange* for a paltry £400 four years back;
but there again the English rights of *Waiting for Godot* went for half that.

Mr. Burgess himself was not too happy with Kubrick's explicitly
horrorful angle, and was alarmed by the resultant murders, following
screenings. *CHAOS ODER ANARCHIE,* the wall graffiti proclaimed. *LEV
LESBISK. GLOO IS LUVE.* Gobbledegook was on the rise, the eye radi-
antly preparing for death.

Mr. Burgess, unsolicited, recalls early days of poverty, as if it had not
been his very own bread and dripping. School-master Devar brought
two copies of *Ulysses* into Manchester, secreted upon his person in order
to pass undetected through customs, the same customs that burnt 2,000
copies in 1922.

In 1959 he was given a year to live; overwork had taken its toll, a
suspected tumour of the brain. He had churned out five novels at the
rate of 2,000 words a day in one year. 'Fecundity is not a good sign?'
The eyes narrow behind a cloud of Daneman, cigar-smoke. 'You've got
to write—keep at it.

He was teaching in Borneo then, couldn't find a job in England, pen-
sioned off. 'A thousand pounds was a lot in 1957.' He believes in the
Word. In 1965 his first wife died. He soon remarried, to the Italian Contessa; they make their own deals, rumoured to be stiff. His work—some
fifty titles now—goes into translations. Publishers may speak of a continuing slump, but Mr. Burgess goes on churning it out, novels, oratorios,
reviews and articles, screenplays.

He had thought to take a sabbatical in Dublin, show his Italian wife
'another kind of Catholicism'; nothing came of that. He accepted no state
grants, Arts Council handouts; all revenue came via his strong right
hand. He was with Jack McGowran the day before he died, of a heart-
attack in the Algonquin. A fund for the Irish actor was started, funds
collected, but it was 'too late anyway.'

He would like to write a play about John Calvin; tried to set up a
film based on John Hawkes's *The Lime Twig.* Composed music for the
bassoon, spoke with Borges in Middle English to baffle the Peron spies.
He is sixty-three but doesn't look it, fears his memory is going, but it
isn't. His son Andreas wears a kilt, wants to be a Scotsman, doesn't
wish to write.

Cranks phone in the middle of the night—another *Clockwork Orange*-type murder—your comment? 'People like war. It's like art, has a beginning and an end.' The ghosted book with Ingrid Bergman was just a rumour; Anthony Burgess is no ghost. I complain that there are no meals in *Earthly Powers*; a real book of fiction must have a meal in it. He reaches out, finds a page, shows me a meal; well, a list of stuff to eat. It seems ungracious to dislike the novel, but the author does not much concern himself with this. It was a year's work, discarded before, taken up again, finished; there are other books to be written. I pick a page at random:

> Hellsmoke curled from the gratings. Red and yellow light flashed on and off faces of gratuitous malevolence.

He admires the gentle Svevo, Corvo's *Hadrian the Seventh*, Faulkner's 'harmonics,' Joyce for his everything. The T. S. Eliot Memorial Lecture at Kent was delivered extempore, *con brio*, broadcast. He can be witty, but the fun comes grimly enough.

The host is standing now, fingers clamped rigid like Beckett's on the cigar (Beckett's brand too), the noble head still enveloped in cigar smoke.

A kind man withal, considerate of others, with few bad words to say of his fellow scribes. He fell foul of Professor Ricks and Saul Bellow, for reasons unclear. Mr. Burgess shows me politely to the door of his high suite, offers a firm handclasp, specific advice. 'Work! . . . Work!' his last words on the slowly closing door, the narrowed Burgess eyes. The entourage are silent still in another room, holding their collective breath.

In the murky Strand a peevish voice cries out: 'You flash cunt you, I 'ope yow wreck yow fukken caw!'

I wish Mr. Burgess well in the rough times ahead. Our times.

Sunday Tribune, October 1980

III

The Small Neurosis

The smaller the island, the bigger the neurosis.

69

Fire in the Hills

Ann Saddlemyer (ed.), *The Collected Letters of John Millington Synge, 1871-1907*, vol.1
(Oxford University Press)

Those who knew him spoke of reserve, even gloom. A delicate child had become a man in poor health. But Synge was about as staid as a raging bonfire. It would all go into the work. He had something of Red Hanrahan in him; cycled 750 miles, broke the springs of his typewriter—a Blickensdorfer; spoke four languages, studied Hebrew, musical theory and counterpoint.

Riders to the Sea would prove much too sad, even for the Czechs. Much of the early correspondence was lost; these here are culled from fair copies in the notebooks. He wrote 'Under Ether,' did not care much for the English, was in the great tradition of Congreve, Sheridan, Goldsmith. He would always be a little removed from life. His fiancée, the actress Molly Allgood, had prophetic dreams of his approaching end.

His plays are riddled with the death-wish, in particular *The Playboy of the Western World*. But then again playing skittles with skulls had long been an Irish game. He had something of Kafka and Keats in him, though not as frolicsome a correspondent as either; he was no Flaubert, no Byron.

Hodgkin's disease, lympathtic carcinoma, was to kill him at thirty-seven. His letters give little enough away. Not for him the acerbities and astringent wit of the joker Joyce, the outbursts of joy directed at Shem's own children. John Millington Synge (the additional surname had been grafted in the time of the first Elizabeth because the Millingtons 'sang so sweetly') had none; his barrister and land-owning father having passed away when John, youngest of eight, was but a year old. His issue would be his plays. Was he celibate? Yeats thought highly of him, wrote with customary prescience:

Irish national literature, though it has produced many fine ballads
and many novels written in the objective spirit of the ballad, has
never produced an artistic personality in the modern sense of the
word. Tom Moore was merely an incarnate social ambition. And
Clarence Mangan differed merely from the impersonal ballad writers about him in being miserable. He was not a personality as Edgar
Poe was. He had not thought out or felt out a way of looking at the
world peculiar to himself. We will have a hard fight in Ireland
before we get the right for every man to see the world in his own
way admitted.'

Letter to John Quinn, 15 February 1905

The truth is the objection to Synge is not mainly that he makes
the country people unpleasant or immoral, but that he has a standard of morals and intellect . . . They [the Abbey audiences] shrink
from Synge's harsh, independent, heroical, clean, wind-swept view
of things. They want their clerical conservatory where the air is
warm and damp.

Letter to John Quinn, October 1907

What was to emerge: the *Playboy* riots, Yeats's *Plays for Dancers*, *Ulysses*.
Stirrings. A bakereen dozen or so years on would come *En attendant Godot*
and *Fin de Partie* via Paris; after a false start by Wilde—*Salome*. Drama
personal as a lyric. Beckett's immobilised hero, the bawdy innuendoes of
eternity; an exiguous affirmation that contained sneers against the tradition, the peasantry, the Turdy Madonna, the consolations of a folklore
beyond compare. Diarmuid and Dervorgilla, Cuchulain and the hosts of
the Sidhe were things of the past.

The present volume comprises about three hundred and fifty letters;
the scholarship, one may assume, is exemplary, though the lode is thin.
A sequel follows.

The Guardian, 11 August 1983

70

Fires from Gehenna

Dorothy Nelson, *Tar and Feathers* (Hutchinson)

The older way in Irish writing, so prone to please, was to show a world where everything was familiar, if mundane; the indulgently raised forefinger, winsomeness. Hold hard; knackery became *kitsch*.

The modern style attempts the opposite: to discredit such complacency and show a world where virtually nothing is secure. Unfolding history is now perceived as a tattered concordat, like Murphy's mind, all dying falls. That melancholy Kraut Adorno argued that today it is part of morality not to be at home in one's home: 'wrong life cannot be lived rightly.'

The Bray shown here and in Dorothy Nelson's first novel (*In Night's City*, Wolfhound Press, 1982) is as ferocious in embryo as Faulkner's Memphis, give or take some roasted mile of arid grid-patterning, urban stew and disorganised crime. Scale hardly matters. Bray main street tilts from the fake Tudor Town Hall to the Starlight Hotel; down by the harbour James Joyce's family once lived poorly. Seamus Costello lies buried in the cemetery under an expensive gravestone; Provo sympathisers prefer bellicose blasts from The Dubliners, the Council Estate spawns a large unemployed youth problem, murderous punks look for trouble on the esplanade:

> One lad has a crowbar and his friend has a knuckle duster and they go down to the toilets on the seafront and wait for someone to come in. If he's able to crawl back its his lucky day.

The afflicted mother speaks in tongues, sees in a vision the headless body of God floating in the Dargle: 'When I caught sight of this stately corpse, he's cut in half, so that's what the confusion is all about. God's in flitters. Have you seen my earrings?'

Bourgeois citizens expect always to be surrounded by love, family life being an arrangement of possessions. Expectations may diminish further down the social scale, at the bottom, total deprivation, a torture-chamber of helplessness, vide *Hunger* and *As I Lay Dying.*

Apparently Mrs. Nelson reads no fiction, preferring Marie Louise von Franz, a Jungean lady (not Karen Horney). Her preferred subject-matter is the outré, the family shambles; pain and terror without prophylactic. Treated in this manner, her material—incest, exhibitionism, murder—is new to Irish fiction, whatever about Irish life.

Her two novels read like case-histories, in the manner of Roy A. K. Heath, late of Guyana (*The Murderer*), or English Alan Burns, the former criminal lawyer (*Celebrations, The Day Daddy Died*). She is unpopular with the Feminists, who cannot object to the brutal wife-beating husbands, but might object to the weak wives. Both blurbs are misleading. The Crawford family are anything but 'fiercely loyal to their religion and country'; and a second novel can hardly be a debut.

Her father ran Bray Wanderers FC, the Bray carnival, later Bingo Halls. The subject is shabby as can be.

'I will be the green fly on the roses,' Sara Kavanagh counsels herself. 'I will become a race-horse . . . I'm in the jungle . . . the sun heats me with its heat like a whip.' Four feet space separates her from the wife-thrashing incestuous father: 'Bloody and four feet space between your bed and mine for the past twenty years.' She invents an alter ego, Maggie, who lives in the wall over their bed, suffers recurring outrage.

The harm done to daughter and wife in the first novel reaches its apotheosis in the second, where murder is done outside the family. Half the town is out of work, and misfortune, when it does arrive, comes like an old friend; the idle men rise late and later, the punks wait in the Gents. The 'brother in arms' goes under different names, Augustus Kinley then Sylvester, then Daniel, coming and going from the North. The unemployed father is hired as a Provo hit-man. The 'grass' has become a 'gorilla,' described after the manner of Jem Casey, Bard of Booterstown, or the Citizen in *Ulysses:* 'a man with a song in his heart and a brain to beat all brains.' But the part-time executioner is disowned by the Organisation, because political prisoners are not allowed to have prison records (flasher in the nearby woods). Put away for life, he passes the time inside practicing the waltz and foxtrot.

The son Ben, aspiring to show business, has given up nicking things ('I did not want to spoil my image'). The grisly spectre of modern Ireland rises up with Band Aid and Bono, Ballinspittle, suffering Ethiopia part of Croke Park razzmatazz. Comics have replaced the Bible, God is 'the arsehole in the sky.' Just offstage jibber the men of violence, hate intensifies. The wives *expect* to be hammered:

> Once I stood on the landing half the night rather than lie beside him [thinks the beaten wife of the first extraordinary novel]. I watched the sky turning black the way it does before the heavens open. I listened to the dull shapeless sounds coming out of the night and the sky getting ready to swamp them under a torrent of rain. As I stood there I thought, quite suddenly too because I was beginning to feel cold and I was going back to bed, 'What is is,' I thought, 'and there's nothing I or anyone else can do to change that.'

The two novels are damaging to all parties concerned, mordant texts graved in acid.

Hibernia, 21 October 1987

71

Cantraps of Fermented Words

Dermot Healy, *Fighting with Shadows* (Allison & Busby)

Folksong—ever on the endless theme of ancestral wrong—is transformed by the singer into pure joy. The folk tune 'Banish Misfortune' had no words to it; only a tune in the singer's head. Folklore vaporised into folk music, fast airs, a non-acceptance of the norm: Irish misery.

> It's the hurt mind, you see. The hurt mind. 'Are we putting on airs again?' the ganger said.

The energy of Irish writing is dependent largely upon the vernacular and idiomatic; street language in *Ulysses*; the frequently forked-tongued natives found they had another hidden lingo at their disposal. Which relates to the Citizen with his hurley medals and rabid jingoism, his cur, all the way back to Earwicker the sleeping giant, and onward to William Trevor. And now Dermot Healy, who takes his rightful place in the first rank, a beady eye fixed on what's what in the here-and-now.

In this case the Irish war in the North and its lamentable effects on the prototypal Irish (Fermanagh) family, moving south and north, then south again like a weathercock out of control. The forked barbs fly. Even truth itself is often bitter. And no better man to record it.

The trials and tribulations of the unfortunate Allen family are observed as coldly as Tisse shooting footage for Eisenstein's Russian Revolution; though the partisan clench is there too, locally painful as the bursting of a boil, or razor to knee-rear, without a local anaesthetic.

Unsatisfied ghosts peer in the window. The yard would turn your stomach. A 'grim drenched raucous' air permeates the pubs. The quick lines spiral up, deft as motets, a merry mixture of joy and scepticism, jibe and jest, with the pictorial element rampant. The novel takes off from where the stories, particularly the title story, ended. The grandson screams out in nightmare, the wrong brother is murdered, the river runs north and south, the killing goes on.

For a longish novel, thrice rewritten, it stands remarkably well on its own two feet, excepting perhaps the mid-section where the skeleton does show through. Paragraphing is odd, single lines isolated for emphasis in the manner of Max Frisch. Odd? Well, characteristically devious.

> January frost sparkled on the horns of the cattle. They tore at the raw hoary grass. Their beards filled with dew. The sun was gone and rusted transparent clouds steadied in the light blue water above the blackening mist. The clouds went under the water. The water was grey. I was tirelessly alone. I could feel everything . . .

Margaret writes to her brother-in-law Joseph. Even if armed British soldiers stare out from inside concrete observation posts, the prevailing mood is gay (the frantic jig before the drop), gaiety transfiguring all that dread. It departs signally from anything else being written hereabouts today, strangely sure of its own effects. Hard to define precedents—*The Third Policeman* (Ireland as revolving Hell), Beckett's acerbic *Mercier and Camier?* Something too of Jack Yeats's 1938 novel, *The Charmed Life.* Prickly as a hedgehog, slippery as an eel, it goes its own sweet way. The vulgarities of emergent Republican Ireland, with its micro-ovens, spin-dryers and vote seeking politicians, come in for a good deal of stick:

> The North was hibernating. There was sleet in Belfast. Force nine on the radioactive Irish Sea. A rock band, backing the Fianna Fail party, set up their gear on the back of a lorry in the square. From such platforms throughout the country the future would be decided.

North Magazine, Autumn/Winter 1985-86

72

Uric Acid

William Trevor, *Miss Gomez and the Brethren* (Bodley Head)

His work is not known to me, apart from a piece on Strindberg's second marriage in *Atlantis 2* and the television play *One Fat Woman* that owed more to Lindsay Anderson's *If* than to Frances Cornford's poem.

William Trevor (born Cox, of Cork) is the author of five novels and a collection of short stories, *The Day We Got Drunk on Cake*. Another collection, *The Ballroom of Romance*, is due next spring. *Miss Gomez and the Brethren* is his fifth novel in seven years, a labour that began late. A boarding-house or decayed hotel, an old boys reunion, a street under demolition, a dream gone awry, the semi-moribund in their last pockets of resistance—this is his subject-matter. A particular area of London life comes through: the London of *Angel Pavement*, *Adventures in the Skin Trade*, *It's a Battlefield*:

> Beyond Crow Street, and unaware of the crime that was forecast there, London's natives and exiles continued their lives, some sleeping, some awake. The Maltese stood about the streets of Soho; Chinese girls from the good-time clubs came and went in Lisle Street; Russians, elsewhere, spoke of politics . . .

Marietta biscuits, Urney chocolate, barley sugar and Peggy's leg betray the author's age, that and a pointed mistrust of the hairy young ('the young didn't like the world . . . four schoolgirls had killed themselves while experimenting with their minds under the influence of an unnamed drug').

> Men who had visited Miss Gomez in Mrs. Idle's pleasure house talked of their wives, or slept beside them, or slept alone. The man who'd given her the Canadian Pacific bag with the cheese in it remarked in a bedroom in Hampstead that no break in the weather could be seen by the television forecasters . . . The man who had asked Miss Gomez to lie in a grave with him made the same request to another girl and was told to leave her room at once. The man who'd asked Tina von Hippel to string him up on a pulley found himself in better luck.

The song of the spirits over the water; a dream set somewhere in Jamaica—messages and consoling thoughts come in Tacas from a drunkard and swindler. A red-headed Irish labourer from the demolition squad interferes with a fleshly woman, a deaf war veteran recalls an aircraft flying into clouds ('Ludendorff wouldn't stand for this; Ludendorff, they said, played games with the dead'), a dream-bar is 'knicker-pink,' an old woman dies and a sex-crime is averted, a band of pseudo-Tibetans perform a dance in Oxford Street.

> Youths had battered to death a perverted man on Wimbledon Common. Children were hourly enticed to motor cars. Women were set upon. Even animals weren't safe. All over London, it was the same; all over the world, as far as she [Miss Gomez] could see. Every newspaper she perused contained details of violence and uninhibited sensuality, or sensuality that was in some way strange. A man who had been arrested for interfering with the brakes of a model girls's MGB sports car, 'having conceived some sort of desire for her . . .' Other men had been found at night in the trees . . . wearing masks and eccentric clothes, all for some sensual purpose.

She saw the incurable man on his way to the crime. Crow Street comes down, the cats run wild, set upon by an Alsatian dog, Atlas Flynn of the demolition squad takes Mrs. Tuke far gone in gin.

> Cave's hardware, where Mr. Batt had stood for much of his adult life, fell easily beneath the blows. So did the disused Palace Cinema, and the Snow White Laundry, and in Bassett's Petstore pictures framed in *passepartout* came down with the walls of an upper room and were not noticed.

From the battered terrain, it sounds like war; the subjects like survivors. Alban Roche with long thin hands, a hint of tautness under his face—'black hair reached his shoulders, which was the fashion that summer . . . holding a guinea-pig in his arms.'

West Indian writers such as Hearne, Lamming or Harris would hardly perceive London as such a decaying old forest.

VD—who cares?

Hibernia, 3 December 1971

73

Stratafiction

William Trevor, *Beyond the Pale and Other Stories* (Bodley Head)
Bernard MacLaverty, *A Time to Dance and Other Stories* (Blackstaff)
Brendan Behan, *After the Wake* (O'Brien)

Here are three collections of stories and random prose, dealing with impoverished Catholic Belfast and environs or the lives of some of its citizenry elsewhere; poor Catholic North Dublin at the mid-century; and ampler terrain of the urbane and prolific ex-TCD man and ex-sculptor William Trevor Cox, who is not of their persuasion, their senior by some twelve years, and by far the superior talent. Tosspot Behan was only forty-one years of age when he died; the living MacLaverty is forty.

In the ten MacLaverty stories featuring teabags and relatives who die off, the lavatory is frequently visited, pubic hair clots the shower-stall, gunge gets in the eye, Liz O'Prey the undernourished Catholic sells herself to a Unionist employer, a Polish piano-teacher is given her walking-papers, the vivacious young Mrs. Skelly dances go-go in a sleazy bar in Scotland, unemployed Eamonn drinks in the Provos's club, Sadie and stout Agnes show definite Sapphic tendencies, Father Lynch is on the booze again, the hard Liam copulates 'the way other people rodded drains,' and halitosis is everywhere rampant.

The short tendentious sentences build up to nothing much ('she woke like a coiled spring'). It is a dire style favoured by Morrow, Leitch and Boyle from the North, and found too in the more thickheaded fictions of Patrick Kavanagh. The author as *voyeur* is intrusively present, bodily functions itemised; but the low life fails to stir.

With all due respects to editor Peter Fallon, it's a palpable absurdity to claim 'genius' for Behan; he had a genius for getting into trouble, but has no place in 'classic Irish fiction,' whatever that may be. *The Quare Fellow* and *The Hostage* just about measure up to the pretensions of middle-of-the-road O'Casey (*The Silver Tassie* or *Red Roses for Me*) or the sentimental

jingoism of O'Connor's story 'Guests of the Nation.' The fiction recalls
the more tired diurnal jokes of the 'Cruiskeen Lawn' column in the *Irish
Times* on one of Myles's off-days. The homosexual element carefully
omitted in *Borstal Boy*, concerned with the institution where the practice
presumably originated for the author, is broadly hinted at here in the
description of the hand-guns and the nocturnal killing. (Compare Behan's
story 'The Executioner' with the murders in Capote's repulsive *In Cold
Blood*). Specifically in the attempted seduction of the blond English husband in the title story:

> The supplely muscled thighs, the stomach flat as an altar boy's . . .
> the golden smoothness of the blond hair on every part of his firm
> white flesh.

The introduction causes some winces ('By this time, Dublin's darling
boy had become the whole world's roaring fellow'). The glossary is super-
fluous (a checklist taken at random gives Aughrim, Shinners, B Specials,
Clann na Gael, Ulster Protestant, Easter 1916, Michael Dwyer, Tans), like
Republican bigotry itself. The now obligatory sneers at the noncatho-
lic J.M. Synge originated with the waspish Flann O'Brien, echoed by
Kavanagh, whom I suspect feared the other's sharp wit. The name of the
subtle Elizabethan pederast Marlowe is misspelt on page 48. Gunmen
are drawn to terrorism by what Jacobo Timerman called its sensuality.
Perhaps Behan wrote better in Irish?

The manifold tomfooleries of the gurrier style serves only to remind
us how much better was James Joyce over this same grubby ground, pace
Dubliners, Monto and Roto and all, though now and then the authentic
voice of the Coombe is heard: 'What's this the name of that crowd owns
this child is?'

As a palliative to the soggy fiction, the 'classic' text is 'laced' (Fallon
dixit) with songs, puns and . . . *jokes*, to keep the reader happy.

To come to better things. More is revealed in the 22 pp. of Trevor's
'Mulvihill's Memoir' than in the combined afflatus of Behan and MacLaverty. It is told from a dozen different angles, by narrator, by an unmar-
ried sister from Purley, by a Hungarian colleague, through Smithson,
through Strathers, by the sister again, again by the Hungarian ('It isn't
very nice,' Wilkinski said again, quietly in the middle of the night. 'But
no one heard him, for though he addressed his wife, she was dreaming

at the time of something else'), by the narrator again ('Then two things happened at once'), Ox-Bonham, by Bloody Smithson, once more by Wilkinski ('It seemed to Wilkinski that the dead face of Mulvihill was being rubbed in the dirt he left behind him'), by the Market Research expert, once more by Bloody Smithson ('The messages that murmured at them were rich in sexual innuendo'), lastly by the narrator, who deals out the penultimate nostrum, like the ace in a poker game. Then the clincher:

> To a few at least it seemed that Mulvihill had dealt in an honesty that just for a moment made the glamour of the images appear to be a little soiled.

But not so fast: Wilkinski writes to the sister in Purley. But Trevor himself has the last word:

> It was not exactly a lie and it seemed less of a one as the day wore on, as the glamour glittered again, undefeated when it came to the point.

Here a complexity and wit beyond the reach of the other two. Trevor is most adroit when dealing with the duplicity of people; an unmasker of hypocrisy, the Irish disease.

Books Ireland, no. 65, July/August 1982

74

A Purple Glow

William Trevor, *Fools of Fortune* (Bodley Head)
Bruce Arnold, *Running in Paradise* (Hamish Hamilton)
Clare Boylan, *Holy Pictures* (Hamish Hamilton)

'I was just trying to find out what turned people into what you have to call murderers, terrorists. How their psychology changes, if it does change, how pressed you have to be.' Thus William Trevor in a recent *Guardian* review. He has been living in a farmhouse outside Exeter for more than thirty years, sending home these dispatches. This his ninth novel since *The Old Boys* (1964). In the novels, as in the texts of his devious stories, he buries the plot as a dog its bone; it is for the reader to dig it up.

No Protestant Irish writer has written as sympathetically of his Catholic brothers and sisters since Synge. The plot takes in sixty years of Ireland's slow ascent towards the light; Collins walks again, ambushed and killed, becomes part of history. Hero Willie Quinton kills Sergeant Rudkin of the Black and Tans over his vegetable shop in Liverpool, goes into hiding, is next heard of in Puntarenas, then Italy.

It's as if moments of Irish history were recurring in different forms: Joyce in exile in Italy, his daughter insane; Lord Edward Fitzgerald killed again on orders from Major Sirr. What springs to mind are other yarns of houses burning and ancestral wrongs readdressed by murdering again: *Jane Eyre,* Faulkner's story of Sutpen's Hundred, Yeats's *Purgatory*, the acting out of what has to be acted out: *Absalom, Absalom!* The 'miasmic and spirit-ridden forest' is present in the form of Ireland's woes, the present turning into the past, and vice versa. Coole Park rises again, is burnt down once more. The sanguivorous bugaboos gibber, a traitor has his tongue cut out, is hanged from an old oak tree, Kilneagh House goes up in flames. Two daughters with very Catholic names die in the fire: Geraldine and Deirdre. The grim conclusion: 'There's not much left in life when murder has been committed.'

On the map, Ireland and England, closely conjoined, are likened to lovers; but the Dorset cousin cannot marry Willie Quinton, and the child of their union goes insane. In the child's disturbed mind the murdered ones come to life again, the gondola in the green picture of Venice, seemed 'just for an instant, to give the slightest of shivers, as if about to begin its journey. But the figures outside the church by the bridge remained motionless.'

The *Shan Bhean Bhocht* appears in disguised forms: a servant with raincoat thrown over her head. And in a more sinister emanation: 'An old woman with bad eyes lifted three knives tied together from the shop window, and he undid the hairy string.' This in a shop like a pawnbroker's at the bottom of the steep hill in Cork. It would be a pity to betray any of the plot; two generations and sixty years occupy around 230 pages. The unappeasable hosts seem to be in good battle order.

Trevor's collected stories are now available in Penguin and take an honoured place among the remarkable collections of recent years: John Cheever and Eudora Welty, V. S. Pritchett and Isaac Singer.

From the subtleties of Trevor to the pseudo-subtleties of Bruce Arnold, who writes, at his worst, like Henry James with migraine. Father and son are gnawing away at each other again here, and finding little comfort in their tribulations. This is the fourth and final volume of the Coppinger novels. Kennedy is assassinated in Dallas. Breakfast at the Cavendish (champagne and treble brandies), a visit to the Chelsea Flower Show, old Commander George starts in dying with a suppurating leg, eyebrows are raised, sighs heaved, garden paths trodden, the rose beds tremble, in fragile exercises in construction. The narrator cycles along a Somerset road in June sunshine, pondering (no doubt) on the devious mechanisms by which the memory is activated. The trivia of day-to-day Muddle Class life is faithfully recorded. Benign muzziness? The usual chaos of living well? It's a mild November in Worthing.

Holy Pictures is Clare Boylan's first novel. We are back into oppressed Catholic Ireland with a vengeance, circa 1925 in Dublin, where the mother does not act against the father's wishes and no windows were ever opened, *Ave Maria* is played loudly on a gramophone, women work a ten-hour day at the factory, putrified horsemeat festers on the plates of the inmates at the Union, on the bridge at Sullivan's Cross the corner-boys are waiting for gruesome things to float by; they will not be disappointed. Best Wigan coal is selling at 49 shillings a ton, Cantwell corsets are being manufactured, the daughter bandages her growing breasts, the mothers look bemused, the ancestors creak and murmur in their frames: do not give impudence when talking to your betters. The immodestly contoured older girls in class were 'putty in the hands of the devil.' The gentry were said to devour worms in Gorgonzola cheese. Cow pluck suspended from the clothes-line attracts stray cats. On the South Circular Road the Jewish traders are making a living where the natives would certainly starve: Wertzberger, Weinronk (real name Schweitzer, known as 'Shyster the Jew'), Buchalter, rag merchants, wine merchants and bakers, of the five thousand Jews living around Clanbrassil Street, in those days of yore. 'To your womanhood,' the Jews teased.

The damaged hearts (mostly female) here cannot even begin to dream of a post-de Valera capital of whores and pimps, protection rackets and 'saunas,' in a thoroughly liberated Ireland some fifty-eight years on. 'They felt for one another's hands and began to find their trail out of the forest.'

Books Ireland, no. 74, June 1983

75

The Blackrock Cosmology

Adrian Kenny (ed.), *The Journal of Arland Ussher* (Raven Arts)

Ussher dearly loved theoretical complexities, the more complex the better; question him about Heraclitus or Klopstock, Boehme or Swedenborg; Ussher was ready, his mind was not narrow. Maybe he loved his home-comforts too much, loathe to leave his library and references. Somehow one never saw him as a father; he seemed to be the perennial bachelor. His passing closes a genteel if more impoverished era; whether or not he was a true philosopher remains to be seen. He liked to insinuate and modestly infer with much shy tittering that *some* system or other had been evolved in the Blackrock study, some post-Tar Water schematics involving graphs and obscure pointers in coloured inks hung over his desk—the Blackrock Cosmology.

But it might have been one of his jokes. A more gregarious anchorite you wouldn't meet on a day's march. He liked to flatter his hearers, being himself somewhat vain, and attributed intelligence where it was not. He froze in the presence of belligerent rudeness and wasn't there for the sceptic and the hostile. He had acolytes of course, shy as himself; all his long life he was engaged in that most unIrish of occupations: thinking.

Oppressed Ireland has produced few painters of international class, while for the philosophers, you would have to go back to Bishop Berkeley and Duns Scotus. Ussher published very little and used to say that he had no philosophy, for the times were out of joint and wisdom would fall on deaf ears. 'No one that ever lived ever thought as crooked as we,' moans blind Hamm from his shrouded throne.

Flann O'Brien was invited to Ussher's retreat just once and kicked the ancestral furniture about the small sittingroom, demanding to know how anybody could live amid 'such junk'—the grandfather's antique hand-carved stool! The Sunday soirées were peculiar affairs: Constantine

Fitzgibbon squatted toad-like in a corner, the Butlers came from Bologna, the drinks tray was whisked away before the glasses were replenished, the genial host kept tittering away like a tap dripping.

He should have worn a peruke or a wig, not the latter-day toupee (real hair but a dead man's), claimed to be distantly related to Nell Gwyn and thus in line to the throne of England, offered his services as an Irish hangman. He would have made a benign judge; none would be punished in Ussher's Court of Justice—even if his grandfather had ridden down Croppies at Cappagh. The grandson could converse in Gaelic with the ploughman, perhaps his subtle way of trying to make amends, level things out. His Protestant sympathy for Irish Catholicism—not the narrowly practiced variety—came as a surprise. A Catholic Ussher would have been impossible, an abomination like Wilde's three-headed ogre that devoured itself. No more obscure claimant to the English throne ever sipped dry sherry.

The railwaymen in the signal-box above Merrion Gates level-crossing trembled for his safety—Ussher alone and plunged in thought on the tracks, and the Wexford train pounding in. I told them that he was a philosopher looking for a lost philosophy.

This narrow and ill-gummed-together volume is difficult to keep open, the contents culled from a 14-volume diary covering the period 1943-77, detailed as those of Thoreau or Emerson or Captain Cookes's log. He was not in the class of Chateaubriand or Kafka as an aphorist, though pithy sayings can improve with age, like vintage wine. Chesterton and Wilde were public men in a way that Ussher never aspired to be; W. B. Yeats had trained himself to be a public man, but Ussher lived the life of a recluse, aghast at what he saw about him—the increasing vulgarity and violence in the world, himself gentle and passive, an ascetic of passion like Yeats's Proud Costello.

'I am a practical person,' I read with some amazement, remembering Emily Ussher leading the tittering philosopher into the kitchen and showing him the large boiler, which he had roundly declared did not exist in the house, where he had been resident for two-score years and more.

Curious how such sedentary men fall for the deeply absurd philosopher-novelist D.H. Lawrence.

I am saddened not to receive any more letters in tight single-spacing on the red ribbon, the signature taking a dive when Ussher was depressed or indisposed; for in a damp house overlooking Sandycove

Beach he did not enjoy much good health. 'The Irish never die,' he declared once; 'they just drop off':

> It is evident that this race—little inclined as it is to revolution, but rather deeply and warily conservative—must make a powerful appeal to revolutionaries. The Irishman has real scorn and life-rejection—even though the gesture is barren and negative, it is not mischievous and perverse. Synge's Playboy, Christy Mahon, is an idiot who becomes a bully; yet just because we see him so very much alone, he has become one of the few quixotic figures in modern literature. Because he is apart and uncommitted, he is disposable, because he is timid, he blusters his way into poetry; because he has no belief in anything but chance, chance can seem to lift him—for a brief moment—above other men. For a moment only! The Irishman cannot believe in himself sufficiently for real success, and seems, when most successful, to court Nemesis like a player. Oscar Wilde must stand his hopeless trial, Parnell throw away himself and his country's cause; these men are like somnambulists . . .

It's Arland Ussher's very voice. All that old gentility now gone; this residue is part of the larger detritus in fourteen volumes, here cast upon the Finglas foreshore.

The Irish Times, 20 February 1981

76

The Bosky Dew

From the catalogue of the Patrick Collins Retrospective Exhibition
at Douglas Hyde Gallery, Trinity College Dublin. Summer 1983.

Ulysses was his Bible. He called it Üley-says, liked to quote two lines from it; of Stephen 'rear regardant' and of 'The weedy waterways of Ireland.' These were the lodes, the fern seed hexagonals, the *Cephalanthera* and *Epipactis*, the bosky dew.

He knew Ellmann, onto whose surname he insisted on grafting a third syllable, showed him where Bloom might have pitched from Ben Howth, tore the great ensuing biography in twain, all 842 pages of it.

He lived in Ireland for most of his life, went abroad reluctantly, took it with him. In a London restaurant he gave his order in atrocious French; waiting in the reception area at breakfast time, was appalled to see one hundred identical men come downstairs in dark suits, bowler hats, with rolled umbrellas, carrying briefcases. In Turkey once on the steps of the station (Istanbul?) he saw a strange bug, studied it all day. He was a lover of the visible world.

His letters when they came were much like his conversation, tart, the telling phrase (he wanted to be a writer; I wanted to be a painter), a sort of dandy Irish Degas; once in Normandy he had threatened to knock me down for dismissing the Frenchman's work. Self-educated, his mind was not narrow. He liked to talk, liked French wine and tobacco (Diskey Blew), congenial company, preferably Irish (the major and minor premise). He always had plenty of words when he wanted them, appeared to know a lot of people but had few close friends; whom his *intimados* were I never knew. He saw things that others less perceptive would have missed.

Once in winter after a shower when we were crossing transversally the wet Ranelagh triangle, heading for James Russell's godless pub, a thin young beauty in high heels stepped off the curb, seen for a moment in the act of crossing a narrow-road-become-stream-after-shower, and he glancing quickly said: 'Sandpiper.' He liked the jenny wrens in the low Normandy ditches.

Once he whistled a robin-hen out of a bush on the Howth Road, pretending to be a cock-robin at the start of the mating season. In his youth he affected a Latin Quarter hat, sunk deep in Celtic gloom, was Stephen Dedalus. He loved wild birds, first and last light, mystical nature who is commanded by obeying her; he fancied a spicey brand of Findlater's rasher which he cooked by dropping it into an open wood fire. He was rarely in low spirits, or hid it, never morose, a traveller who had remained at home. He liked the company of women. Once in a bosky wood with a tall lady, she noticed how his nostrils expanded. After many years of confident bachelorhood, he came to late fatherhood in middle age. He was never stingy, did not go in for our national sport: mudslinging.

His fragile art had something of the *muscae volitantes* to it, threads seen before the eyes, opaque fragments floating in the vitreous humour, flying clouds. He painted Howth Castle as though adrift on the outgoing tide, in unnerving hydrotherapy. He should have been a sailor in Melville's day. His art was circumscribed, as the Eskimos,' but not for him le Brocquy's white spaces. His palette was feminine, pink, grey and faint blue, early-morning sky colours. He admired the work of Cezanne, Leger, Pollock, Bacon, wild men with oils, his opposites. And Nano Reid, Camille Souter, his likes. He had something of Izaak Walton in him ('Everything is alive . . . birds and animals are as interesting as men and women'), or witty Lamb in a boisterous mood. There was something of the dandy there. No shrewder judge of character trod shoeleather. He was (still is) his own man. 'Any painting I did in my life,' he told the *Irish Times* lady, 'has got forty paintings underneath it . . . or maybe only five.'

He was touched by the sight of the prehistoric standing stone in a brake of trees in the Castle grounds, as later by the menhirs of Brittany. Underneath them lay the everlasting forms. He painted the shadow of things, avoiding the direct face, the later lies of Rembrandt. Opposites greatly appealed. He introduced me to Donne's poetry, the stories of Eudora Welty, Chief Ikkemotubbe and Yoknapatawpha County, Flagstad singing Wagner's *Liebestod* on an old 78, Flamenco music, Maire ni Scollig, bottled and draught Guinness. When thickheaded from the drink, he could be brilliant. We walked on Sunday mornings in the damp Castle grounds, smoked Diskey Blew up in trees. He had a grand laugh, low and personal, the Stuart love-locks nodding. He had, one shouldn't wonder, something of the Shane O'Neill nature: hot royal blood; yet he was good-natured. False position induces cant; and of this he was refreshingly free.

When I knew him first in his Howth Castle days, he was working in an insurance office in O'Connell Street, and spent six months or more on a painting, reworking over it with a dry brush, layer upon layer of paint with little or no geometric perspective, like the inside of a faintly luminous box; the outside, the damp countryside, was all flux and flying cloud. A technique like the lacquered nature painting of the Edo period in Japan, long after Musashi the champion painter-swordsman, or Jaku-chu, who spent eight years on a series of thirty dyed silk scrolls called 'The Colourful World of Living Beings.' One looked into the details for a sight of Basho bound for some secret shrine, his stomach shrunken, ill with dysentery, living on black rice and *sake*. I was in my middle twenties; the savant-painter in his middle forties. His landlord was a Lord, related to a great Catholic family expelled into Connacht by Cromwell. Another attendant Lord lived in the bird sanctuary on Ireland's Eye. You spoke of the difficulty of getting any breakfast there, the profusion of daffodils in the grounds.

I first met Paddy Collins in Arthur Power's hospitable house behind the monkey-puzzle in Sandymount; 1950 it might have been. I'd met Power through Ussher, whose name had been given me by Sam Beckett. The Powers had said: 'Higgins must meet Paddy.' A monk, Doris said, a mystic, who lived alone in a wing of Howth Castle: Kenelm's Tower. It was arranged. It must have been winter, I recall a coal fire burning in the grate. Brinsley MacNamara was there. Collins arrived later with a gorgeous girl, Carmen. I knew no one in Dublin in those days, had written Beckett in praise of *Murphy*, and he had given me Ussher's address on Strand Road.

Lord Talbot de Malahide allowed him the dead timber in the grounds. I took to spending weekends there, sawing and hauling wood, sleeping on the sofa before the fire at night, listening to Collins speak. His boyhood had been spent in some strict religious teaching institution, he had been to Paris. Early on Monday morning the door banged below and he was off to the insurance office in O'Connell Street. I put some of that time into a story called 'Tower and Angels' (from Donne's 'Aire and Angels') ten years later, and some more into a novel (*Balcony of Europe*) twenty years later, and more again into another novel (*Scenes from a Receding Past*) twenty-seven years later. For Heidelberg read Howth, for Neckar read Liffey, for Fishback read Millionaire's Cove, for Schloss Park Schwitzingen read St. Stephen's Green, for 'Pastern' (the man who came to look at a horse and stayed as tenant) and 'Ruttle' read Collins, with an admixture of Ussher—the former objecting to the 'emaciated buttocks' of the latter. The Yeats family had once lived in Balscadden Cottage, John Butler taking Willie into Amiens Street and across to his studio in the Green. Collins had walked in the opposite direction across the Green to his office in O'Connell Street. I have come across a Merlin Revue of Winter 1952-53 which he borrowed once. *Godot* has just opened in Paris; corpses are being exhumed from 10 Rillington Place. Collins is living in Kenelm's Tower.

Of those finished times and friends, now so many gone to ground—Ussher, Terry Butler, Dillon and Campbell, Knudsen and Gerda Schurmann, Ralph Cusack, Behan, MacNamara, Billy of Davey Byrne's—what remains?

These canvases offer some kind of testimony. Painting, that most rigorous of arts, attempts the impossible: to arrest time. Now for a while the episodic labour of a lifetime is gathered together here; but its creator I trust has not yet finished.

Collins himself is not by nature a modest man; he knows too well what he has. He already praised in print Hone and Paul Henry ('a modest man who painted Ireland like an Irishman'), strangely omitting Orpen; but more gifted Irish landscapers (seers of sorts) were to arrive later—himself, Nano Reid, Camille Souter (an errie Grand Canal in the Municipal Gallery is fine as anything by Corot).

Jack Yeats in his later years applied oil thickly with a knife as if spreading butter, and his human figures are treated as sentimentally as any by Keating. As for Paul Henry, he had much to be modest about; instead of painting what was there before him he seemed to be employing knitting needles (large wooden ones), and worked it out in grey-blue wool; not painting but wool-gathering. Those absurd clouds and uninhabited cottages existed only in his head. The fierce cirrocumulus towering over Mayo, lit from within and behind, was beyond him.

But Collins's landscapes are quite another thing, the real thing, his own, and yours and mine, thankfully. Those remote images brought close seem to emerge from the point of a hypodermic. Superfine. But, speaking of suffering, you cannot take his Stations of the Cross too seriously. He was never a figure painter.

From Johannesburg I once ordered a Collins landscape from Ritchie Hendrick's Gallery on the Green; it arrived in due course at Jan Smuts Airport, with an old copy of *Ulysses* strapped onto its back. Back in Dublin and throttled by pecuniary limits, I was obliged to sell it, the artist himself kindly finding a buyer in Sir Basil Goulding.

Paddy Collins has come a long way from Dromore West, from George Collie's Life Class, from Dermot O'Brien's old studio in Pembroke Lane, from Kenelm's Tower and the paintings of that time, Rain Lake and Moorland Water, Children in a Legend, Stephen Hero; and yet not so far. This roundelay makes it all contemporaneous. The good things are not yet gone. Painter of *plein-air*, paint on!

77

Glencree *Knackwurst*

Francis Stuart, *The High Consistory* (Martin, Brian & O'Keeffe)

The air dimmed under the cloudless sky in the form of a wave of doubt. I stopped to reflect and find out its cause, which it didn't take long to determine was the realisation that in the face of my fantasy even the other festival happenings would be totally effaced.

Grammatical niceties, and indeed logic, have never been this author's strong card; he thinks nothing of ending a sentence on a preposition. His tormented characters indulge in back-chat with themselves, of which the digression above is fairly representative: 'I think,' Claire surmised, 'that I as yet did not!'

The verbal infelicities and scrambling attack recall Warwick Deeping, or our own dear Maurice Walsh. Novels with narrators purporting to be painters, and good ones at that, seldom convince—neither *The Horse's Mouth* nor *Islands in the Stream* nor *The Razor's Edge* begin to approximate to *Cher Theo* or *Mahu Mahu,* real painters' diaries.

Our author had always shown concern for 'the creative and prophetic spirit' in whatever bottle it might be corked up. Your critic first encountered his work in the defunct *Envoy* and took it to be of German origin, ill-translated into an English full of redundancy and wooden dialogue with a very German propensity to justify and explain his characters' motives at length; which did nothing to raise our spirits. Hans Fallada, by comparison, seemed sharp as a whip.

A reading of *Pillar of Cloud* (1948, reissued by Martin, Brian & O'Keefe, 1974) and *Redemption* (1949, reissued by Martin, Brian & O'Keefe, 1974) already reveal martyr complex and stained shroud—precisely what Joyce attacked, and Beckett attacks. Ireland has no further use for these manifold tomfooleries; it has gone on too long already. *Black List, Section H* fails because of the pseudonyms; leaving aside the high content of cliché.

In this his twenty-third novel, published at the ripe old age of seventy-nine, the narrator is a painter called Simeon Grimes, commissioned to paint a portrait of the Führer, who is too busy to sit, having other fish to fry (in the early 1940s). His agent, thought to be Jewish, accepts the large fee.

Grimes is then commissioned to paint 'The Little Flower' for the convent of the Little Sisters of the Holy Face in Minneapolis, falls for a French-Canadian lady, who is later ravished by a pet ocelot. Chronology is deliberately jumbled as the diaries and papers from which it is reassembled are scattered in a jet crash.

Grimes is questioned by an improbable pair from MI5 in Berlin in 1942, invites the famous American writer Robert Banim to the holy island of Inisheask, after offering arms to Pearse in the GPO, declines the services of a black call-girl called Pacella (wink, wink), is then given a hot tip for Chantilly by Therese of Lisieux, drops a packet but is consoled by a Polish lady, mistress of Gascon de Many Paloner.

All splendid stuff in the picaresque vein, like the 48A bus bowling along towards Bray, until the plot runs aground around page 167 with a visit to the National Gallery of Ireland and the introduction of some Dublin bowsies, but when Grimes & Co. set off for the Holy Island all is reduced to pathos.

Within this *pons asinorum* of plot, there are a few felicities. The stableman who worked for Noel Murless is 'an elderly man, the skin of his face like pale mud from which a flock of starlings had lately taken off, bearing the imprint of their feet.' If you can call that felicity. Leaving aside for the moment that mighty elusive element, The Creative & Prophetic Spirit, with which some Irish critics claim his work is imbued, Stuart has lately praised the later work of Mr. Cronin (to whom this volume is dedicated), while dismissing *Company*, Mr. Beckett's latest work in English—a revealing misjudgement. The blunt attestations and ambiguous decorum of this fundamentally old-style novelist are a very far cry from Beckett's near-speechless misgivings. But the novel will appeal strongly to Irish readers for it is crammed with familiar lies.

The Irish Times, 7 February 1981

78

The Corn Is Green

Liam O'Flaherty, *Famine* (Wolfhound)

Devouring Time swallows us whole. As deep-freeze processed food replaces fresh beans or carrots dug from the ground, so too coronaries replace gout and dropsy. Now read on.

It's difficult to get through *The Islandman* with a perfectly straight face if you have first read Flann O'Brien's wicked parody, *The Poor Mouth*; as it is difficult to stomach *Stephen Hero* after reading *Ulysses*, difficult to get through Gorman's biography after reading Ellmann, or to read O'Flaherty after Joyce, particularly if you encounter *Famine* after Mrs Woodham-Smith.

O'Flaherty's first novel was published in 1923, the year after *Ulysses* appeared, eleven years before Beckett's *More Pricks Than Kicks*, when Hemingway's first novel *Fiesta* was ten years into re-reprinting. O'Flaherty calmly proceeds along his sedately outmoded way as though *Ulysses* had never astonished us. This being a reissue of the 1937 blockbuster. Its plot is rocky as Aran itself, following the plight of three generations of the Kilmartin family in a small village on the Mayo-Galway border in the period 1845-46 during the potato blight and subsequent famine.

It is a free and meandering tale in the way *Thy Tears Might Cease* and Plunkett's *Strumpet City* meander, massive only in bulk, epic only in name ('panting with the effort of thought'), dedicated to another famous Aran-man, the movie legend John Ford. Even Ford himself at his most winsome could not make much sense of Fr. Roche and his curate conferring on the sacred ground and the subsequent march against the constabulary ('God bless Father Tom,' shouted the people).

Character delineation is paper-thin, or prejudice-deep; situations are contrived and cannot develop in any logical or (as with Faulkner) illogical way; but are content to go rattling along like a stagecoach full of garrulous starving Irishery, masters of implausible dialect. The villains, as often happens in Hollywood, get all the best lines; Chadwick is the only realised character in the novel. In India, ambushed by 'heathens,' he had half his *shame* cut off. The inexhaustible virtue and sufferings of the rest of the Irish cast creates a vacuum ('Easy now, John . . .') into which the whole narrative collapses. The picaresque form is perhaps unsuited to such a grim theme.

Steinbeck's destitute ones at least spoke convincingly, as did the parasitic Snopes clan in Faulkner's trilogy. The first person singular appears mysteriously thrice at widely separated intervals (cf. pages 237, 257, 393) as though the troubled author was lost in there somewhere, struggling to write a different novel. Towards the end (page 442) the diction changes and *Famine* briefly becomes a better novel:

> Three horsemen came riding from the east, along the edge of the tall shore grass. The hooves of their horses threw up little blobs of sand. At the same time a Spanish ass came trotting from the west, drawing a cart on which sat a man, who wore a tall hat and a grey cape.

The biblical undertones have come full circle; a new Ireland is about to be born. But somewhere along the way O'Flaherty lost himself, levitating too far off the ground.

The Wolfhound Press has done a fine job, as have the Trowbridge printers, though the boards creak a little when abruptly parted, though scarcely more so than the plot itself.

Hibernia, 18 January 1981

79

Blood Brothers

Eugene McCabe, *Heritage and Other Stories* (Gollancz)

PREAMBLE: 'it is a proverb of an old date,' quoth a Sixteenth Century English savant with polished acumen, 'that the pride of France, and the war of Ireland, shall never have an end. Which proverb, touching the war of Ireland, is always likely to continue, without God set in men's hearts to find some new remedy that was never found before.'

Dr. Whyte of Queen's University, Belfast, argues that anyone who studies the Northern conflict must be struck by the intensity of feeling there; which seems to go beyond what is required by a rational defence of the divergent interests which undoubtedly exist: there is an irrational element, a 'welling up of deep unconscious forces which can only be explained by an appeal to social psychology.' He suggested a three-year moratorium on discussions. But not talking of it will not make it go away. The conflict is so intense, not just because Protestants mistrust Catholics; but because they also mistrust each other. The closed circuit of 'an eternity of public fawning and private snarls' has come full circle and the nostrums of Hume and Fitt grow knottier by the hour.

The American historian Professor David Miller proposes a new theory of Protestant identity, suggesting that the Northern Protestants 'missed out' on the great nationalist movement in Europe through the last century and, as a result, their fixed attitudes are 'pre-national.' whatever that may mean. Today Protestants are more deeply divided than at any time since the 1880s. They are not looking for nationhood but for themselves; an alternative life that existed nowhere is being considered. You do terrible things to prove that you are a real person. Expert appraisers have signally failed to agree on what has gone wrong.

Half a century ago, before such killing had become institutionalised, Yeats, ever perceptive where Irish feelings were concerned, detected evidence of 'our Irish cruelty' in the opening passages of *Ulysses*. Joyce himself had detected a past riddled with treachery—our own. The 'British' soldier from Belfast dying on the Western Front in Longley's extraordinary poem 'Wounds,' cries 'Give them one for the Shankhill!' At which Longley's father marvels: 'Savage as Ghurkas.'

NOW READ ON. Hot on the heels of Kiely's *cri de coeur Proxopera*, comes Eugene McCabe's grim collection of border moralities, in a vein not hitherto attempted: controlled bile. There is a leery Irish saying to the effect that you cannot kill a bad thing; McCabe suggests that it kills itself. The metaphor used most often is of caged animals (rats?). Belief in fire as curative prevails; from the damp piano that won't function in 'Music in Annahullion,' on to TNT and the fire-bomb. The dull red glow over Fermanagh may be sun trying to rise, or more property burning.

The dropped commas in the dialogue are most ingenious, like links slipped from chains. The text is riddled with checkpoints. At Glasgow in the 1880s seasonal migrants from Northern Ireland offer themselves at the hiring fair with large numbers of pigs and poultry. A child lies to save a Catholic servant, the servant is sacked, takes the Belfast boat. 'If they take anything, they'll take everything . . . they're all the same; they lie as they breathe.' The infection returns to the source.

The second story, 'Victoria Fields,' is taken from depositions made at Petty Sessions held in 1872 and concerns two brothers and a wife whom they are attempting to have certified in Monaghan Asylum in order to inherit a small parcel of land and four cows.

In 'Roma,' a simpleton is enamoured of the young daughter of an Italian fish-and-chip shop, whom he confuses with the Blessed Virgin, sees the Holy Family in a field in Knockatallon and promptly departs for Leitrim.

The two remaining stories, 'Cancer' and the novella that gives the collection its title, take off into a region hitherto unexplored by Irish pen-pushers of whatever persuasion. The incorrigible hardness of the North adheres to them. Hawthorn's grave is trim and neat, showing evidence of Protestant order and need for privacy. The Catholic progenitive capacity is seen as a threat, hence the sneers at 'hedge whore Papists' and a reference to Protestant brother Sam's 'whorey Papist wife,' meaning Southern (Roman-Catholic) fecklessness. The senile mother is raving. The quaint County Armagh of rural copulators encountered in Leitch's *Stamping Ground* cannot stand up to scrutiny when compared to this. And even such excellent new work as Neil Jordan's *Night in Tunisia* or Healy's *Banished Misfortune*—work which one takes to be a new and fruitful departure

away from the old certainties, the Abbey antics and the *Irish Press* school of
scribbling—are here possibly surpassed, by an ear closer to the ground. At
all events Val Mulkerns's *Antiquities* or the stories of Kate Cruise O'Brien are
merely themes of fashionable self-absorption that have gone on too long.

Here the Catholic-Protestant impasse is set forth in fugal form: *Anglo-Celt*
versus *Protestant-Telegraph*, the two sainted Johns (assassinated Kennedy and
the second-last-ex-Pope) versus 'smokey portraits of the Queen' and Paisley
alongside a row of 'faded sashes' in the murderous blacksmith's forge. 'I'll
shoe no Catholic ass, my boot in his hole.' No symbols except unless express-
ly intended. The dialogue is as alarming as gunfire. 'Cancer could be in the
blood fifty years and then all of a shot it boils up and you're a gonner.'

The illegitimate progeny of Protestant-Catholic unions turn out to be
halfwits. Willy Reilly wears a knitted cap like a tea cosy. The otter-hunt
is memorable:

> From their gaunt lands they looked down on the green border
> country below, watching, waiting. To them a hundred years was
> yesterday, two hundred years the day before.

The burden of the argument would seem to be that men who don't
wish to hate are pushed to it. The murderer lies in his own vomit—'raving
about Christ in the fields.'

Wasn't it Céline who wrote that the crimes of which a people is
ashamed constitute its real history and the same is true of man? Here
the onstage bloodshed rivals a Shakespearean shambles. A British soldier
with a Yorkshire accent speaks the epilogue: 'Christ knows, he's Irish
mate. They're all fucking mad over here; shoot first, ask after.'

The lurid text is mercifully free of that untranslatable German
word *Schöngeistig*, or poetry with a capital P. Local scribblers take note.
The tribal formulae of human existence—irrevocability, unrealisabil-
ity, inevitability—is known to McCabe. The sombre dictate *blood tells*
tolls over Tatnagone, Oakfield, Latgallon and the fond hope of an Irish
brotherhood of man would seem as remote as ever.

Irish History? A servant sharpening knives: *Gael versus Gall,* Orange
versus Green, Catholic versus Protestant; the sectarian killer, the bullet in
the back, the Irish confusion, the old Irish cruelty directed against itself.

Hibernia, 11 November 1976

80

Buck Mulligan

J. B. Lyons, *Oliver St. John Gogarty: The Man of Many Talents* (Blackwater)

He loved yellow, wore yellow handmade boots, drove a yellow Mercedes, later a butter-coloured Rolls, famously fell out with James Joyce. One of the chronically impecunious Joyce brothers sent him a begging letter in 1918: 'Dear Dr. Gogarty, Can you lend me £11? I feel I am treating you badly but the pressure is very great. Charles Joyce.' He had somehow offended brother James, a bad man to cross, whom Gogarty would later dismiss as being 'not a gentleman.'

Both were touchy, both seeking a new colour for Irish art; snot-green would not serve. Both composed fragile verse, frail villanelles, had heated imaginations; their paths were to diverge. Joyce's revenge for the cut, real or imaginary, was a cruel one: Gogarty was trapped for perpetuity in the *Joyzewerks* as 'Buck Mulligan.'

Their last years were equally wretched, dying respectively in Zurich and New York. Gogarty had feared the 'Celtic chloroform'; Joyce thought that the Celt had 'contributed nothing but a whine to Europe.' My mother knew Gogarty and thought him a witty fellow; he sent her inscribed copies of his books from America. Some were not for sale in the Saorstat, by request of the author. I read them as a lad and found them far from salacious, despite the titillating promise of some titles—*Tumbling in the Hay* and *Rolling Down the Leer. As I Was Going Down Sackville Street* was intensely arch and not much different in kind from the mild-mannered tittle-tattle and inane social gossip of *The Irish Tatler & Sketch*.

The Gogertys or Gogartys were a branch of the County Tipperary ruling sept, MacFogarty, which on moving to County Meath (Nobber) changed its name to O'Gogarty or Gogarty. Richard ('Uncle Dick') Howard Aloysius Gogarty was the Dublin agent for Argyll Motor Company before emigrating to Argentina where he styled himself Señor Ricardo O'Gogarty; when last heard of he was working for Cook's.

Dr. Gogarty had strong views on the value of preventative medicine; in August 1924 there were 250 children's deaths out of every thousand born, one out of every four died. He said that the prevention of disease must begin in the schools. The Dublin slums were 'Out-Patients' departments of the nineteen Dublin hospitals . . . It is monstrous to have this city splattered over with lazar houses.'

He urged that one large central hospital be built up in the mountains near Kilbride. His fidelity to Arthur Griffith led him into a kind of hysteria against the Republican party; he had a very great dislike of Mr. de Valera, as had my own father. Dr. Gogarty was elected onto the first Senate by the Cosgrave Government on account of his literary attainments. During the Civil War he was kidnapped from his home in Ely Place and taken to a boathouse on the Liffey to be shot. But Gogarty escaped and swam the Liffey to safety; he vowed that if he got away he would donate two swans to Anna Livia. They were liberated at the Trinity Boat Club with Yeats in attendance. The Clonskeagh tram-conductor responsible for his capture was later murdered and Gogarty took possession of a keepsake—a bullet dug out of the body of the victim.

For de Valera the Senator had only contempt: 'The President ran the Irish treasureship on the rocks in spite of many warnings from the Seanad and he wants it to be applauded because he gets away in a lifeboat with a quarter of beef and a lump of coal.'

Gogarty argued that it is bad to hate anybody, but worse to hate England, not for fear of reprisal—'for how can she possibly imagine we have any hate left over when we have done so strangely by ourselves?' For him, England had become identified with all that came from Europe and civilisation; humanitarianism and all those things which are indispensable for human life were pilloried in the general hate:

> Everything becomes anathema save ruin and vulgarity. We are to be fed on the negations of a progressive people—pauperism and plainness. Is there any other way of not being English? Is there no other way of being Irish?

Seamus O'Sullivan stood at the window of his house on Morehampton Road, watching a man pass with a cart of manure. 'I see Paddy Kavanagh is moving house. There go his furniture and effects.'

The celebrated Gogarty wit is not much in evidence in this untidy compilation, which gives little idea of the progress of his life; nothing is said of the Bailey nights, the bawdy verse omitted, while a long bad war poem is given *in toto*. Penultimate paragraphs tend to subside onto their sequels, the chapter-heads are disconcerting; a lacuna occurs after page 80, followed immediately by page 161 through to page 178; the following page is given as 97 and from there on the numbering is carried through chronologically to the end, duplicating pages 161-76 but omitting Chapters 7 and 8, *videlicet* 'With Flowers and Wine and Cakes Divine' and 'Learn Your Trade.' Lines, like converging train tracks, sometimes merge; overprinting creates a muzzy effect of double vision, and transposed sections intrude into the text proper. It must have been a wild night in the printing works of the Blackwater Press.

Bleached-out photographs of parents and grandfather show stuffed stiff figures from a waxworks. 'He never got under the surface,' he remarked after Orpen's funeral, 'until he got under the ground.' Molly Colum, wife of the poet, 'was one of those rancid women who shake one's belief in the juniper berry.' And there is a further wounding reference to the 'tame flesh of the convent-cooled wife' of the small, self-satisfied poet who wrote *Wild Earth*.

His particular bugbear (Dev) was 'a cross between a corpse and a cormorant.' At the end the specialist is smiling behind the oxygen mask, Renvyle House long gone up in flames, rebuilt, in other hands, 'Damn the vulture dead who left us nothing but a heritage of hatred.'

Persuaded that a 'major contributor to Anglo-Irish literature was being short-changed,' this frothy pseudo-scholarship sets out to mend the omission but this makes sorry reading.

Hibernia, 17 April 1981

81

Recurring Refrain

Kathleen Worth (ed.), *Beckett the Shape Changer: A Symposium*
(Routledge & Keegan Paul)

The erstwhile publishers of *Murphy* (1938) have brought forth this collection of critical residua on the Master's *oeuvre,* though the insights here paraded are slight:

> Getting to know Mr. Beckett could seem a rather formidable business [gushes the Editoress], How best to approach him, how to read him, how to get closer to the concrete experience, these were the questions we pursued; perhaps they may be thought sufficiently real [?!] and pressing [!!] to justify our following them up in print [!!!].

The cool effrontery of that 'perhaps' is rich. Settle back in your armchairs, gentle browser, we are in the presence of bores, *arch* bores, academics trimming their fingernails.

The said symposium 'grew' out of a series of five lectures delivered at the University of London Extramural Department, here dreadfully augmented by an additional three papers. All this dubious bounty from the delicate hands of university lecturers and teachers. In a word, individuals with cultural axes to grind; and grind them they surely do.

Barbara Hardy's piece ('The Dubious Consolations in Beckett's Fiction: Art, Love and Nature') invites the hot blush. Brian Finney rambles on about the shorter fiction, some of it unpublished. 'There is no better commentary on the work of Beckett's than the rest of his writing,' leaving aside the awkward grammar, comes curiously off the page.

Exegesis breeds exegesis; soon they are at it hammer and tongs, Driver and Gruen, Fletcher and Federman, Kenner and Sage; the checklist oddly echoes the coupled surnames of Lucky's ravings in *Godot.*

All is explained. Victor Sage is . . . sage on *How It Is*, mud and all. Martin Dodsworth strikes a bold dissenting note in seeing *Film* as a total failure, which throws the ladies into a dither:

> Looked at together, *Film* and *Eh Joe* remind us of the continual temptation for Beckett of falling back on the schematic and dogmatic and the difficulty he has in resisting it.

Stoutly spoken, Dodsworth! Kathleen Worth contrives to add nothing new in an 'argument' spread loosely over threescore pages of *intuit*, on the teasing subject of the theatre of deprivation. Perhaps *Happy Days* (*Ah les beaux jours*) is indeed unperformable, unless played in the dark by deaf mutes.

Who, in their right minds, would buy this book, which is not cheap? Would it not have the effect, contrary to that intended, of putting potential readers right *off* Beckett's work? It reeks of the seminar. 'How Beckett renews and reshapes himself, the freshness, variety, inventiveness of the process is our recurring refrain,' warbles the intro.

It's not a very sunny symposium; but then again, few symposia are, given their nature, and audience. The work itself, liberally quoted, breathes like a great lung, far removed from these arcane researchers. The face of Samuel Beckett glares through a mesh of stippled dots on the dustjacket. Precise intent of fixed scrutiny difficult to gauge, but at all events in full retreat from the schematic. *Nich ich!*

Hibernia, 18 July 1977

82

Cark

The Collected Stories of Sean O'Faolain, vol. 2 (Constable)

The prolific ex-Corkman, present incumbent of some place designated 'Dunlaoire,' seems self-exiled in his native land, itself riven by sectarian killings; is this perchance an *Irish* form of suicide?

Two old IRA cronies carry a corpse across the border, after a botched raid, engaged on a discussion about Goethe's *Faust*: 'the open mouth showed fine white teeth smiling at them.' The relentlessly joshing manner—surrogate sincerity—might not be to all tastes. His gabby natives perceive Ireland in Tourist Brochure prose: 'The heather streamed past them like kangaroos . . . to their right they heard the lisping bay.' Clouds are likened to soapsuds, to human hair; waves to worms. The *obiter dictum* is generally awful, wise priests and solemn Monsignori abound.

The benevolent despotism of the plots will not allow the characters to live an inch beyond that permitted—Donna, Biddy, Patrick, Tommy Morgan, Molly Cardew, Carrie Brindle and the Jewish girl from Buffalo, Fr. Saturnius (a good old Irish name) perform as they are bid. Is the Irish vacuum a fictional convention or does it really exist? Cork is not, admittedly, Vienna of yesterday, or West Berlin of today. 'Love is a sedative disguised as a stimulant' seems a poor mot from a sometimes witty Corkman. The reverse might be truer. 'The gay, bubbling over, have no time for the pitiful.'

Only in the story of Lord Carew's lake is there any respite, enough to let the real people, and the land, through. Of the thirty odd stories, some novella size, covering the period 1958-66, not one even begins to hint at the upheavals that lie ahead.

Hibernia, 18 March 1978

83

Poolbeg Flashers

David Marcus (ed.), *Body and Soul: Irish Short Stories of Sexual Love*
(Poolbeg Press)

Isn't it rude to have no clothes on, isn't it, daddy? They should have
put their clothes on, shouldn't they, daddy? That's where the fire
was, wasn' it, daddy?

'The Compromise'

David Marcus, *eminence grise* of New Irish Writing, has fathered a further
short-story collection with the bold subtitle appended above and a daring
Ballagh cover of a supine nude to startle the natives. It's a Cahill Printers
rough job, with grateful acknowledgements to the Arts Council.

A baker's dozen taken from already published (but here undated)
collections or from magazines, the *Irish Press* grab-bag, with only three
from hands of the unfair sex, yields nothing much in the way of sharp
surprises.

O'Faolain's old chestnut 'The Talking Trees' has a pathetic fallacy in
the title, Edna O'Brien has one in her first line. No great matter; Joyce's
'Araby' has three on the first page.

Two of the stories (Trevor and O'Faolain) are set in Cork, four in
Dublin, one in Belfast, one in the ghost village of Kilcreeshla (four
schoolchildren, forty old folks), one in Meath, one in an unnamed rural
town, only one outside Ireland—Edna O'Brien in Vermont, dreaming of
the Blackwater.

For an island nation ferocious as Corsicans when it comes to *crime
passionel*—contributory factors being land-hunger and plain honest-to-God
ignorance—these yarns are genial enough. Tommy Flynn's 'Da' recalls
the black flag flying over Cork Jail for the murderer of the woman among
the laurels on the Mardyke. Period catch-phrases and slang tend to date
the older stories. The girls behind the Mardyke trees whisper 'Oh no, oh

no!' the escorts pant, 'But yes, but yes!' The trams are still running out at Sunday's Well, and somebody's father is playing Haydn, when today he would be gaping at televised football.

In 'The Talking Trees' four randy lads from Red Abbey School pool together and for £1 old currency the bold Daisy Bolster reveals her all; towards the end the story swerves away to an implied perpetuation of guilt in the classical Irish mould—all lies. O'Connor's old tear-jerker 'News for the Church' suggests, among other things, how much damage the Catholic Church and its well-meaning but ignorant priests have done Ireland. Bluff Fr. Cassidy puts probing questions, fitter for a doctor to ask his female patient ('He knew he was hitting below the belt') than a priest his penitent:

> 'But you're making it sound so beastly!' she wailed.
> 'And wasn't it?' he whispered. He had her now, he knew.

After hearing her confession (carnal intercourse with Terry) he needs air, walks down the aisle 'creaking in his heavy policemans's feet.' The penitent, a nineteen-year-old teacher, is described rather oddly: 'What struck him most was the long pale slightly freckled cheeks, pinned high up behind the grey-blue eyes, giving them a curiously oriental slant,' but no doubt captivating Terry.

A Hell-raising Mission priest features in Casey's old-fashioned story 'Priest and People.' where the internal monologue is used in a dishonest way; as again in Tim Pat Coogan's 'The Compromise' where an Irish XV wing forward 'thinks,' improbably, of other things while sprinting for the English line.

The child conceived without love is not normal, one of eight; if that were really so, half the Irish population would be loonies.

Diehard McGahern tells it again in the old style, of two poor will-o'-the-wisps, dark-haired Geraldine and the fair-haired narrator, suffering for love all over darkest Fairview, in 'Getting Through.'

The most adroit story, the funniest, is William Trevor's, given as 'Dempsey' in the contents, 'An Evening with John Joe Dempsey' from *The Ballroom of Romance*. Among names new to me, the best comes from Helen Lucy Burke, who has some of the willed madness of Lucille Redmond or Dorothy Nelson: in 'Trio,' a Boy Scout leads a blind man into the house of a large woman who removes her clothes to strains of a

Bach cello suite. Some hidden resources in the story excuse improbabilities in the plot. Miss Moore, all six foot three of her, dances alone, dreaming of a partner six foot six. For the rest, the formula is as before, tried and untrue.

Perhaps the new force in our writing will come from the women, them same women, much put-upon, in the new emergent Ireland of call-girls and massage parlours, noonday murder, a £3 million daily alcohol bill (your brain simply swirls), here hardly touched upon at all.

'Vomit and pastels fought in the revolutionary space,' Lucille Redmond wrote elsewhere. Natures wrung by obscure abstract hatreds must come by the most devious ways to mayhem, with us almost a family affair; and all in the name of thwarted love. The female chroniclers will be tenderhearted but tougher-minded than the males—a drift of chosen females standing in their shifts itself.

Hibernia, 5 April 1979

84

Paradiddle and Paradigm

Bernard MacLaverty, *The Great Profundo and Other Stories* (Blackstaff)
John Montague, *The Lost Notebook* (Mercier)

Bernard MacLaverty is a master of scrupulous meanness, having at his command an authentically Irish parochial touch. The squalor of the parts is matched only by the patented accidie of the whole. There isn't a great deal to be said in favour of low life, as such, but he does his level best to fill us in. Metaphors fidget, uneasy as sheep with a dog around. The model is surely *Dubliners,* James Joyce at his least joyful, or Stephen Hero in Mullingar. You'll just have to take us as we are. 'They walked awkwardly on a beach of apple-sized stones hearing them clunk hollowly beneath their feet.' Elsewhere the snow 'kept up an irregular ticking at the window,' as the Cardinal's old Da tells him he has lost the faith. ('The snow was getting heavier and finer and was hissing at the window'). *Sic &* *stet.* The snowfall from 'The Dead' falls now like confetti on some peasant melodrama.

The eleven stories here creak in their ethos as our author assays desperate shifts to make them flow: an aged priest, locked into his own church, sees ghosts, passes away; a blind homosexual painter instructs Jordan how to apply colour (tennis balls dipped in paint) while sneering at the prose of Beckett ('almost impossible to read aloud and quite, quite meaningless'), a father and son solve the Northern Problem on a walk up a hill ('The British Government are on the same side as the terrorists now. They're beating us with the stick *and* the bloody carrot'), Dad and Roy.

The only approach to this difficult terrain, over which hangs the pall of defeat, would have to be unsentimental, imposing some strict order on formlessness. You might anticipate freakishness: cf. Eugene McCabe's *Heritage and Other Stories*, Maurice Leitch's *The Hands of Cheryl Boyd*, and a novella concerning the inmates of an asylum.

Three stories here seem to belong in a better collection by a better writer: 'End of Season,' 'Across the Street' and the title story, or 44 out of 143 pages:

> The silver paper glittered in the street lights as the men angled the stretcher into the ambulance. Her face was white as a candle. A voice crackled from a radio in the police car. Mrs. Payne stood with both hands over her mouth. The doors slammed shut and the ambulance took off in silence and at speed with the blue light flashing. The police officer came out of the house and they drove off after the ambulance.

The unsubtle but useful art of freeloading (learnt in the drab school of Dublin pub life in the late 1940s) is recorded in Montague's novella, his first fiction since *Death of a Chieftain* in 1964. It is by no means in the class of MacNeice's long-lost partial autobiography, *The Strings are False*, much less *Giacomo Joyce*; and one wonders why it was published.

Our Armagh anchorite shacks up with the 'sexual meteor' Wandy Lang in 1950 at his coming-of-age in, yes!, Florence, and learns a thing or two. Stumbling towards fulfilment while chatty Italians 'flowed in and out'; and down in the Piazza Della Signora, 'happy tourists were tucking in, under the partly coloured awnings.'

The *Catholic Standard* film 'critic' dispatched to Florence for the International Conference on Catholic Cinema is befriended by 'a famous Irish actor' who feeds him at a number of *trattorias*, observed by *carabinieri*: is taken under the wing of Wandy, buggers her before departing, learns a thing or two about the painting brother, a practicing sodomite of New York. Erotic love is a game with secret rules; and in that time a closed book to these inhibited types, frozen out of their very nature by censorship.

No symbolic snowflakes fall here, no sneers at Monsieur Beckett, though the clichés rain down thick and fast.

Might not he have written a novella as frank and honest as the late Cheever's *Oh What a Paradise it Seems*? But apparently not. *This* happens in another country, and besides the wench is dead. The *Notebook* is not even opened here; the characters paper-thin, strolling archetypes, inane figurines.

Here again the sad aroma of defeat, congeries of stinks, *polvo enamorado*. The Mercier Press, taking no chances, disclaims any resemblance to real persons, living or dead ('purely coincidental'). 'I was in true spirits,' wrote Emerson years ago and in yet another country, 'I surveyed nature with a noble eye' Not this one:

> Red wine flowed, *pastasciutta*, and liquid syllables of Italian that sounded splendid even if I only dimly understood. And when our host began to quote Dante, with all the sonorous intimacy of a Florentine, I responded with Yeats, boom answering boom, like church bells ringing across the city.

Basta!

Dark thoughts, carnal desires beset our 'horn mad celibate with a bright red comb and a roving eye' who once stood 'within spitting distance' of the pale bespectacled Pacelli, *Pio Dodicesimo*.

The text itself is ill-supported by John Verling's b&w illustrations, mostly smudgy nudes engaged in lewd practices; in one case the picture is inverted.

The Irish Review, no 5, Autumn 1998

85

Old Porn and Corn-Plasters

John McGahern, *Amongst Women* (Faber & Faber)
Aidan Matthews, *Muesli at Midnight* (Secker)

'Did you make much hay in your parts, Sean?' he asked pleas-
antly as he picked carefully at the black pudding and sausage.
'Hay and some silage when the summers were bad.'
'You must be well used to it then?'

A familiar prosaic wholesomeness instantly recognisable, as the fetid
reek of old socks, permeates the McGahern *oeuvre*; to which he has just
added this melancholy 'Monaghan' novel, his first since *The Pornographer*
of eleven years ago.

'I think a writer is stuck with his world,' he told the *Irish Times* lady
interviewer phlegmatically. Himself once sadly notorious among the
pious Irish as the author of a dirty book, following hard upon the ban-
ning of his second innocent novel, *The Dark*, in 1965 by the Irish Censorship Board, presumably acting upon instructions handed down from the
Grand Inquisitor himself, Archbishop McQuaid. Due to a legal loophole
or episcopal oversight, the Irish blind (ill-sighted) could safely read it in
Braille.

McGahern was dismissed forthwith from his government-sponsored
teaching post in Clontarf, to which he had brought some distinction,
winning over his thick pupils by lying on the flat of his back on the
classroom floor. The offence was further compounded by his marrying
Anniki Laaski in a Finnish registry office.

Almost half a century before that, Brinsley MacNamara has his novel
The Valley of the Squinting Windows publicly burned in Delvin, County
Westmeath; his father's school was boycotted and the parish priest sued
without success; the son left the place in fear of his life. 'Sink log! All find
their way to the dirty hollow!' cried the coarse onlookers. Such coarse

shouts from the Rev. Ian Paisley followed Seamus Heaney into County Wicklow (Papist flees!), following death threats made against his family a lifetime later.

We may assume that the dire, fear-ridden family life recorded here in a place purporting to be County Monaghan (Presbyterian badlands, bandit country, Clogher and Newbliss, the dregs!) is in reality a cover for McGahern's own home-county, Leitrim, where he farms.

The rural idioms suggest the 1950s, a period wherein the spirit of McGahern still abides, with its feck-all, haven't a frigging clue, blackguard, topper, suggesting those tamed times under Dev and McQuaid 'The talk turned to easier waters as they drank tea.'

Stepmother Rose drinking coffee (presumably Irel?) and smoking a cigarette with the two girls (page 149) seems an error in the Time-Space Continuum. But heifers (and wives) are still bought in the cattle-fair at Mohill.

On one of those annual 'Monaghan Days' who comes to Great Meadow but an old comrade-in-arms, Jimmy McQuaid, Moran's lieutenant in a flying column during the Black and Tan fracas, now driving a white Mercedes—a rich and gross Monaghan cattleman with yellow boots laced halfway up 'stout thighs,' come to put a hole in a bottle of Redbreast and talk of old times.

His old commander, Moran, having refused an IRA pension and been dismissed from the regular army, is now giving his three daughters hell.

Michael the second son is off tomcatting after Nell Morahan, one of the Morahans of the Plains over on vacation from the Bronx and fairly loose, by Monaghan standards; while the eldest lad Luke is doing well for himself in London. The gross old patriot is thought to be dying. 'As he weakened, Moran became afraid of his daughters' the novel opens. I saw no evidence of it, the father is a representative ugly type; as for 'coming to terms with the past,' I see no evidence of that either. The blurbwriter lies.

'Moran was too complicated to let anyone know what he thought of anything'—but once only are we privy to the secret thoughts of this farmer, complex as a carrot. The novel itself is plotless, ever subsiding like silage settling itself in a soggy dyke. Barefaced honesty was ever the McGahern style; the 'claustrophobia of the interminable day' is well captured even if without much joy.

Mitching from school to fly to Nell, the silly son is found out and told to go to his room and strip for a flogging; Moran addresses daughter

Sheila as 'pig.' The Holy Rosary is offered up in the muddy Ford travelling through Dromad, Drumsna, Jamestown, the last Hail Mary ending as they come to the bridge at Carrick ('I'm dying for a cup of tea').

Sheila marries Sean Flynn and off with them honeymooning in Majorca but before you can say condom or coil they have three dotey children and begun a new life in a Dublin Bungalow estate 'among a couple of hundred bungalows exactly the same.' The raw new hedonism is coming in. Sean believes that there's more to life than security. Good on you, Sean.

Meanwhile Moran, that surly old brute, dies and is buried in a brown Franciscan habit, the expensive oaken coffin draped with a worn tricolour. We are spared the regulation graveside homily and rifle salute for this truly awful hypocrite.

* * *

> Felicity was enthralled. Or, rather, she was elated. No, not elated, because, of course, elation was one side of a psychiatric coin, the other being depression; and that would not do. The nearest Felicity had ever come to a depression was when she shared a Fairy cake with an Akela at a brownie brunch in a glacial moraine. On the other hand, enthralled was wrong, as well.

Muesli at Midnight is a first novel and its incessant grammatical tics and attempted verbal frolics may remind older readers of the pyrotechnics of Beckett's *More Pricks Than Kicks*, with perhaps a knowing nod toward Nicholson Baker or the cycling freaks of Jarry's *Supermale*, though the hits are less concussive. A strong weakness for oxymoron is displayed, the antic manner in danger of running away with its own conceits.

The plot might be compared to one of those dinky toys that, once wound up, can proceed only in circles, until the spring gives out. Theo and Felicity, two second year medical students from the College of Surgeons in Dublin set out on a tandem spin around Ireland in search of funds for the Surgeons Conquer Cancer Campaign.

The 'chateau wines of language, the sex of words' all yours in some 288 fairly randy pages in the manner (bogus jocose) already familiar to those who saw *Exit/Entrance* on the stage. *Tush* or *kitsch* ('bottoms and sniggers'), the *schmaltzy* manner can become wearisome.

Theo, with single earring but no Walkman—Felicity 'is switched into Pink Floyd'—annotates the *Kama Sutra* and the dubious philosopher Sartre.

Felicity, we are informed, 'got into hash' at the school sports when just fifteen, won the sack race (wink, wink) and kept on going, adorable she. Her dad is a Dublin barrister, mum suitably emancipated. Felicity has a gerbil named 'Spartacus,' did a year in Arts and was debauched by a Dominican. The dog of the Dominican's sister choked to death of a Bisodol tablet, was christened Pride of Place but answered to Shit or Faeces (Latin).

The hearse-driver talks and thinks too much. The fake mirthfulness begins to pall, no pun intended. It reads like the special pleading encountered in the more sophisticated advertising copy where it's hard to tell *what* exactly is being advertised, Purple Silk cut or Slazenger golf balls. Perhaps he tries too hard to be engaging?

London Magazine, August/September 1990

IV

From Numina to Nowhere

No one was present in the past. But there is no living present
with a dead past. No one has been present in the future.
—Carlos Fuentes, Harvard Commencement, 7 June 1983

There once was; there once is.
There will have been again.
—Günter Grass, *Headbirths, or, the Germans Are Dying Out*
(*Kopfgeburten, oder, die Deutschen Sterben Aus*), 1979

86

Dream-Zoo

Jorge Luis Borges, *The Book of Imaginary Beings* (Cape)

Pascal wrote: 'Nature is an infinite sphere whose centre is everywhere, whose circumference is nowhere.' Borges set out to hunt down the metaphor through the centuries. He traces it to Giordano Bruno (1584): 'We can assert with certainty that the universe is everywhere and its circumference nowhere.'

But Bruno had been able to read in a twelfth century French theologian, Alain de Lille, a formulation lifted from the work of *Corpus Hermeticum* (Third Century): 'God is an intelligible sphere whose centre is everywhere and whose circumference is nowhere.'

He finds the metaphor again in the last chapter of the last book of Rabelais's *Pantagruel;* in Empedocles, in Parmenedes, in Olaf Gigon (*Ursprung dergriechischen Philosophie*, AD 183), who had it from Xenophanes six centuries before Christ, when he offered to the Greeks a single God, a god who was an eternal sphere.

> The metaphor runs on. I found it again in Beckett's *Murphy* (1938) 'Not know her is it,' said Wylie, 'when there is no single aspect of her natural body with which I am not familiar . . . What a bust! . . . All centre and no circumference!'

Metaphysics as a branch of the literature of phantasy? Maurois said that Borges was a great writer who composed only little essays or short narratives. His sources were innumerable and unexpected; 'he has read everything, and especially what nobody reads anymore: the Cabalists, the Alexandrine Greeks, Beowulf, De Quincey. His erudition is not profound, but it is vast' (preface to *Labyrinths*).

He sees Lord Dunsany as a precursor to Kafka, which would have astonished his Lordship. The Browning poem 'Fears and Scruples' also foretold Kafka; in this correlation the identity or plurality of the man involved is unimportant:

> The early Kafka of *Betrachtung* is no less a precursor of the Kafka
> of sombre myths and atrocious institutions than is Browning or
> Lord Dunsany.

Borges quotes Yeats, Wilde, Shaw unexpectedly self-effacing ('I understand everything and everybody and I am nothing and no one') in a letter to Frank Harris. Irish surnames crop up in the sub texts, Nolan, Kilpatrick, Ryan odd looking as Malone, Molloy and Macmann amid Beckett's French.

Beckett and Borges shared the 1961 International Publishers Prize, the *Prix Formentor,* and a year later New Directions brought out *Labyrinths* and Grove Press *Ficciones.* Borges began as a poet and essayist in the 1920s; came to short prose texts in the late 1930s, subsequently collected in the volumes *Ficciones* and *El Aleph.*

The texts here are rendered into lean unlovely English by a variety of hands, of varying competence in rendering the pure original, as might be expected; the nature of that reality which the original Spanish reflects waveringly 'like an old greening mirror,' being captured best by Señor Kerrigan—one more Irish surname—the self-styled *Ohlerite-Trotskyite* sometimes resident in a topmost flat in Fitzwilliam Square, formerly servants' quarters.

Borges quotes Conrad in his foreword to *The Shadow Line* to the effect that when one wrote, even in a realistic way, one was writing a fantastic story; because the world itself is fantastic and unfathomable and mysterious.

> Nobody knows whether the world is realistic or fantastic, that is to
> say, whether the world is a natural process or whether it is a kind of
> dream, a dream that we may or may not share with others.

The Idealists maintain that the verbs 'to live' and 'to be' are strictly synonymous; the idea being that since the whole universe is one living thing, then there must be a hidden kinship between things that seem far off and unconnected. The Stoic philosophers believed in signs and omens, as did the Romans after them, as did James Joyce and primitive people scattered about the world in out-of-the-way islands.

Five years after his rumoured death (*muerto en noviembre de 1957*) and a year after receiving the *Prix Formentor*, Borges lectured on Wordsworth in Madrid, in Spanish; and ten years later lectured at Harvard on English poetry.

The first edition of *Manual de zoologia fantastica* or *Handbook of Fantastic Zoology* containing 82 pieces appeared in Mexico in 1957. Ten years later a second edition was published in Buenos Aires with 34 additions—*El libro de los seres imaginarios*. This present handsome Cape edition contains 120 pieces, the two previous Spanish editions added to and revised and rendered into English by Thomas di Giovanni the doyen of Borges translators, in collaboration with the author.

The Rain Bird, The Lunar Hare, the Norns, Kafka's Lamb-cat, together with some of Herr Rudolf Steiner's thermal beings, all cavort together in this Zoo of Dreams.

Thomas Mann wrote of the genesis of the novel: 'My own growing conviction, which I discovered was not mine alone, was to look upon all life as a cultural product taking the form of mythic cliché, and to prefer quotation to independent invention.'

What transpires here then? The fortuitous concourse of the atoms of Democritus? Thomas Hardy's obscure surgings of eternity? Or Señor Borges's own vertiginous symmetries, the secret laws? Who can say. Henry James asserted that fictional invention is neither evasive nor tautological: 'Every novel is an ideal plane inserted into the realm of reality.' Let Borges have the final word:

> It may be that universal history is the history of different intonations given a handful of metaphors . . . I have felt them [his parables] so deeply that people might not find out that they were all more or less autobiographical. The stories were about myself.

'The dream is you' (Joseph Conrad, *Lord Jim*).

Hibernia, 1 November 1976

87

Our Hero, After Babel

Introduction to Carl, Julien and Elwin Higgins's
Colossal Gongorr & the Turkes of Mars (Cape)

Just before the publication of *Ulysses*, James Joyce was walking in the Bois de Boulogne with his wife and Djuna Barnes, when a man brushed by them muttering darkly, whereupon Joyce turned pale. Questioned by Miss Barnes, he said that the Unknown One had muttered in Latin, 'You are an abominable writer!' A dire omen on the eve of publication, James Joyce feared.

Nine years later he persuaded George Moore to read some pages in a French translation; but Moore could not go on. 'It cannot be a novel, for there isn't a tree in it,' he complained to Janet Flanner. An odd *demeure*. Only family trees? He would not have known that the Irish alphabet is made up of the names of trees; the eighth letter *ioda* (i) signifying yew tree. 'Fik yew! I'm through!' (*Finnegans Wake*).

Joyce admitted, 'I'd like to have seven tongues and put them all into my cheek at once.' He did his best, knew many languages, could speak a number fluently, though not all simultaneously ('The chief spoke his native tung'). He loved and understood children and thus could not, as sometimes claimed by the Irish, not the least vindictive of peoples, be a Bad Hat. He battled with language all his life, married one of the Barnacles of Galway.

The child, who knows nothing, invents the world, and is haunted by it. A child's secret scribblings and scrawlings are a vatic spreading of the inks. Early terrors, induced by reading, are perhaps premonitions of later realities, rendered in symbolic form; the form of the Tale. The movies and television, the latter regurgitating the former in an insatiable greed for perpetuation, are in the way to destroy storytelling; and storytelling may be the base of language. The Noun today can no longer name (nail) its Object; verbs, the energy of a sentence, are machine-made.

The text here was firmly founded on a general ignorance of the English language, the rules of its grammar and the generally accepted usages of spelling. It seems to be in a hurry. Where? To tell its tale. Just beyond lay the murky, depthless region of Unthought or whatever lies beyond the realm of Words.

The later fierce storytelling freely dispenses with punctuation as we understand it: commas and periods are dropped along with paragraph spacings (useful for breathing purposes), as sense outruns syntax, in an effort to say the impossible, and the whole races on towards its close, multiplying its own multiples forever, with heroes and heroines reduced to lower case versions of themselves. The method employed: The Continuous Overflow.

The icy wastes are testing grounds for valour and extraordinary deeds. The monsters may be ill-defined but are true monsters ('There wos this ophill creature who could eat people'). When a sheet of paper is being burnt, Baroness Blixen observed, 'after all the other sparks have run along the edge and died away, one last little spark will appear and hurry after them.'

The Floating World, the kingdom where children play, seeking astonishment but menaced by monsters, is reached by crossing the line at noontide, entering the Land of the Unicorns. The path progresses sometimes through the mother (Proust?), sometimes through the father; the signposts to it are marked Solicitude.

Jean Genet wrote:

> The ryefield was bounded on the Polish side by a wood at whose edge was nothing but motionless birches; on the Czech side, by another wood, but of fir trees. I remained a long time squatting by the edge, intently wondering what lay hidden in the field. What if I crossed it? Were customs officers hidden in the rye? I was uneasy. At noon, beneath a pure sky, all nature was offering me a puzzle, and offering it to me blandly. If nothing happens, I said to myself, it will be the appearance of a unicorn. Such a moment and such a place can only produce a unicorn. Fear, and the kind of emotion I always feel when I cross a border, conjured up at noon, beneath a leaden sun, the first fairy-land. I ventured into the golden sea as one enters water. I went through the rye standing up. I advanced slowly, surely, with the certainty of being the heraldic character for whom a natural blazon had been shaped: azure, field of gold, sun,

forests. This imagery, of which I was a part, was complicated by the Polish imagery . . . When I got to the birches, I was in Poland. An enchantment of another order was about to be offered to me. The 'Lady with the Unicorn' is to me the lofty expression of this crossing the line at noontide. I had just come to know, as a result of fear, an uneasiness in the presence of the mystery of diurnal nature, at a time when the French countryside where I wandered about, chiefly at night, was peopled all over with the ghost of Vacher, the killer of shepherds. As I walked through it, I would listen within me to the accordion tunes he must have played there, and I would mentally invite the children come and offer themselves to the cut-throat's hands. However, I have just referred to this in order to try to tell you at what period of my life nature disturbed me, giving rise within me to the spontaneous creation of a fabulous fauna, or of situations and accidents whose fearful and enchanted prisoner I was. The crossing of the border and the excitement it aroused in me were to enable me to apprehend directly the essence of the nature I was entering. I was penetrating less into a country than to the interior of an image.

The Thief's Journal

Early terrors: Noah and his Ark in the Deluge (the nightmare of being born), Jack and the Beanstalk (falling nightmare), Three Blind Mice (disguised infanticide?), Dick Whittington and his Cat (banishment, exile), Dr. Hoffman's Struwelpeter, much of Hans Anderson, most of the Brothers Grimm, Rapunzel in particular (nightmare after nightmare).

The child has not at his disposal the adult barrier—the barrier of forgetting—*what you are doing now and something identical in the past*. The child has no past. Today the past has disappeared, while the future has never been so close, within touching distance. Or, better still, future and remote past merge into a present of irredeemable decadence; apes from outer space mounted on horses drag human infants through the streets of New York in A.D. 2022. Conan.

As parents spend less and less time with their children and are replaced by the television set, 'living memory' must lose much of its meaning. What meaning, if any, will 'living memory' have in the minds of our grandchildren? Every family had its terrible sentence. Not any more.

The child too feels the growing emptiness about him. 'Around the shore of the pool a bundle of apes were jumping.' A handful of phrases gather and the lightning strikes. 'Suddenly there was a loud shout from the shore.'

The furious Christ who expelled the buyers and sellers from the Temple two thousand years ago has returned whip in hand to chastise wrongdoers—'in the graspe of their hands was pistols.'

I say that that which is is. I say that which is not also is. The remote past and the future have never been so close together and the present has disappeared as the world shrinks and the imagination of man dwindles away. The weakening began in language itself. Maybe it continues, roughly, in the din of Rock; certainly no other century has been as loud as ours. Meditation ('think-tanks') becomes more difficult by the hour.

The disturbed child, that is to say the modern urban child, makes a baboon in plasticine, then a snake-charmer, then a man dressed in animal skins with a parrot on his shoulder and a fowling-piece cocked by his knee, with an umbrella also made of skins for protection against the fierce island sun—Crusoe. Somewhere, just out of sight, the savages are howling.

Heraldic beasts guard the fictive way to come—Kafka's martens, leopards, jaguars, the tiger in Bursen's training cage. A hero becomes a cockroach overnight, sickens, expires, is thrown out on the refuse-dump.

Gone are the old source-books—Wynken de Worde's *A Lyttel Gest of Robyn Hode* (initiation rites), Finnemore's *His First Term: A Story of Slapton School* (ritual flogging), *The Giant Mole*, or *The Mime of Mick, Nick and the Maggies*, to make way for Hergé's faceless boy-detective, Jean de Brunhoff's Babar, King of the Elephants and his court, Pom, Flora, Zephir, composed and illustrated in a Swiss sanatorium by a man dying of cancer, as a memoir for his children.

The brink, the abyss itself, is very close in a child's early feelings, experienced as a condition of convalescence. The blue-shadowed wall towards the end of a long summer's day, the emptied city and the deserted home; the sense of dread, things in abeyance. In the silence that settles over nature, human cries go straight up like hair rising on a terrified scalp.

A word about the composition of these yarns. They were written in English after three years' schooling in Spanish and one year in a West Berlin school. The stories have been filtered through strictly limited vocabularies in these two languages, and were written in four different countries by my three sons at ages varying from five to fifteen, covering a period of perhaps ten years. I assembled them from Spanish *cuadernos* and

Berliner Hefte, retitled here and there and put together in the Connemara Gaeltacht during the worst winter in living memory, through weeks of penitential rain, looking out of a cottage window at the Maamturks, and they have afforded me more pleasure than any of my own enfeebled efforts.

To convey something straight from the heart in a familiar tongue—in this case Hardiman's 'comen English tong'—is no easy matter. To convey something strong and straight from the heart in a lost tongue (one's own) is more difficult. From the pre-verbal chaos of unnaming, go on without false emphasis or hesitation to the later exemplary truths of the Primer. Why do children love to hear stories of the beginning of the world?

I first saw West Berlin, that half-city, in 1956 when touring with a marionette group out from London, bound for Rhodesia and the Copper Belt; then a father-to-be. Sixteen years later I returned, now the father of three sons, and in the dark cellar Quasimodo next to the Delphi Cinema on Kantstrasse, spoke to Martin Kluger of a possible children's book that would be different, a Boyes Buke for Grown Boys. This is that book, eight years on. No, twenty-three years on. I have lost count of the years.

Jonah Mackol suffering for Linda, and in a P.O.W. camp at that, assumes the old form of the knightly vigil, chivalry. Slay the dragon (or the ape) and the reward is not Linda but 'all the proteins of a good square meal.' After the raw fish and water, the beatings. The Tarzan-Linda saga is a reworking of The Sleeping Beauty. The illustrations are by the three authors.

Why, asks Eleanor of Worms, does the child forget? Because if he did not forget, the course of this world would drive it into madness, if it thought about it in the light of what it knew.

Children might just as well play as not. The ogre will come in any case. *Dia guive.*

1979

88

Tellers of Tales

Introduction to *A Century of Short Stories* compiled by Aidan Higgins
for Book Club Associates (Cape)

A phrase, wrote Isaac Babel, is born into the world both good and bad at
the same time. And, as a stiff corollary, 'no iron can stab the heart with
such force as a full stop put just at the right place.'

The combination of letters is not something to fool around with (*pace*
Isaac Bashevis Singer). An error in one word or one vowel accent can
'destroy the earth.' In the beginning was the Logos. The imagination,
avoiding the hegemony of the banal word, goes in search of a fabulous
world.

Stories have their oldest roots in folklore, the common dreams of
all language: an oral tradition. The West of Ireland stories that open
this collection may belong more properly to Paddy Flynn, not to Lady
Gregory or even to Yeats, who later transcribed and retranscribed them,
searching for a purer diction. The poet saw the storyteller asleep under
a bush, smiling.

The prescription 'I dreamed . . .' tilted the Tower of Babel. Some stories have no beginning, others no middle (*Mosby's Memoirs?*), and there is
a Gogol story that has no end. Transcribed, because of Gogol's defective
memory, the pages were baked into a pie.

Nursery rhymes, laying-on of curses, trance-speech, the Little Language
of Lovers (*Journal to Stella*) where the loved one is likened to monkey or
snake, are all perhaps akin; as are rhyming slang, prison argot—all secret
languages. The sedulous dreamers always refused to be psychoanalysed.
Hence Nabokov's obligatory sneers at the Viennese witchdoctor and
Freudian 'mystics,' Joyce's dismissal of Drs. Jung and Freud as Tweedle-
dum and Tweedledee. The *Brüder* Grimm were always anthropologists.

Here then is an idiosyncratic collection of middle and early twentieth
century short stories and aperçus published in English during the period

1890-1970. Eighty years, a lifespan. A look askance at people and things perishing, talents and vanished cities, the slow decay of manners, time's afflictions. From the groves of United States Academe Nabokov sees a lost white St. Petersburg, a misty Fialta, written at a time when his talent was perhaps purer. Djuna Barnes invokes a Berlin that no longer exists. Singer, another Warsaw; James Joyce, starting out on a career of notoriously straitened circumstances, looks back from Trieste towards Dublin at the turn of the century.

Some of the American stories might be regarded as *post hoc* European writing; a branch that sank underground for a generation, transmuted into a newly emergent language. Bellow might have written in Russian; Singer's English is coloured by its Polish-Yiddish origins; Beckett's French has to some degree modified and pared his austere English.

Behind the London clubmen, the swells and hearties, rowing men and athletes with single-sticks and boxing-gloves, dukes and baronets, names to conjure with, racehorse owners and scoundrels, lawyers and surgeons, sinister non-English persons, criminals and low fellows, wronged women, 'Penang lawyers' (a stick that could fell an ox), growlers, nice bits of blood between the shafts, that infest the pages of Conan Doyle, in a London of cabs and Bow Street runners or an unspoilt countryside sometimes luridly lit, lay another England: a land of dead bare-fist champions, ostlers and seconds, *more* Penang lawyers, and the hangman; and behind them stood the Empire, Bloemfontein, India, Gurkhas and the Raj—Sir Arthur Conan Doyle's land, boy's land. An exhumed Egyptian mummy sprints down an Oxfordshire lane, after Abercrombie Smith of all men. Elsewhere, a gigantic hellhound roams the moors.

Unmasker of the outré and the bizarre, Doyle's work is tinged with a certain Edwardian bluntness and brutality. A text teeming with the minutiae of keen observation is notable for the energy of its verbs and the springy marksmanship of its adjectival clauses ('A spray of half-clad deep breathing runners shot past him, and craning over their shoulders, he saw Hastie pulling a steady thirty-six . . .'), combined with an overall inventiveness that is hard to resist. His output was huge, Balzacian; the sheer energy prodigious. H.G. Wells, who once played a game of fives against Nabokov's father, had it also. Human dynamos.

V. S. Pritchett's writing has the mark of the just, decorous, law-abiding English mind. Passion induces responsibility. How English couples interact, the men shady, the women a cross between boa-constrictor and angel. ('They spend half their lives in the bathroom.') A self-effacing talent that does not draw attention to itself.

William Trevor, like Pritchett, and Dickens before them, is a sly recorder of London, its inner life and outer fringes. Very good on middle-aged despair (The English Disease), progressive inebriation at cocktail parties, the fog of cigarette smoke and the warm smell of brandy, the fearful Mrs. Fitch ('that man up to his tricks with women while the beauty drains from my face'), the edgy diction of distress is well caught. Dukelow, Belhatchet, Angusthorpe, Dutts, Miss Efoss, Matera, Marshalsea, Abbott, Da Tanka, the Lowhrs, Digby-Hunter, Wraggett, Buller Achen ('reputed to take sensual interest in the sheep that roamed the mountainsides'), no telephone directory can hold them. Echoes of early Eliot, curious congeries. 'I looked in a window,' admits the halfwit dwarf Quigley, 'I saw a man and woman without their clothes on.' Voices garrulous as Mr. Jingle, sinister as Quilp. His characters talk because they are unhappy. Stories of Ireland too, refreshingly free of the turgidity and rank complacency that characterises the Older Cork School. Free also of the insidious self-pity that mars the work of his co-practicioners, he was born Cox, son of a bank manager.

John Hawkes is a crafty manipulator of chilly details, not in the contemporary American grain, but more 'European' in approach. The Sicilian Vittorini, ('Erica') the German Robert Musil ('Tonka'), or the Austrian Robert Walser ('Kleist in Thun') spring to mind; mordant ambience of Bierce or Poe, among the illustrious dead; or the surrealist Harry Mathews among the living, he is admired by Bellow.

Saul Bellow's own dramas of ideas (*Herzog, Mr Sammler's Planet*) show the anecdotal and discursive held in a vice-like grip. Exegeses proliferate. Imbued with fluctuating hope, the short declarative sentence has rarely been worked to better effect. Recapitulative epistolary forms, letters to the dead. Updated versions of *Les Liaisons Dangereuses*. Chronicler of sexual intrigues and vexations, generally Jewish. A touch of Chateaubriand; Leclos.

Few writing today can match his descriptions, both acid and tender, of the tarnished Modern Megalopolis and the dire condition of its citizenry. The trembling energy of the modern city (tumescent Chicago, rotting New York): 'a strip of beautifying and dramatic filth.' A keen ear for argot and slang has gone into the making of an abrasively idiomatic high style.

Hemingway by comparison is ill-mannered, when not insane (*Islands in the Stream*).

William Faulkner, after a false start as poet, came to his main theme early on: the back country and woods of Mississippi, its garrulous *habitués* and clientele of 'freed niggers.' The stories exhumed from the New Orleans *Times-Picayune* reads as though written on shipboard, adrift on a tumultuous sea.

Faulkner made early supererogatory claims to being 'sole owner and proprietor' of Yoknapatawpha County, Mississippi. Here already, escaped from chronology, is one loose horse troubling Mis' Harmon as its brother would trouble Mrs. Littlejohn in *The Hamlet*, dispute right of way with Ratliff himself, and a whole herd of wild spotted horses go rampaging on through Frenchman's Bend. Gibson's store, give or take a prop, would become Will Varner's, all ready for the usurping Snopes dynasty.

Faulkner was already at work on his first novel, *Soldier's Pay*, to be published by Boni & Liveright through the good graces of Sherwood Anderson; the same publishers would bring out Hemingway's *In Our Time* and early work by Djuna Barnes. Faulkner was travelling in Europe that summer.

The second story given here, 'Delta Autumn,' is from *Go Down, Moses* (1942). 'The Liar' is notable for much preliminary spittin' and whittlin,' the 'prodigious' yellow of an outbuilding, the description of a pistol shot, with other intimations of latent powers ('the others sat in reft and silent amaze, watching the stranger leaping down the path'). Only in the back country would his imagination take off. Those Mississippi farmers and traders spoke Elizabethan English with a tinge of Baptist fatalism. Faulkner's English would always be odd and curious, a vocabulary replete with archaicisms ('yon,' 'ere,' 'dasnt') and Bible tones. 'Myriad,' 'doomed,' 'avatar,' 'apotheosis,' 'redeem' and 'chastisement' recur and recur, particularly 'doomed.' 'God knows I hate for my own blooden children to reproach me,' says the atrocious father in *As I Lay Dying*. Jefferson is 'a fair piece.' In rural Ireland it would be a fair stretch, or step. Where a metal sign designates Jefferson, Corporate Limit, the pavement ends.

It is curious to compare Faulkner's early work with Joyce's, both into their first novels while engaged on short stories. Office girls took home seven shillings a week, a deckhand a pound a month, porter cost a penny a pint, and it was possible to dine on peas and a bottle of ginger beer for twopence halfpenny old currency in Dublin at the turn of the century, when James Joyce came of age. Little evidence here of the later all-in-oneness of *Ulysses* (1922) or the wholesale discarding of the wide-awake language of cut and dry grammar and go-ahead plot as discovered in *Finnegans Wake* (1939). Language topples as Europe itself topples. A sequel to *Dubliners* (1914)–*Provincials*–was never to be written.

Sponge cakes, raised umbrellas, old gentility, dusty cretonne, waltzes, unheated rooms, poorly paid servants, foul weather, crestfallen daughters, tedious aunts, craw-thumpers, *Mignon*, *The Bohemian Girl*, descant singing, the human voice, music, tenors, the dead—these stories, written at the suggestion of the middle-class mystic George Russell for *The Irish Homestead*, and later included as the third and ninth in order of composition of the fifteen that made up *Dubliners*, were rejected by thirty publishers; the 'blackguard production' must since have been reprinted in as many different languages.

Written mostly in Trieste when Joyce was working on his first novel, *Stephen Hero*, it reads today more like *Little Dorrit* than Chekhov. The ground already seems exhausted. Jack Mooney climbs upstairs for ever and ever, with two bottles of Bass under one arm. Prototypes of Gerty McDowell proliferate. Dublin *circa* 1906: a circumscribed area in which to settle old grievances:

> I remarked their English accents and listened vaguely to their conversation.
> 'O, I never said such a thing!'
> 'O, but you did!'
> 'O, but I didn't!'
> 'Araby,' *Dubliners*

A gap of some twenty years divides *La Fin* as written by Beckett, in French, and its appearance in English; thirty-three years yawns between some minor re-titling and rephrasing in the two Barnes stories subjoined here.

> Whatever happened, it happened in extraordinary times, in a season of dreams. These stories, begun at Rosses Point and ending in a rowing boat on Dublin Bay, have gone almost full circle, in three quarters of a century's patiently accumulated recording.

1977

89

Tintin

Benoît Peeters, *Tintin and the World of Hergé* (Methuen)

His *nom de plume* meant nothing in French or English, nor in Walloon for that matter. Georges Remi drew, left-handed, from the time he could hold a pencil, fled from the Ecole Saint-Luc and vowed never to set foot in another art school. As with Steadman and Ungerer after him, he invented his own style.

Some of his inventions turned out to be real: the Jewish Blumenstein. Remi had changed Blumenstein into Bohlwinkle after *Bollewinkle*, Brussel dialect for a small confectioner's shop. But he was again out of luck—another Jewish name.

He worked for *Le Soir* a Nazi-supported paper, learnt other early bad habits from American comic strips syndicated in Mexican newspapers forwarded to Brussels by Leon Degrelle, future Belgian fascist leader and friend of Hitler.

The influence of *Bringing up Father*, *Krazy Kat* and the *Katzenjammer Kids*, which Gertrude Stein lent to Picasso in Paris, can be seen in his 'prentice work for *Le Petit Vingtieme*; even a touch of Thurber is detectable in *Quick et Flupke*. From Hollywood shorts he learnt the reactionshot, Edgar Kennedy's slow burn became Haddock's rages.

Nobody is ever killed in a Tintin adventure, although guns are constantly popping. For Hergé, clean lines and the absence of cross-hatching with squiggles was part of the visionary *élan*, the brave conception of human life as a continually developing adventure. Even strangeness would be presented in meticulous detail, the wonderful (Tibet) brought close, the fabulous made familiar, as in a vision.

Few comic strips were ever *lit* so well. Hold the page away from you and it could be stained glass glowing; charm (the curse of the Disney Studios) was resolutely bypassed. Regard the mysterious Egyptian twilight in *Cigars of the Pharaoh*, the sunset clouds above the Scottish port in *The Black Island* when Tintin and Snowy arrive at the rural pub at dusk.

He—who liked to invent things—invented new countries. San Theodoros, Nuevo-Rico, Syldavia, Borduria, São Rico, Tapiocapolis. These places were hyper-real, aglow like a Burne-Jones canvas long deliberated and worked upon—*The Light of the World*. The strips fairly glow. The mise-en-scène was as important as the story.

'I've got an idea, or rather a place, a setting . . . now I have to find a name,' he told Numa Sadoul (what a splendid Hergé name!) in an interview. The Hotel Cornavin in Geneva was subjected to the closest scrutiny; than the Cervens Road out and the nondescript town of Nyon (another Hergé name); though nothing was ever nondescript for Hergé.

His first assistant, with the fine Hergéan moniker of Bob de Moor, was dispatched into Scotland to check out details. Long black Citroëns glide by in the rain.

Born in Brussels, Hergé was in his quiet and restrained way as fired-up a visionary as Magritte himself. Not for him the relentless charm of Disney, the bogus goofiness of Goofy, nor the cosying up displayed in the adipose Asterix the Gaul with their little puffs of dust; he was Hergé.

Tintin is no simpleton, but a Joseph at loggerheads with his brothers, in perpetual exile in his own land. English cartooning from Lear to Posy Simmonds, via Kent and Heath (cross-hatching gone berserk), tends to avoid the uncomfortable truth that ours is indeed a Vale of Tears. It's a long way from Christopher Robin to the ferocious graphics of *Raw* magazine, Spiegelman's *Maus* (Jews as mice in a Poland ruled by Gestapo Cats, the unspeakable approached through the diminutive); behind whom lurks Three Blind Mice and Strewelpeter, intimidating Prussian disciplinary forms.

This political cartooning is a far cry from the inept graphics and feeble jokes of *Private Eye*, or the verbose and flatulent *Doonesbury* committed to the dinky and the coy—*petit bourgeois* helplessness? Edward Lear gives us some idea of the depth of English reserve, Giles a good idea of post-war austerity and working-class bellyaching, as does Raymond Briggs today, as did Cruickshank illustrating Dickens.

Alex in the *Independent* and Posy Simmonds in the *Spectator* belong to a softer school; the father of this type of voluble winsomeness was presumably Feiffer.

Fantasy apart, the archetypes found in Tintin's three and twenty adventures are so true to life that twenty-three different nationalities recognise themselves in Monsieur Tryphon Tournesol, *radiesthesiste*, who, lo and behold, becomes Balduin Bienlein in German, Kalkyl in Swedish, Trifolic Gisassol in Portuguese, Tertius Phosfatus in Afrikaanse, Vandratur in Icelandic.

The original of all this miscegenation was Professor Auguste Piccard, of bathysphere fame, whom Remi sometimes encountered in the street. The Professor has an 'unending' neck that emerged from a collar that was too big for him. Hergé scaled him down but enlarged the collar.

Tryphon was the name of a Brussels carpenter; the long-necked Professor Piccard became the absent-minded Cuthbert Calculus in the English version, lost to his surroundings, inseparable from his plumbline.

The Everlasting Forms would go under different names. Tintin himself, the most absurd of all unlikely detectives with the expressionless face of a turnip, had evolved from Totor, Patrol Leader of the Hannetons in the Belgian Catholic Boy Scouts, rather distantly connected with the *Wandervogel* movement in Nazi Germany.

Tintin, the greatest living cypher, evolved from the larvae of *Les Aventures de Jo, Zette et Jocke,* where he sports a sinister black eyepatch but is already togged out loose-fitting knickerbockers of a distinctly *Wandervogelish* cut. Milou, the white fox terrier with a partiality for Scotch whiskey becomes Snowy in English. The twin detectives so uniquely inept, Dupont et Dupond, become Thompson and Thomson in English, O Ntupont O Ntupon in Greek, Tik-Tak in Arabic, Skapti in Icelandic.

Somehow Iceland seems the perfect land on which to gorge on Tintin adventures, with walrus herds and seals, alcoholic fishermen seated patiently at holes cut in the ice, lingering twilights lit up by the *aurora borealis.*

Moulinsart, ech Sarmoulin, the name of a small country town, derived from Chederny, a chateau on the Loire, becomes Captain Haddock's grand country seat, Marlinspike Hall, shorn of its grandiose wings to make it more comfortable for its irascible new owner, who has taken to wearing riding britches and a monocle, ordering about his imperturbable butler Nestor, who is subjected to many a prat-fall. The *mise-en-scène* is as important as the story; the characters were built up naturally over the years.

'One must kill the demon of purity in you,' purred Professor Ricklin, a satrap of Jung's. Remi was suffering from 'white nightmares.' Ricklin advised Remi to stop working; but he flatly refused. How could he not go on?

He created some imperishable types, the twenty-three adventures of Tintin have sold more than 120 million copies in forty languages and have been selling for sixty years, with a range of appeal that goes from small children being read to, to the most geriatric of amiable pensioners.

General de Gaulle told Malraux that in the end his only international rival was Tintin. Herge never finished the last adventure, *Tintin and Alpha-Art*: suffering from anaemia for several years, he went into hospital in late February 1983, as a result of pulmonary failure, and died there on 3 March (oddly enough, my birthday) in the intensive care unit of the St. Luc University Clinic on the outskirts of Brussels.

I could have met him once at a signing session in Hachette's, in London, for I was around the corner in a bar. I missed the chance and have always regretted that. My three sons were raised on Tintin books. This Benoît Peeters compilation, a sort of variorum Tintin in Foundation Hergé colours, should delight all addicts. No translator's name is supplied, but the copyright belongs to Carlsen of Copenhagen, printed by Casterman of Belgium in French.

London Magazine, October 1989

90

Torquemada

Benito Perez Galdos, *Torquemada*, translated from the Spanish by F.M. Lopez-Morillas (Deutsch)

Nineteenth century realism cannot but appear mannered and subfusc to jaundiced late twentieth-century eyes blinded by TV spume of things and agitprop newsprint. *Silas Marner* at least had the virtue of brevity.

Not so Galdos, on the evidence of this turgid tetrology. The first English 'version' of *Torquemada* comes to us via Columbia University Press in a translation made possible (so the credits unroll) by a grant from the Translations Program of the National Endowment for the Humanities. Columbia also acknowledges a grant from the Program for Cultural Cooperation between the Spanish ministry of Culture and North American Universities, for their aid in publication.

A nameless narrator chronicles the four parts. Torquemada on the Cross, in Purgatory, at the Stake, with St. Peter, where we meet Father Gamborena (well named and almost as great a bore as Dostoevesky's Father Zossima, of sainted memory). The real culprit, however, is the lady translator, who cannot quite capture the odours of exhaled onion at bedtime.

Indeed it comes as a surprise to read of horse-drawn carriages in Retiro Park, of lamp-lighters igniting the gas lamps of the Paseo de Atocha; for all this is filtered through a diction relentlessly modern, and contemporary American at that: *vide*, to earn so much dough, to sweet-talk, big-shot lawyer, driving me crazy, fixing a snack, gosh that was a dandy little battle. Are you getting the picture? Have fun.

Arturo Berea brought a later Madrid more vividly to life on the page. Here the great Spanish capital with its scorching days and freezing nights, its fountains, parading citizens, tremble uncertainly as on an ill-painted backcloth. Galdos goes in for a deal of preaching through his makeshift characters; the shift from Calle de Toledo and the Cacaféel Gallo to the

Palace in uptown Madrid is chronicled in painstaking detail but leaves us unmoved, as would not happen in a novel by (say) Balzac:

> On the morning of the burial, and half an hour before the procession set out, all the balconies on the street were replete with people.

Replete? An intolerable digressiveness prevails throughout.

The Financial Times, 30 January 1988

91

Hallucinations

Reinaldo Arenas, *Hallucinations: Being an Account of the Life and Adventures of Friar Servando Teresa de Mier*, translated from the Spanish by Gordon Brotherston
(Cape)

It was far more to discover that you and I are the same person . . .
Only your memoirs and nothing else appear in this book, and they
appear not as quotations from another text, but as a fundamental
part of this one, so that I need not emphasise that they belong to
you; but finally they don't, being like all great and grotesque things
the property of time, whose brutal passage will shortly make you
two hundred years old.

Arenas was twenty-three years of age when this ur-novel was published
in Mexico and France, but not in Cuba, his own country. His views
of New Spain are circumscribed by La Cabana and La Esquina Chata
Prisons, *Gachupins*, the Holy Inquisition. He was the first Dominican ever
to be jailed by his own order in a prison which they hadn't intended for
their own members.

'You've come at last' the voices said. And suddenly everything was
a great onrush of rats embracing him and taking him by the hand
'this is your cell,' said the rats.

Friar Servando was a Mexican who preached a heretical sermon
on the apparition of Our Lady of Guadalupe, an indiscretion that
resulted in lifelong persecution. Arenas uses the uncomfortable life of
this Mexican revolutionary rather as Buñuel used the unknown saint
Viridiana—unknown in the sense that her name is not mentioned in religious calendars.

The pseudofiction exhumes famous personages from European history:
Chateaubriand, Madame Recamier, Lady Hamilton, Benjamin Constant,

Napoleon—described alternatively as scoundrel and gangster—bold Simon Bolivar, Madame de Staël with the complete *oeuvre* of Voltaire bound in gold; that odd woman Orlando. The wily Friar is offered a position at the Institute, then on the Grand Concile National by the scoundrel, but refuses both. 'It became clear that the people might have changed rulers but in fact had only changed tyrants . . . I then realized that everything is a fraud in the world of politics. And I felt a great pity for the French people.'

Be that as it may, here Mexican history begins to repeat itself, or to swallow itself; the Conquistadors ride again, blood flows. 'You need such a store of hatred, so many sword thrusts and punches in the face, to be able at last to set in motion that unending and ascendant process of collapse . . . I was trampling around on the skeletons of those who had once been prisoners.'

Friar Servando dies. His coffin is desecrated by a certain Carreon looking for Dominican remains. The mummified body is bought by an Italian and removed to the Argentine, where it is sold to a circus manager who exhibits it in Buenos Aires as a victim of the Inquisition. The corpse is shifted around like the remains of Francis Xavier, or Philip the Fair. Mexico—Graham Greene's 'grim, bright, goaty land'—has not been observed so well since Lowry's *Under the Volcano*.

The construction is as odd as the contents; individual chapters have three variants, tenses shift from third to first person and back again, chapters repeat incidents (as if they could hardly believe the first telling), evidence is omitted in the repeats, added later. Conjunctions are itchy as ants. Incidents proliferate in the inspired manner of Garcia Marquez. The translation appears slipshod. 'Jumping the queue,' 'bog' for WC, 'fuzz' (police), 'Lets call it quits.'

Friar Servando found himself in the Battle of Trafalgar, heard Nelson's stricken cry. 'I tried to get away from that reddish patch of sea, under which sea creatures were dying of indigestion.' This Cuban missile comes in at a very steep trajectory, bang on target.

Hibernia, 15 August 1972

92

Kundera

Milan Kundera, *The Art of the Novel* (Faber & Faber)

In the larger context of the ineffable, epistemology gives me the creeps. It is not good for man to keep reminding himself that he is man. Lukacs, Adorno, Benjamin, Goldmann, Karl Kraus, Chomsky, what good did they ever do us?

The late Arland Ussher (philosopher *sans* philosophy) used to argue that Germans couldn't write novels because they couldn't stop explaining. He was surely thinking of the desolate stagnancy of Herr Mann's *Doktor Faustus*, in the times before Grass got going. Our unburdened philosopher defined the artistic process as a 'howl of anguish, suitably modified.'

In the winter of 1979 Kundera was deprived of Czech citizenship by the Prague government and now lives in Paris, where he teaches in the Sorbonne. In April 1969 Czech democratic socialism had been formally buried and, a grim Communist-style joke, Dubček became a trolley-car inspector in Slovakia. The totalitarian state laughs at its victims and perpetuates its own jokes; but laughter is crushed when the joke becomes codified by the law.

As with Buñuel's films, Kundera's novels only exist fully if we can open the windows of the dream. In seven essays here he presents his personal conception of the European novel. The message comes via Czech and French into English with emphatic italics. The *meisterwerks* that Kundera admires most are the very ones that least appeal to me: *Don Quixote*, *The Man Without Qualities*, *The Good Soldier Schweik*, *The Sleepwalkers*, *Doctor Faustus*, anything by the ghastly Gombrowicz.

Writers concerned with 'greatness,' more particularly their own, must make readers uneasy; and Kundera setting out to explain and furnish a gloss on his own emerging *oeuvre*, no less so. It is hardly fitting that authors should theorise in print about their own work, for if it's any good, the writing itself constitutes a theory. Part of the argument here is recycled from *The Paris Review* interview given in 1983 where Kundera comes over as very snappish with Christian Salmon. His piece on Broch cannot compare with Carlos Fuentes (say) on Gogol: nor can his Jerusalem Address of spring 1985 compare with Fuentes's Harvard Commencement of June 1983, published in *Myself with Others*, written in English, a corrective to the pushy Mailer.

Fuentes is a pal of Kundera's and recalls him bellowing in a Prague sauna, emerging from a hole cut in ice; Marquez was there. The illusion of the future has been the idyll of modern history; Kundera dares to say that the future has already taken place under our noses, and it stinks.

Hibernia, 13 June 1978

93

Bore-Holes

Jillian Becker, *The Union* (Chatto & Windus)

The explorers are all dead. Stanley and Livingstone, Major Dixon Denham and MacGregor Laird ('Among other annoyances, they thrust a disgusting Albino close to me and asked if he was my brother'); Scotsmen all, of inflexible rectitude. The finger writes and moves on.

After Doris Lessing and Harry Bloom, indifferent chroniclers of different parts of the subcontinent and what were the Rhodesias. From Johannesburg Mrs. Becker now enters the lists, already launched into the second volume of an ambitious trilogy.

The Union takes us back a pace in time to 1948 and the coming to power of Afrikaaner Nationalism. Her characters speak in tendentious sub-Jamesian periods and sub-clauses that might have been discards from *Guy Domville*, but were never heard on either bank of the wide Limpopo:

> 'Do sit down, Mr. Budge,' Rayful boomed, and resuming his own chair he clicked his fingers at the coffee-boy, an old Malay in a red fez.

South African writing with its one miserable theme, *Blanke* versus *Nie-Blanke*, has yet to produce any singular talent, apart from Athol Fugard; how odd that resistance to the regime should come from the Afrikaans side and not the English.

Mrs. Becker at her best has an eye and an ear quick to catch nuance, that gives the writing an irrefutably hard edge, when on line with the subject-matter and not trying to out-James Henry James himself; for when she is tempted to overwrite, her quick senses desert her.

There is no feeling of the city here—Johannesburg's seediness down Long Street and Jeppe as if both were already mouldering away; and the desert and wild country at the end are just *papier-mâché*. Here and there psychological complexities begin to look like fine crochet-work and the last forty pages are as forced and far-fetched as anything in Paul Bowles's *Sheltering Sky*.

The white overseer is as unlikely and absurd as the 'Irishman' Boneparte Blenkins in Olive Schreiner's *The Story of an African Farm* (1883) can be when she examines a class below her, her black servants will never be quite human as Farah the Somali or the cook Esa or the Kikuyu in Karen Blixen's *Out of Africa*; only she can write of the cruelly deprived without patronage, contrary to what Shiva Naipaul may believe; aristocrat though she, the Baroness, may be. Africa in slow turmoil will certainly change, and Mrs. Becker, who is Jewish, is no mean recorder of that shift:

> One must give to the blacks. Whose activities, however, were invariably extramural to one's own. Who clung, as it were, in never exactly computable numbers, to the skirts of one's property. They were to be helped. They belong to one's life, one's family life, to one's outbuildings.

Hibernia, 17 July 1973

94

Marx-Time

C. L. R. James, *Spheres of Existence: Selected Writings* (Allison & Busby)

The profusion of initials hints that he was once an amateur gentleman cricketer, and indeed his first job was as cricket correspondent for *The Manchester Guardian* under the aegis of that arch-Tory Neville Cardus. His big book, *Beyond a Boundary*, was only superficially about West Indian cricket; for how national sports evolve and are conducted affords clues to national character, and the great coloured cricketers tend to end up as political appointees—only the colours of their blazers have changed.

A slave-caste has evolved this proud man of Barbados with his acid jibes at West Indian politicians, their hands still out for British bribes. Like a fellow at a fair pitching coconuts at a cockshy, he quotes Hegel, Michelet, Toussaint L'Ouverture, praises Fanon, Stokely Carmichael, Rapp Brown and Dr. Castro—'one of the greatest revolutionaries history has ever known.' Paul Robeson was 'one of the most remarkable men of the twentieth century,' Sobers and Constantine demi-gods.

He praises Mailer for having an imagination active in social terms and Wilson Harris for being a black Hegelian, and novelists George Lamming and Vidia Naipaul, though giving effusive praise to the pseudo-philosophy of Sartre, whose lugubrious prolaxatives fail to reassure.

His encomia tend to be large and sweeping like George Headley clouting a sudden six over the square leg boundary. Yet the essential emptiness of Existentialism led to nothing but the *nouvelle vague* (Madame Sarraute devoting an entire 'novel' to describing a small hole in one wall of her Paris apartment), the movies of Godard (the Dead Hand), Lelouche and Agnes Varda, white maggots emerging from the corpse of Collaboration.

Some bad books later and Mailer himself was up to his neck in the very Mammon that an earlier Mailer had affected to despise; he became a part of the New York Establishment as inevitably as the sun comes up. As inevitably as Kingsley Amis in London had moved from left to extreme right within a few titles that were getting progressively worse, ending up being just as bigoted as Evelyn Waugh, who had never pretended to be on the side of any but those who had, as opposed to the have-nots, whom he despised.

C. L. R. James (evidently a fast runner between the wickets, a stealer of singles) evolved an independent Marxism that broke with Trotsky, with whom he had discussions in Mexico in 1938. But thinking in absolutes is a game to which all Marxists of whatever stripe are prone. The very terminology makes me uneasy ('Let X equal . . .'), as the surds and factors, the vulgar fractions and the whole notion of abstract equations as set forth on the blackboard in the old punitive days of the terrible maths class and inevitable punishment resulting from blank and ineradicable ignorance. Revolutionary sophistication, revolutionary initiative, rampant factionalism; these 'factors' convey nothing but the lie of a controllable world. When in fact neither close analysis of the here-and-now nor the gift of prophecy can throw much light into the murk ahead; and who can tell how the world will be in 2020? Let alone 2050? Perhaps by then mankind will have changed and live a life inconceivably different to that of today; as certain fish deceived by the light-source in marine grottos live permanently upside-down.

James's own fiction, to judge by the two stories appended, was always too highly organised, too concerned to prove its point, to move us or work well as fiction.

He spent fifteen years in the United States, studying the enemy. As a lecturer he was bellicose and witty; an imperious autodidact in the proud lineage of Huizinga, Cioran and Cobb. The proletarian front never had a more articulate defender. Intellectual strategist of West Indian independence, James arguably had a greater influence on the underlying thinking of independent movements in the West Indies and Africa than any other writer. A stranger in the house of his masters, he saw the way out before others.

Hibernia, 25 September 1980

95

Gasoline

Ilya Ehrenburg, *The Life of the Automobile*, translated from the Russian by
Joachim Neugroschel (Urizen Books)

This exhumed work first published by Petropolis Verlag in Berlin in 1929
and brought out in German in the same year, was published in English
last year by Urizen Books of New York in a lively translation made from
the extended German text, written and translated as if through clenched
teeth.

Where *The Road to Rome* left off, Ehrenburg goes on, cursing, protesting that it's not fiction. It's better than most fiction, an oddity to place
beside Jarry's *Supermale*—the shower of red roses, the raped corpse, the
ecstatic record, the ten thousand-mile race between a four-man bicycle
and an express train. The text splutters and ignites.

The villains are Monsieur Andre Citroën, old man Ford of Detroit,
Herr Gottlieb Daimler, Monsieur Andre Michelin and various *dei ex
machina* and fly-by-nights: Fiat and Peugeot, Renault and Anacondra,
Astra-Romana. Brazilian forests are decimated, oilfields and rubber plantations flourish; the stockbrokers are in a hurry to get dividends. Church-
hill and Hoover are there, Tex Oxborrow of the *New York Herald*; in rush
the rubber cartels, Shell and General Motors, the Stevenson Plan, Royal
Dutch and the brokers of Mincing Lane.

People were in a hurry to live. A new car was born every minute.

Monsieur Michelin was sometimes overcome by fatigue. Tricky deals
are made on the stock market, coolies flogged in the rubber plantations,
Matteotti is murdered in a chocolate-coloured automobile by Mussolini's
hitmen, an unknown passenger dies of a heart attack in a Berlin taxi, oil
stocks begin to fluctuate, auto salesmen disperse, iron is costly, paint is
costly, coal is costly. A retired manufacturer of cigarette papers takes out

an automobile hire purchase agreement for eighteen-month installments but crashes his car fatally en route to his sister's home in Perigeuex.

> There are no people anywhere. Citroën is stocks, it's lightbulbs on the Eiffel Tower, it's the iron belt, acids, Michelin tires, Deterding gasoline, it's the dust and howling on the straight highway, the trembling of needles and dials, the heartbeat of engines, but there are no people anywhere—people are just a fabrication. . . .

Outside Alhama, at Los Banos, bubbles a hot spring favoured by sufferers from arthritis. In 1974 when I was there, some 37,552 cars were stolen in Spain, 22,821 belonged to tourists.

> The automobile has come to show even the slowest minds that the earth is truly round, that the heart is just a poetic relic, that a human being contains two standard gauges: one indicates miles, the other minutes. . . .

Rubber trees bleed. Oil gushes from the underground. Man threw away his pitchfork or his smoothing plane. He became a driver. The acid emigrant Nabokov refused to sit at the same dinner table as Ehrenburg.

Hibernia, 18 March 1977

96

The Regimented Numbers Flow

Alain Robbe-Grillet, *Snapshots*, translated from the French by
Barbara Wright (Calder & Boyars)
Alain Robbe-Grillet, *Towards a New Novel*, translated from the French by
Barbara Wright (Calder & Boyars)

You either take to him or you don't.

He asserts that the novel of character belongs to the past, its life intimately bound up with that bygone society, and attempts to dispense with straightforward narrative as such.

He substitutes the solemn Froggy pie-jawing of invented characters (supposing it possible to invent characters *ab ovo*) with some solemn pie-jawing of his own. The former agronomist examines his characters under a microscope, as if they were tropical fruit of the Antilles.

La Jalousie set out to improve upon Graham Greene's *The Heart of the Matter*, the narrative as impersonal as Godard shooting a movie, the camera's protracted stare fixed on the back of Anna Karina's head, alternating with close-ups of a cup of coffee. At the centre of it all (there is no heart, only centre) a vague disquiet, a disquieting vagueness—the *nouvelle vague?*

The Coterie published by Jerome Lindon at *Les Editions de Minuit* (Sarraute, Pinget, Claude Simon, who was later to liberate himself with the help of Faulknerean pyrotechnics) were all deficient in that useful solvent (Bergson thought that art was incomplete without it), humour, the yeast that made the bread rise.

I once asked Beckett what he made of Robbe-Grillet's work. 'He has his place,' purred the Master of the Boulevard St. Jacques diplomatically. *La Jalousie* follows *Les Gommes* and *Le Voyeur* and others as cryptic.

Some tightlipped theorising follows on the characterless narrative, the plotless play (*En attendant Godot*); Raymond Roussel is praised for saying little and saying it badly. Camus of Oran, Joe Bousquet, Pinget, the Italian

Svevo (the hunter who mercilessly chases his quarry—himself—down to earth) are considered.

This is a paperback reissue of the 1965 casebound edition, itself an Englished version of matters thoroughly French as set forth through *Instantanes* (1963) and *Pour un Nouveau Roman* of the year preceding. More will undoubtedly follow.

New Statesman

97

Black Mischief

Shiva Naipaul, *North of South: An African Journey*

The cheapest way to get from London to Nairobi is to fly Air Zaire via Brussels and Kinshasa. Shiva Naipaul flew out in the company of a financial delegation returning from Washington; the charade, begun at a fairly high level of absurdity, never descends into mundanity. He makes a bizarre journey from the Marrakesh bazaar to the Kenyan highlands.

Only marginally less troubled by mess and dirt than his fastidious brother, these forays yield up insightful clues into human confusion, the perplexities of other races. He sees little future for the Asian in emergent black Africa; transitional states are full of pain and progressive ideas travel slowly, as the deadly harmonies of Zairian pop-music drift dismally through the air-conditioned gloom.

Tinned food and canned music, Africa 'swaddled in lies,' the lies of an aborted European civilisation, the lies of 'liberation,' are grafted onto the Dark Continent. He is, if that were possible, an even greater pessimist than his brother.

Tanzanians will tell you that their wild animals are the best in the world: it's only here that you see lions sleeping in trees. In Kenya lions don't sleep in trees. And if by any chance you get to Ngorongoro, make sure you don't miss the Masai in the crater—they really are value for money.

In Zambia, in Kenya and Tanzania the word 'South' means of course South Africa. The last white imperialists had hoped to retreat into the Southern Sudan; for the English in Kenya by turning 'Englishness and whiteness into a commodity had enslaved himself.' General Amin had done more damage in his lifetime to his own country than the slaughtering Mongols and the Huns in the long centuries before.

Overburdened buses of Romanian origin run in Dar es Salaam. Mini-skirted whores window-shop on Kenyatta Avenue in Nairobi, rustling up custom. In Uganda, General Idi Amin had 'totally destroyed any hope for a long-time future for Asians in Africa.'

'We are non-persons,' Ashraf said 'They only see us when they want to hate us.'

Naipaul argues that the Indian in Africa had not evolved a picture of himself in keeping with his changed circumstances, unlike the European; reacting neither to the land nor the people among whom he lived. He has no use for Baroness Blixen's notions of a mystical kinship with the land—'Karen' is now the name of a swank suburb on the outskirts of Nairobi ('and it stinks').

Saddening and often absurd, the white smile of universal brotherhood is a frightened mask; witness the incident of the lady in the train leaving Lusaka. Wole Soyinka may be Africa's Shakespeare but the preferred light reading is Robert Ruarke.

The Wabenzi, middle-class black *nouveau riche*, travel grandly in Mercedes; while on the far side of the Limpopo the Afrikaaners drive autos big as battle tanks. All over the huge sprawling continent, pyromaniacal techniques are being sharpened as the coloured races begin to retrench themselves into new bigotry, fresh disorders. 'In time Africa will close over their heads and they will drown in it,' the sceptic sourly concludes.

Hibernia, 6 September 1979

98

Sinewy Dreams

Roy A. K. Heath, *The Murderer* (Allison & Busby)

Some mighty eerie murder novels spring to mind on reading this account of a wife murdered in Guyana. Gadda's *That Awful Mess on Via Merulana*. Durrenmatt's *The Pledge,* James M. Cain's *The Postman Always Rings Twice*; in that the murderer's heart is unknown, the grimness of the surroundings is all.

Mr. Heath has lived in England since the age of twenty-four and is a schoolmaster in a London comprehensive school, itself a splendid breeding ground for young felons. He was called to the English Bar in 1964 and to the Guyana Bar in 1973. This being his second novel, full of dialect, the narrator's life snarled up with thwarted good intentions gone bad.

He is doomed to act out the love lost between his parents, who died when he was young. We are told little of his motives, probably unknown even to himself, but by the end of two short chapters, nine pages, we are deep into it.

The murder occurs midway through the novel, from there the murderer slides into insanity or something close to it, rising in the middle of the night to return again to Lombard Street where he had lived with his murdered wife Gemma. He suffers little remorse, only bad dreams: the murdered Gemma risen from the river has his mother's face. The apparition attacks the father, plate-glass intervenes on which he beats with his fists, 'but can only remain a powerless observer of his father's distress, and when the latter fell forward into the river his mother pursued him, hacking away with the stick.'

The ancestral home is there again, the hovel with mounds of bauxite excavations ('he has left Georgetown because he could no longer live in the home of his birth').

He moved, worked as a watchman in a sawmill, brought his wife to the tenement. They lived in a room vacated by the sewerman above the police informer and the old man ill with cancer who coughs in the night. He is assailed by recurring dreams of the murdered wife. His return to the scene of the crime and being observed there in the rain by the man who had a child by his wife is as disturbing as the shooting of the corrupt detective Hank Quinlan at the end of Orson Welles's *Touch of Evil*. Seven swift shots, seven refusals to enter the murderer's mind:

> He dips his hand in the water, wondering whether Gemma's dress-es are still hanging on the nail, thinks 'the new tenant must have removed them.'
> Recalls a night in his childhood.
> Remembers what his mother had said to him (deluge).
> Prayer for his father.
> Image of his father cycling hatless and making little headway.
> Sees a man standing above him on the ramp.

He returns to where he had disposed of the body, the nut vendors having long since gone home. Gemma Burrows had 'lived most vividly,' writing him love letters that began 'Dear Tormentor.' The reader recognises that he has lost someone who might have been his salvation, that he is a doomed man. Or perhaps they are both doomed. She had written to him: 'You men lock women up in small places and expect them to be normal. These fires burning inside me are not normal.'

Mr. Heath, the schoolmaster, lawyer and novelist could have written of Galton Flood's two years in the bush among the orchids and venomous labaria; what he offers us is odd enough, in all conscience now.

The informer, the Walk-Man, Theophile Giles, all come strangely alive to the sensitive touch; all participants in this disturbing *crime passionel* from Guyana.

Hibernia, 29 March 1979

99
Blood in the Morning

V. S. Naipaul, *The Return of Eva Peron, with The Killings in Trinidad* (Deutsch)

When words, *qua* fiction, fail him, V. S. Naipaul takes to travel, keeping a leery eye open ('from the end of 1970 to the end of 1973 no novel offered itself to me') and from the travel notes—Argentina in the second reign of Peron to the killer cars of 1977, Zaire under Mobutu, commune killing in Trinidad—come the new novels, if novels they be, for a second reading of *A Bend in the River* leaves this open to question.

He himself has begun to doubt the evidence of his own eyes. The world's sore spots attract him and pessimism comes naturally to this fastidious sourpuss. Disputatious arguing ensues, on that most nebulous of subjects, The National Identity, here replacing characters. In an earlier collection of stories, *A Flag on the Island* (1967), a character complains of not being real.

Here characterisation is suppressed under the authorial thumb; the characters have no outline because of the tar-and-feathering to which they are subjected; a mood of bleak panic is caught and held. 'I felt that the make-believe had turned horrible and that I had come to a horrible place,' he wrote in his Zaire novel. 'We went on. Darkness fell. Thousands of insects had become white in the white light of the searchlight.'

White men have had their chances in Africa and blown it; emerging black Africa will follow their white brethren into disastrous courses. Nobody has learnt anything. Nihilist Pierre Mulele, a former minister of education, had established a reign of terror in Stanleyville; anyone who could read and write had been taken out and shot, everyone with a tie had been shot.

Conrad's fictionalised 'Kurtz,' an amalgam of wretches known to Conrad, had human heads around his stockade. Casement and Gide (who had their own reasons to be there) had been in the Congo before him, the former noting 'the ghastly tally of severed hands.' 'African wars are bothersome things,' wrote explorer Stanley, who had shot sixteen savages before breakfast.

Stanleyville is now Kinshasa, the domain already rotting, as the six tractors standing in a row. The President or Mr. Big Shot is here derisively named Mobutu Sese KukuNgbendu Wz Za Banga, King of the Congo.

The great Congo is now the river Zaire; Zaire also being the debased local currency, 'which is almost worthless.' The rancorous tone mimics Waugh's *Black Mischief,* with its credulous savages and lordly white interlopers ('I know these people'). The whole place is trapped and static, a true home for sadomasochists such as Casement, fascinated and appalled by the whips and severed hands. It is Conrad's world of illusion on the edge of the outer darkness; or what Naipaul prefers to call 'the African sense of the void.'

The students at the University at the end of the highway are reading Stendhal and Fanon with the enthusiasm of those to whom everything is new; while not too far away lies General Amin's slaughter ground and Ugandan progress thrown back three centuries.

If a jaundiced view comes naturally to this author, who is to blame him? Things have always been bad, only now they are worse. He always chooses the very worst time to arrive and depart, even if he flies First Class or chugs down the river Zaire in a *cabin de luxe,* passing the ghost of Captain Konrad Korzeniowski beating upriver in the old log-burning *Roi des Belges.*

Naipaul writes with grim relish of 'good' and 'bad' torture; a father is informed that his son's case is closed, a mother receives her daughter's hands in the post. Nor has he any high opinion of the great Argentinian polymath Borges, as man or writer, and the same goes for Argentina; its failure being one of the mysteries of our time. The brothels charge by the hour.

> History in Argentina is less an attempt to record and understand than a habit of recording inconvenient facts; it is a process of forgetting.

But a particular bile is reserved for his own home, Trinidad; the 1972 double murder in Christina Gardens commune is taken as symptomatic of the whole: 'Michael X and the Black Power Killings in Trinidad.' The murders are described in graphic detail, evidently culled from court proceedings; and a more unsavoury parcel of rapists, psychopaths and hitmen you would not care to meet outside the fiction of Chandler, who had troubles of his own. The 'red bastard' of Portuguese blood whose mother ran a bawdy-house and flung boiling water on her sleeping husband is the familiar 'crap-shooting spook'; the commune a breeding ground for murder. Michael de Freitas, the Trinidad seaman become Michael Abdul Malik, become Michael X, founder-member of an imaginary Black Liberation Army, calls to mind other such communes and freakish saviours (Manson and Jones), the wild and whirling words of pseudo-redeemers. Freitas-Malik is writing a novel about a certain Lena Boyd-Richardson and her friend Sir Harold; 'Mike' (Malik himself) is seen 'leaning against the Coconut tree like some statue on a pedestal.'

But soon the dream becomes real, becomes nightmare, and he descends into the pit, cutlass in hand, to wreak bloody vengeance. A real woman is murdered, for no better reason than 'she didn't look good' with a black man in Trinidad in 1971. Her father, Captain Leonard Plug, with an ex-Bulgaria address, is mailing off translations of Lamartine from California.

John Lennon donates a £400 piano to the cause; Laing and Trocchi are among august names invoked, when Balial and Behemoth might be more apt. Large subscriptions are extracted from American philanthropic foundations and a French-style mansion redecorated against the imminent arrival of no less a luminary than Ringo Starr.

But soon the victims are shovelled under the earth, the hired killer gone back to Boston, the house burnt down; and the great leader, armed with part of a cutlass, sets out on foot for the Brazilian border. Brecht himself could not have parodied so effectively the rise and fall of Adolf Hitler and loaded the stage with such bizarre details. Naipaul's baleful asides are waspish. When jargon ends by competing with jargon, people don't have causes; they only have enemies.

Malik's career proves how much of Black Power—away from its United States source—is jargon, how much a sentimental hoax. In a place like Trinidad, racial redemption is as irrelevant for the negro as for anybody else. It obscures the problem of a small independent country with a lopsided economy, the problems of a fully 'consumer' society that is yet technologically untrained and without the intellectual means to comprehend the deficiency. It perpetuates the negative, colonial politics of protest. It is, in the end, a deep corruption.

100

In the Polluted Desert

V. S. Naipaul, *Among the Believers: An Islamic Journey* (Deutsch)

You must not expect glad tidings from a misanthrope; the only abandon-
ment can be to even gloomier moods. This is V. S. Naipaul's seventeenth
published work, the seventh travel book coming hard upon last year's
The Return of Eva Peron which dealt with Michael X and the Black Power
killings in Trinidad.

He directs his attention now to the vexing question of Islam: Iran after
the Shah, Ayatollah Khomeini's revolution, Tehran, the settlement 'in a
polluted desert.'

He travels into Pakistan, Malaysia and Indonesia, quotes Polybius (d.
118 BC) on the rise of Rome: 'The affairs of Italy and Greece are connected with those of Asia and Greece, and all events bear a relationship
and contribute to a single end.' He seems to imply an unhappy modern
application.

The reticence noticable in his fiction carries through into the travel
books, a hangman's grimness. The hanging of Bhutto is described or
imagined in some detail with evident relish, and the shooting of Hov-
eyda. Racial religious animosities are sometimes hard to figure out and it
is not always easy to follow what is being explained as calamity follows
calamity. The tone is always acerbic:

> The Bengal Muslims had Bangladesh; the people of West Pakistan
> had Pakistan. The Bihari Muslims had nothing.

Behind the Ayatollah Khomeini stands Khalkhalli his hanging judge,
behind him the Koran. A fine description of bear-baiting in the interior
of Sind, the bear squeezing a dog to death with its forward slump and
'the dog being killed looked out with a sudden blank mildness from the
brown-black fur of the bear. . . . The fight lasted three minutes. It was a

village entertainment and, like the faith, part of the complete, old life of the desert.'

Otherwise he keeps very poker-faced behind queries on the discipline of the Koran, the *haram* and *harus* of the matter. Naipaul found Muslims individually and collectively elusive and secretive, lovers of conspiracies. He watched the director-teacher Darme-Sastro picking his nose during Ramadan in the holy city of Qom. Little escapes him, little is forgiven.

In Bandung the Imaduddin reads an emotional poem written in Urdu and translated into Arabic, from Arabic into Indonesian by Mohommed Natsir, once leader of the banned Moslim party of Indonesia.

The trainees were the children of the Jakarta middle class, people faced with the special Indonesian threat of the loss of personality. 'In Islam, the life of the mosque, with its rules and rituals, they found again, or reconstructed, something like the old feudal or rural community that for them no longer existed':

> It was the late twentieth century—and not the faith—that could supply the answers—in institutions, legislation, economic systems. And, paradoxically, out of the Islamic revival, Islamic fundamentalism, that appeared to look backwards, there would remain in many Moslim countries, with all the emotional charge from the Prophet's faith, the idea of modern revolution.

But why is our man, born in static colonial times, found in bed wearing Marks & Spencer winceyette pyjamas at seven thirty in the evening?

Hibernia, 11 October 1974

101

Cautionary Tales

Djanet Lachmet, *Lallia (Le Cow-boy)*, translated from the French by Judith Still
(Carcanet)

History as a family quarrel writ big? Family feud as the quarrel fixed into a pattern; vendetta, a never-ending family blood-feud? Here in Algeria before Independence, the humid nights are 'streaming with scorpions,' a big green wooden door is decorated with huge nails, a snake bars the way at the foot of the stairs, and Princess Loundja is shut up in the tower, fearfully awaiting the ogre-father. That filthy war is seen through the eyes of innocence; for 'Lallia' read Djanet, the OAS and the cut-throat brothers are true to life, as is the wholesale butchery on both sides. A French soldier and his Algerian girlfriend are laid down side-by-side and their throats opened in a single retaliatory slash.

This alarming first novel shows the break-up of a Muslim family, middle-class and nameless, the violent deaths of all its male members, the slaughter that brought about Algeria's freedom. Mme. Lachmet has taken her time in preparing the evidence and omits to mention how Algeria fared in the decades since Independence—squalidly as Cuba?

> I thought that hell was in the desert, very fiery, under the sand. One day at school I saw some little animals who'd died in the desert. They were hollow because the fire had eaten out their insides. Only their carcasses were left. The teacher explained it to us.

Mamessa, the unwed step-mother, begins lactating, squats by the fireplace observing the devil jumping in the flames. It begins to snow. As in a real nightmare, the family has no name. The father, ordered to wipe dried blood from a freedom-fighter's huge knife, leans against the wall, sickened. The head of the murdered grandfather rolls into the river. Schoolchildren are mown down as the black Citroën pulls away. Just prior to Independence it's a bad time for the French settlers; the clauses ring ominous as death-knells.

> My mother decided to go and visit. She found everything changed.
> The orchards were abandoned, soldiers had set up camps all over
> the place to keep watch on the area. They had burnt Grandpa's
> forest down. The French settlers were leaving their farms. The sol-
> diers were raping and pillaging; mothers marrying their daughters
> off to anyone available in an attempt to protect them. . . .

No translation, no matter how inspired, can make the dialogue work, the French slogans on the wall lose their venom when rendered into neutral English, and steamy Algeria recedes. But the sheer feverishness of female childhood—an amorous innocence not quite innocent—is recorded as impartially as Babel's stories of Cossack atrocities in Poland when he rode out with Boudennoy: a touch of Asian cruelty here.

> Some children tried to make their way between the long tanned
> bodies of the country-folk. The frightened lambs could sense their
> death was near. I stroked a kid whose eyes brimmed with tears. It
> made me ill and I had to hold back my anger. Then I ran off, leav-
> ing behind me the powerful odours of flesh and sweat.

Hibernia, 14 April 1980

102

Es muss sein . . .

Thomas Keneally, *Season in Purgatory* (Collins)

This novel is about field surgery during the warfare on the island of Mus and later in the mountains of Bosnia. The atrocities perpetrated by the 'astounding Germans' getting in their hand for rougher dealings against the Jewish civilians in the occupied USSR are answered in kind by the *partisani* with refinements of brutality positively Turkish. The Commissars are there already, meting out mighty peculiar justice; for all is grist to their mill.

A novel that opens with a coronary occlusion and ends with Tito prescribing suppositories for himself ('little pills up the butt end') cannot but fail to be egocentric. And it's all that. Keneally has let himself loose amid medical textbooks, and embolism follows hard upon oedema, tracheotomies follow bursting gastric ulcers, as the night the day. 'She needed cylinders of oxygen and carbon dioxide if she were to have the luxury of a full-scale scream.'

The narrative brio of a 'floor shuddering under his feet with the impact of the Commissar's ammunition boots' comes as a relief after the middle-class turgidities of many novels emanating from England on exclusively English themes.

As the novel progresses the wounds get worse, like life itself; the gun-fire and blood-letting continue apace, the heroics of so many manly men and womanly women (association with Yugoslav girls merits the death penalty) recall to mind Papa Hemingway's unhinged posthumous work, *Islands in the Stream*.

Sex is kept at a discreet remove, which is a distinct relief. The 'wolf-ish smell of death' and the pinched, anxious look of the dying are recorded by one Pelham, who is suffering from a loss of faith in the race of man:

In his bloodstream were two simple propositions: that the savagery
of the Germans did not excuse the savagery of the partisans: that
the savagery of the partisans did not excuse the savagery of the Germans. That the masters of the ideologies, even the bland ideology
of democracy, were blood-crazed. That at the core of their political
fervour, there stood a desire to punish with death anyone who han-
kered for other systems than those approved . . . Those men and
women we mend. Are they so heroic that humanity is guaranteed a
sunny future? Or are they so insane we're all doomed?

Hibernia, 14 July 1975

103

In the Land of the Bitter Macaroon

Thomas Keneally, *Passenger* (Collins)

All is not well in the land of the bitter macaroon. The ego, fashionably suffering and dizzy with self-awareness in the polite English fiction of Fowles and Figes, whines on dreadfully in what remains of the stricken Welfare State.

The latest claimant for our sympathy is, if you please, a rational (thinking) human embryo three inches long and having a poor time of it in the womb (our only good time, you'd suppose).

A thinking foetus capable of rationalisation and with memory (but of what?) intact, is bad enough, in all conscience; but an articulate foetus that can see is an abomination. To make matters worse, *Passenger* speaks familiarly of Veuve Cliquot champagne and Pratt and Whitney jet engines; a tedious fellow even before he was whelped, a know-all like his father before him.

That such a warped creation should be conceived at all, and by the esteemed author twice runner-up for the Booker Prize, tells us more about our decadent democracy, and the Booker Prize, than it does about this author from the Antipodes in this his twelfth novel, if novel indeed it be.

Hibernia, 11 August 1978

104

In Old Trieste

Umberto Saba, *Ernesto*, translated from the Italian by Mark Thompson
(Carcanet)

The love that dare not speak its name can here hardly bring itself to utter words above a whisper. Saba's Ilio joins Mann's Tadzio, E.M. Forster's Maurice, Genet's alarming jail-bait, in the mirthless chronicles of inversion. The tendentious *fin de siecle* manner and fusty rococo call to mind Musil's *Young Torless*, Mann's *Der Tod in Venedig*; Saba could not bring himself to finish it. The densely vernacular work of Carlo Emilio Gadda lies far ahead, *That Awful Mess on Via Merulana*, Umberto Eco's *Lector in fabula*. A contemporary of Ungaretti and Montale, born Umberto Poli, the son of a Jewish mother and a Christian father who abandoned the family, Saba had much going against him. The critical neglect of his work weakened him, early and late sorrows of his own; the Fascists closed down his antiquarian bookshop on Via San Nicolo in Trieste, where the stench of open drains would turn your stomach.

He reads *Ernesto* aloud to a circle of Italian admirers, enjoined Carlo Levi to burn the typescript, was taken aback by the *succes de scandale et d'estime* following publication by Einaudi in 1975; though boy-buggery and bestiality with livestock had long been the stock-in-trade of Italian writing for as far back as Boccaccio. Here again coy references to unnatural acts with a small goat.

Unlike the cruising Pasolini, the older Saba (1883-1957) indulged in only Socratic liaisons, loved and adored from a safe distance; certain tendencies which he had as an adolescent were to return in old age. He thought Alberto Moravia went a bit over the top with *Agostino,* also dealing with a boy's initiation. The *tranquilla innocenza* that he sought for in his poetry would hardly be achievable; from the *Auschwitz caesura* known to Primo Levi he had averted his gaze. He was an armchair socialist.

In the declining years of the last century bankruptcies were common in Trieste, often ending with a pistol-shot in the bankrupt's mouth or temple. Saba put out manifestos to prepare a public accustomed to d'Annunzio's operatic effects. He looked for a leaner and more classical style, published a 337 page 'defense' of his major work, the *Canzoniere*, written in the third person under a transparent pseudonym.

Which recalls to mind (with many a wince) a certain vainglorious Spanish windbag spouting out his dreadful verse in a Madrid bullring; or Camillo Cela being driven about Alcarria in a Silver Rolls with Negro chauffeur in resplendent white livery behind the wheel, heading out for public readings in remote Budia, Gargoles de Alajo and such out-of-the-way places, to the utter amazement of semiliterate yokels. But there again, the self-promoting antics of elderly buffoons making a public spectacle of themselves, whether in Spain or Italy, is well calculated to rise the fastidious gorge.

Only a tougher breed of writer could survive what history, or Musso, had in store for Italy: the likes of Vittorini, the flashy Malaparte, sickly Pavese, Primo Levi the survivor of Monowitz, the Marxist Pasolini in *Lutheran Letters*:

> *Dopo di allora, ad ora incerta . . .*

Why does the name Manzoni remind me of some soft Italian cheese? The older school of Vincenzo Monti, Alfieri, even Lampedusa, had a subfusc air to them. What may have been appealing in Saba's original become very cold mutton in its tranquilised English, though the poetry can hardly be as poor as the translation suggests:

> The little butterfly unfurled its flight
> with potent and unhoped for zest . . .

How little of that vanished irredentist time (1897) in Adriatic Trieste, waiting for Verdi to pass away and James Joyce to arrive, is conveyed here; how much more in Svevo's trilogy! Which do you prefer, Barcola or Sant' Andrea? In her innocence the simple-minded Signora Celestina had supposed sodomy to be the exclusive prerogative of the servant class—like low wages and thick dialect. How wrong can a mother be!

When he was a tiny tot in his Nanny's house, one reason why Umberto was beaten by her was resistance to having his nails cut. As a boy he lived with his mother, who was often out at work; or at Aunty Regina's where his terrible uncle was a regular visitor. His secret book, *Ernesto*, was begun a few weeks after his seventieth birthday. He had never felt accepted by the straitlaced *Triestine borghesia* in the way that Signor Ettore Schmidt ('Italo Svevo') had been, with his motorcar and fur-lined overcoat. Saba was a near orphan, and half-Jewish. As the dust-jacket photo of the old poet suggests, Saba was not—even by Jewish standards—a happy man:

> Oh comeretta, cameretta mia
> che mi fosti campagna del dolor.

He was fond of sweet cakes and pastries, Tuscan cigars, and the company of the witty Svevo, protégé of James Joyce; used dialect sparingly.

Down at the Schiller Club they are most lustily bawling out the Imperial Anthem. Emperor Franz Josef was in control.

Financial Times

105

Period Effects

Stefan Zweig, *The Royal Game and Other Stories*, translated from the German by
Jill Sutcliffe (Cape)

Heavily veiled women hurry to assignations in Vienna. Dreadful secrets
are revealed by night on ocean liners. A coffin in the hold! The dead
go travelling with the living. But a husband is due to arrive in three
days by P&O from Yokohoma. At the Hotel Metropole the solicitor Dr.
B plays imaginary games of chess while under Gestapo interrogation.
Meanwhile Frau Irene is being blackmailed by a poor woman who is not
what she seems to be. 'No one could have suggested what was concealed
in that grey-green glance, and even I did not know.'

These novellas by the Viennese Jewish writer and self-exiled traveller
are riddled with schizophrenia. 'The one chess ego in me was always too
slow for the other.' The plots are as mazelike as the famous sewers. He
belonged to the lost world of Kleist and Georg Kaiser; Hesse exiled in
Switzerland, looked to Eastern religions for salvation, lost his way.

> But there is a flaccidity of atmosphere that effects the senses in a
> similar way to sultry weather or a storm, a well-regulated level
> of happiness that is more maddening than misfortune; and it is
> disastrous for many women, because of their resignation to it, as a
> lasting discontent caused by despair. To have an overabundance is
> no less stimulating than to be hungry, and the secure certainty of
> her life aroused her curiosity about having an affair. There was no
> opposition in her existence.

The Nazi Arms Minister Albert Speer, the only one to admit his guilt
at Nuremberg, now condemned to twenty years in Spandau Prison, took
to walking across and out of an imagined Europe that lay beyond the
high prison walls, walked twice about the perimeter of the earth, crossing

an imaginary frozen Berling Straits in the evening, to the astonishment of Rudolf Hess.

Zweig's work is more overtly traditional than most; the spectral minimalism of Musil's *Drei Frauen* lies ahead. Confidences are hidden within confidences, Frau Wagner longs for the lightning flash that would deliver her, longs to be found out.

Stefan Zweig became a naturalised British citizen in 1940; two years later took his own life in Brazil.

The Guardian, 18 November 1981

106

The Haunted Wood

Mary Butts, *The Crystal Cabinet* (Carcanet)

Some writers are more prone to be crucified on their sensibilities than others, and Mary Butts was one of these. 'It had let me go for a little while, the beast of being alone. The beast which all my life would hunt me into waste places where very few other people went.'

The fruit of solitude breeds such monsters. She is to be seen on the fringes of groups in that time in Paris, silent at the Flore, staring out of the picture at the Rontonde or Deux Magots. She was published by McAlmon in the 1925 anthology that included Joyce, Ford, Pound, Djuna Barnes, Stein, Hemingway, also Norman Douglas and Havelock Ellis. 'It was as though something out of the past, something which I thought had let me go, had come out of the dark and was upon me again.'

The Crystal Cabinet came out in 1937, the painful and embarrassing parts excised; dealing with her childhood at Salterns in Dorset, the rigid Scots Episcopalian schooling on the icy coast of Fife. Written when she was already into her forties, it presents a jaundiced picture of family life in Edwardian times ('Hush, Freddy, that's not a proper story for a child'): the death of the father, the burning of his library by the prudish wife—'I am going to burn those dreadful books of your father's.' Renan and *Fleurs du mal* go up in flames. 'I feel I am washing clean Daddy's hands.'

The casting back in time is in the manner of *Woodbrook*, Anna Wickham's *Fragment of an Autobiography*, Elizabeth Bowen's *Seven Winters: Memories of a Dublin Childhood*, two first-hand accounts of daughters troubled by their times. Add to them *Ryder*, that fell work on polygamy and incest set in an embryonic United States dubbed Cornwall-on-Hudson, 'the shit-house-on-a-distant-hill,' put out by Djuna Barnes.

Matters prudishly omitted from the original edition are replaced: the mother gets it in the neck—as she had got it from her own mother, who had to suffer as the grandchild (Camilla Bag) will be made to suffer, by neglect. The constant visitor, Uncle Freddy, becomes stepfather; fearful accusations are flung.

Underclothes are suspect, as is the menstrual flow, and all bodily functions, calls of nature, particularly the female: *'Undinism!'* The fine rain *spends itself*, say the babbling Asturians. Once every quarter of a century the yucca flowers, sending up a spike (both phallic and indecent) 'rosy and tender, like flesh.' Why even the great macrocarpa is 'standing indecently.' Lingerie has a touch of the pathological about it; Havelock Ellis would have surely agreed. The frustrated only daughter attempts to eat mud, then flowers, 'A state of things to which my mother was as finished a victim—a victim so perfect as not to know what has been done to it.'

Mary Butts married one of Pound's protégés, but this did not last; Aunt Ada took in daughter Camilla. Then, drugs and black magic having failed, Camilla retired to Cornwall, to Celtic *white* magic, dying there in 1937, aged forty-six.

Thirty-two short chapters record the demise of the family Butt and the disfigurement suffered by the land near Salterns as the 'Developers' move in with their tractors. AA guns thunder on the heath. The end of her life must have been as miserable as the end of Charlotte Mew (by Lysol in 1928), or Virginia Woolf's last black depressions before suicide gave release. Or Djuna Barnes's last forty lonely years in Greenwich Village, her health deteriorating—her 'Trappist period.' Her great-grandfather was Thomas Butts, the friend and patron of Blake, whose 'Crystal Cabinet' gave Mary Butts her title. The Journals—resuming where these much-tampered-with Edwardian memoirs leave off, as if appalled by what may yet be revealed—will be worth the wait; promised from Carcanet Press.

Review refused by *Financial Times*

107

Reality's Dark Dream

Franz Kafka, *I am a Memory Come Alive: Autobiographical Writings* edited by
Nahum N. Glatzer (Wildwood House)

His mistresses were out of luck; for he, the kindest of men, could be
cruel. For them he constructed torture-machines. He rather luxuriated in
his Jewishness, burrowed into his Jewish past, summoned his forbears.
He studied law in the German University at Prague, took his degree in
June

1907, was employed with the *Assicurazioni Generali,* an Italian company,
changed to the semi-governmental Workers' Accident Insurance Institute, worked from 8 a.m. to 2 p.m., lived with his parents.

His early writings have not survived, and at his insistence his last
love, Dora Dymant, burned 20 notebooks. Max Brod kept everything.
He wrote of his own 'claw-like hand,' the hand that wrote in German.
Most of these facts are already known. His posthumous reputation has
survived him. Death came to Dr. Kafka on 3 June 1924, about noontime,
as he was correcting the proofs of his last book, *A Hunger Artist,* in the
sanatorium of Dr. Hoffman in Kierling, near Klosternburg. He died of
tuberculosis of the larynx, in fact dying of starvation, was buried in the
Jewish cemetery outside Prague. He wrote of himself as 'a memory come
alive,' as one might speak of pain coming alive.

Nahum N. Glatzer, Professor of Judaic Studies and Religion at Boston
University, has put this compendium together, the ghosted 'autobiography' that Kafka himself never wrote, as culled from diaries, letters and
other close sources. Most of the text would be already familiar to those
who know Kafka's work, though Dora Dymant's memoir is new to me.
His illness he had willed upon himself. There was no cure for it. Tuberculosis was a weapon that continued 'to be of extreme necessity.' 'Sin is
the root of all illness,' he wrote to his friend Janouch. 'That is the reason
for mortality.' He did not have to lash himself to his desk; the desk lashed

itself to him. Writing was 'as important as madness to a madman.' He
was prophetic in that the hour of the Nazi extermination ovens permeates
all his work ('My world is dying away. I am burned out'). He watched the
Jew-baiting from his window. He needed sadness, silence, and to be alone;
Rat und Unrat, tit for tat. He was hard on women because he was hard on
himself; did he enter into affairs, like Beethoven, in order to write about
them? 'The girl's letter is lovely, as lovely as it is abominable.' So too his
own (a weapon that continued to be of extreme necessity). Felice Bauer
sent her friend Grete Bloch as supplicant; correspondence follows, and
an 'intimate relationship' (Glatzer's words) develops. 'I intentionally walk
through the streets where there are whores.'

'Unofficial' engagement to Felice follows, but friendship with her
friend continues; 'official' engagement in Berlin with Grete Bloch present. 'Formal' breaking-off followed by second 'official' engagement he
leaves his parents' home for room at Bilekgasse 10. They were together
in Bodenbach, North Bohemia, in January 1915. He was working in the
factory by 6.30 a.m., encountered the girl from Lemberg. 'A promise of
some kind of happiness,' he noted in his diary, 'resembles the hope of
eternal life.'

In 1915 Grete Bloch became the mother of Kafka's son, who died
before reaching the age of seven, and of whom Kafka knew nothing. In
May of that year he was together with Felice Bauer and Grete Bloch for
a Whitsun holiday in Bohemian Switzerland; the previous day's writing is merely 'filth.' He recalls entering a church in Verona 'with the
heavy compulsion of a man expiring of futility; saw an overgrown dwarf
stooped over the holy water font, walked around a bit, sat down; and as
reluctantly went out again as if just such a church as this one, built door
to door with it, awaited me outside.'

He conducted his own love affairs, or rather they conducted themselves, along much the same fatalistic lines. In spring of 1919, Felice Bauer
married; and Dr. Kafka became engaged to Julie Wohryzek ('a bullet
would be the best solution'). To his friend Brod he wrote: 'But have no
fear, the grim struggle will continue. I have spent my life resisting the
desire to end it.' That year saw the publication of *The Penal Colony* and *A
Country Doctor*. There came a 'crisis' with Julie W., and he met Minze E. at
a sanatorium, the tubercular one hunting for love, or lost for lust ('Seduction on the Graben'). In 1920 Minze E. ('Youth is, of course, always beautiful') was dropped in favour of Milena Jesenska-Polak, a distinguished

Czech translator unhappily married; at the end of that summer Kafka broke off his engagement with Julie Wohryzek, as Milena would in turn give way to the younger Dora Dymant.

He wrote:

> Fresh abundance. Gushing water. Tempestuous, peaceful, high, spreading growth. Blissful oasis. Morning after riotous night. Breast to breast with heaven. Peace, reconciliation. Submerging.

And (doubtless thinking of himself):

> A man who, and this will seem akin to madness, is chained to invisible literature by invisible chains, and screams when approached because, as he claims, someone is touching these chains.
>
> *Letters to Felice*

And:

> The reasons why posterity's judgement of individuals is juster than the contemporary one lies in their being dead. One develops in one's own style only after death, only when one is alone. Death is to the individual what Saturday evening is to the chimney sweep; it washes the dirt from his body. Then it can be seen whether his contemporaries harmed him more, or whether he did the more harm to his contemporaries; in the latter case he was a great man.

Dr. Franz Kafka was a great man.

Hibernia, 30 August 1979

108

Glass Bead Games

Herman Hesse, *The Glass Bead Game* (Cape)

Herman Hesse was born in 1877. Wilhelm I ('a tall, erect military gentle-man who found the masses too vociferous to ignore') was emperor, with Bismarck as Prime Minister, at the start of what was to be the longest period of peace in Europe's troubled history. Kaiser Wilhelm II quar-relled with Bismarck as Hesse grew up. Bismarck went into retirement as Adolf Hitler and then a new century was born. *The Glass Bead Game* was first published in English in 1946, shortly before Herr Hesse won the Nobel Prize.

As a protest against growing, German militancy he went into Swiss retirement in 1919. *Das Glasperlenspiel* appeared in 1943 in the author's twenty-fourth year in exile. It was to be his last book. The story of a man who wants to attain a spiritual province, it has an old-fashioned and rather antiquated air about its musings; more an edifying yarn than a novel, more a yawn than either. It reads like a novice's memoirs from a seminary:

> The monastery of Mariafels, through the many centuries of its existence, had shared in the making and the suffering of the his-tory of the West. Our hero, Joseph Knecht [Magister Ludi] was content with himself and at peace with the world, devoting his days to meditation and the copying of ancient scrolls, whenever he was not occupied with his Bamboo Grove, which sheltered from the north wind a carefully laid out Chinese miniature garden.

> He was shown the garden, the carved slabs, the pond, the gold-fish, and was even told the age of the fish. Until suppertime they sat under the swaying bamboos, exchanging courtesies, verses from the odes, and sayings from the classical writers. The sward was punctuated with stone slabs carved with inscriptions in the classi-cal style.

At his turgid best Hesse is seldom entertaining; at his turgid worst (see above), unendurable. The pace is deadly slow and at 558 pages not lightly undertaken, even as a light read. The Hippies, contemporary exponents of glass bead games, have adopted him, with Timothy Leary, not to mention the Soft Machine and other dubious aids to True Awakening. Much filthy water has flowed down the Rhine since then, and were no nearer to that dream. Dust collects on More's *Utopia*; Orwell's *1984* seems a hotter tip, given the intractable material we must go on.

Come in, Beast 999! Karl von Frisch's work on the bees show how insects order themselves. Don't give me the age of fish. Hesse, whose talent had been on the decline since *Steppenwolf*, died in exile in Switzerland in 1962, aged eighty-four. He has an honoured name.

Hibernia, 30 June 1970

109

Stuffed Grouse

Gregor von Rezzori, *The Snows of Yesteryear*, translated from the German by
H. F. Broch de Rothermann (Chatto & Windus)

Out of Transylvania, homeland of vampires, by definition comes nothing good. It is perilous to be born anywhere near the godforsaken Car-
pathians. Von Rezzori was born in 1914 at Czernovitz (sounds like a
lethal vodka) in Bukovina, an eastern province of the Hapsburg Empire
which became part of Romania and was later absorbed into the Soviet
Ukraine.

As a babe he was pulled on a horse-drawn carriage in a nocturnal
blizzard through the Bargau pass, where Dracula's castle once stood;
with neurasthenic mother, sister and nanny Cassandra, in their flight to
Trieste.

> We lived in the Bukovina . . . as the flotsam of the European class
> struggle, which is what the two great wars really were.

These 'portraits for an autobiography' deal with the Carpathian
nanny, the Pomeranian governess Miss Lina ('Bunchy') Strauss, the
sister who died in a sanatorium in the Tyrol (it bore the somewhat creepy
name of Gnadenwald), the mother and father, the three Rezzoris doomed
to failure and unhappiness. Early-morning showering in icy water with
some off-key singing began the father's day but played havoc with the
mother's nerves. The Cro-Magnon female, Cassandra, romps naked
through the house with the dogs while the family are away—a long journey undertaken for a breath of fresh air.

While on inspection trips to the historic monasteries of the Upper
Moldau, the father takes along his rifles and shotguns. Hunting is an
all-consuming passing, as with Archduke Franz Ferdinand. 'Mother had
a loathing for walls decorated with stag antlers and stuffed grouse.' The

chilly description of his early-morning ablutions recalls Chateaubriand: 'His singing filled the house until noon.' Then the pistol-practice, floriculture, etching and photographic work in his darkroom, the mixing of poisons and the training of young dogs.

His shotguns came from Purdey and custom-made rifles from Mauser; the art materials came in bulk and from the pastel crayons the son (a chip off the old block) catches a whiff of the eighteenth century.

The father walks with deliberate steps, toes turned inward, wearing narrow custom-made shoes 'mirror-polished, rakishly narrow'—a dandy's affectation from the turn of the century, a caricature by Caran d'Ache. He could roll Macedonian tobacco in very thin cigarette papers, with one hand in a doeskin-lined pocket of his jacket. He was fluent in Latin, an anti-Semite who disapproved of Adolf Hitler. He had jumped into an icy river in the depths of winter to recover some game, wanting to spare his dog, and took to his bed with uremia. When he realised he was going blind, he took poison.

Bishop Glondys conveyed the last message to the son. 'Please tell him I'm sorry to be dying in a year in which the wine in Transylvania promises to be so outstanding.' He is the father every son would wish to have.

We are in the forbidding terrain of Joseph Roth and Robert Musil, Thomas Mann's sanatoria. Some of this slides off focus when idiomatic American slang intrudes—'check-list,' 'phoney,' 'those arseholes'—otherwise it is Germanic and humourless. The original title in German, *Blumen im Schnee*, sounds better. Translator Hermann Friedrich Broch de Rothermann was a son of the famous Austrian writer Hermann Broch.

Hibernia, 17 April, 1975

110

1990

Arno Schmidt, *The Egghead Republic: A Short Novel from the Horse Latitudes*, translated from the German by Michael Horovitz (Marion Boyars)

The French seer Nostradamus predicted the doom of Earth in the seventh month of 1999; soured Swift saw the Yahoo pack presided over by wiser horses. Hardly less sanguine, Herr Schmidt forecasts World War in 1990, Europe atomised, German a dead language; Europeans have vanished and with them the cradle of civilisation ('When one's growing up one doesn't need a cradle any more').

Extreme as *Ape and Essence* or *Bend Sinister* or anything by Nathanael West, Arno Schmidt's *Die Gelehrtenrepublik* (Stahlberg Verlag, 1957) comes to us in English twenty years on and purporting to be a manuscript translated into German from a report originally written in American-English through A.D. 2008-2009, a retranslation not simply into American but into an American language spoken thirty years hence.

Charles Henry Winer, born 1978 in Bangor, Maine, now residing in Douglas on the Kalamazoo River, reporter *extraordinaire*, receives permission to visit the jet-propelled island known as the International Republic of Artists and Scientists (IRAS: The Egghead Republic) in the Horse Latitudes, a calm in the Sargasso Sea. The eight Great Powers have settled their 'geniuses' on this man-made island in an attempt to preserve Culture from atomic annihilation.

Before reaching this island for his permitted 50-hour stay, he must cross the Hominid Strip, a huge fenced-off province in the Sierra Nevada. In the Zone he encounters herds of talking Centaurs and an ardent Centauress, Thalia, sixty-foot-high cacti, giant poison spiders with human heads:

> Scorpiomen. A fatally European face stuck out in front: small eyes, long hairy feelers hanging down vertically; the whole tailor-made for a night-fury's career.

He is flown in by balloon at night with a calabash of 93% proof gin and a reversed compass, the permit only granted with insidious proviso that he must never return. The empty gallery forests are shrouded in mist, the Pope has moved to Bahia Blanca where Nueve Roma was immediately proclaimed, a new St. Peter's. He encounters the Great Wall called 'End of the World,' twenty feet high and twice 4,000 miles of concrete 'to shut off our American atomic corridor from both sides.'

Finally he is ferried into IRAS to find the Sacred Island of Humanity ('a Floating Parnassus, a Helicon on the Sargasso Sea') again divided, Portside (good old United States) versus Starboard (funky USSR) with a neutral strip between for diplomatic encounters that come to nothing. Both sides, true to form, are soon thickly plotting to overthrow the other. The 'Bolshies' with organ transplants, the hearts and brains of writers implanted into horses and mares at stud ('Steffan had covered Dshain'), a new Kremlin risen up as a colossal department store with dome.

The Zone Commander General Coffin is there in disguise, the West the first to start up with their confounded tricks, their damned strategies ('technical terms for everything'); the Russians reply with a colony in Siberia (for life apparently goes on as before beyond the Urals) where a specially invented 'security language' is spoken which the ordinary Russian cannot understand. It has a very small specialised vocabulary with no names for many things. They only marry among themselves and never give anything away.

Characters crawl like larvae: Horsemixer the press baron, men turned into women and vice versa; deals can be done in transplanted hostages, some deprived of minds and hearts. The East-West distrust is total, the surrogate Earth in the process of being torn asunder all over again—the Americans ordering Full Speed Reverse, the Russians, 'No Change, Full Speed Ahead,' resulting in *impasse*, the turbo-island rotating on the one spot.

A fearsome future of geiger-counter controls, heart and mind transplants, combat briefing in code, checkpoints, ether-wad and hypodermic is envisaged, grim games. The garrison soldier is in love with his machine-gun. People are not what they seem.

Translator of Poe, Faulkner and Wilkie Collins, his own *oeuvre* likened to Joyce, Queneau and Beckett, Arno Schmidt wrote more than twenty novels, this being the first translated into English. Ernst Krawehl, Herr Schmidt's German editor and publisher, supervised the first draft;

F. Peter Ott, German Professor at the University of Massachusetts, read the proofs and made helpful editorial suggestions.

Arno Schmidt died of apoplexy this summer and had just enough time to read this English version in proof. Berlin Wall and Star Wars have ended; genetic fooling about and gender war begun. One can even get used to Hell—didn't some German say?

'Hell is the devil's paradise.' (Tomi Ungerer)

Hibernia, 23 August 1979

111
Rising Fever

Joseph Roth, *Flight Without End*, translated from the German by
David le Vay in collaboration with Beatrice Musgrave (Peter Owen)
Fred Uhlman, *Reunion* (Collins)

Both Babel and Malaparte have written of war in Galicia, and of Brody
where terrible things happen. Joseph Roth was born there, the only son
of Jewish parents; like Musil, he served in the Austrian Army, then went
into exile. Born in 1894 in the same year as Isaac Babel, he died in Paris in
1939, not long before Babel was done away with. 'O Brody! The mummies
of your crushed passions breath upon me their irremediable poison.'

Their work is not too dissimilar; Kleist and Robert Walser pale by
comparison; Roth's 'extreme laconism' suggests another fatalist, Jewish
in his fatalism: Céline. *Die Flucht ohne Ende* (1927), rendered here as *Flight
Without End,* is like a thermometer thrust into the rising fever of Europe,
European Soviet Russia, in the period August 1916 (Irkutsk)—August
1926 (Paris).

The story hardly matters; it's the exposed nerves that count. The
seduction of the French wife in Baku, Roth's dismembering of the character of the sister-in-law Klara, seeking assistance from the President—these
are memorable incidents in a highly compressed ironic work.

Published at the end of a great literary period, it stands comparison
with the best and is more modern than most work published today.
There are more devastating evocations of Moscow, Berlin and Paris.
One wonders what his characters will say next, as the narrative tense
switches and localities shift; and always a surprise is waiting around the
corner. It put me in mind of Grosz's lithographs from private collections
shown in Berlin, a pen-and-wash of a family of suicides, the mother's possessions on the dressing table; the ferocity in the line, the tenderness in
the aquarelle. Rebecca West in her book on traitors used similar double-
backed metaphors.

The back jacket shows the face of a gambler in a bow-tie, heavy-lidded clever Jewish eyes, 'I have invented nothing, made up nothing. The question of "poetic invention" is no longer relevant; observed fact is all that counts.' The translation never jars, apart from 'opted out,' which is of our time.

Born in Stuttgart in 1901, the anti-Nazi lawyer Uhlman left Germany in 1933 for America, where *Reunion* was written in 1960.

Hans Schwarz, grandson and great-grandson of rabbis, befriends Graf Konradin von Hohenfels at the Karl Alexander Gymnasium in Stuttgart. The time is February 1932 and high-school pupil Eioman has ambitions to be a Reichswehr officer. The Neckar flows by, swastikas sprout on the walls, a Prussian history teacher takes over ('Gentlemen,' he suavely begins his lecture, 'there is history and history'), the PE instructor has taken to wearing a small silver swastika on his jacket.

A fine period evocation of Stuttgart: 'the world utterly secure and certain to last forever.' The narrator is Jewish, the son of a doctor with a modern villa on the *Hoehenlage*, the mother sings *'Heilige Nacht'* at Christmas. Jew-baiting begins as Furtwangler conducts *Fidelio* at the Stuttgart Opera, the narrator's parents gas themselves, he departs for Boston.

'Already the long cruel process of uprooting had begun, already the lights which had guided me had grown dim.'

Perhaps thin in comparison to Babel's 'In the Basement' (the Bank Manager in white flannel trousers reading *The Manchester Guardian* on the terrace, the ladies at poker), though the denouement is most ingenious. It was highly praised by Koestler in his Introduction.

Hibernia, 15 April 1977

112
Culture on the Rocks

Günter Grass, *The Flounder*, translated from the German by Ralph Mannheim
(Secker & Warburg)
Günter Grass, *In the Egg & Other Poems*, translated by from the German by
Michael Hamburger and Christopher Middleton (Secker & Warburg)

How refreshing to be back in the land of freshly killed geese, calf's head in herb vinegar, hog belly with chanterelles, barley and manna grits, eels, Pormeranian dialect *naturlich, und* Neolithic cooking, obligatory references to Danzig-that-was (Gdansk to you), the once-free city on the Vistula estuary thrown in for good measure; and as ever the ups and downs of womankind—Günter Grassland. The swarthy author's mother—wouldn't you know—was the daughter of a wild Kashubian woman.

The man from Friedenau-Berlin has done it again, pressed down and running over. Five years before his fiftieth birthday he decided to write another *Bildungsroman* as a present to himself; and here it is, coming just a year after the German original, Americanised as hitherto in Mannheim's racy translation, the only way to approximate to the energy flow and high jinks of the original.

To the first three extremely odd Danzig novels rendered into American-English as *The Tin Drum, Cat and Mouse, Dog Years* by the same translator, now can be added a fourth: *Der Butt. The Flounder. Local Anaesthetic* (*Ortlich Betaubt*) must be regarded as a dud, a dry-run for the oncoming polemics of *From the Diary of a Snail* and *Speak Out!*

What is common to all four Danzig novels, Vistula tall tales, leaving aside their uncommon energy and narrative brio (compared to which Bellow's *Herzog,* seems slow, more Germanic), is the secret or hidden narrator. In this case the nameless Neolithic fisherman who catches the talking flounder: 'I, down the ages, have been I.'

In *The Tin Drum*, the narrator, Oskar the dwarf, refuses to grow up beyond the age of three, or in Grassjahre just before the Other became

Chancellor. It begins with Oskar Matzerath committed to a mental hospital; 'There's a peephole in the door, and my keeper's eye is the shade of
brown that can never see through a blue-eyed type like me.'

In *Cat and Mouse* (1961) the narrator remains nameless until page 78
when he is reluctantly identified as Pilenz, altar-boy become Parish Hall
secretary. 'What has my name got to do with it?' The Great Mahlke
is the hero: 'I see you, as I've been seeing you for a good fifteen years:
You! I swim, I grip the rust, I see You, the Great Mahlke sits impas-
sive in the shadows.' It's a sour kind of hero-worship. The sunken Polish
minesweeper performs the same function as the Polish Post Office in his
first novel: In Memorium for things lost and Polish; as St. Mary's Chapel
at Marienweg, as the Latin Mass, or Joachim Mahlke's adoration of the
virgin.

In *Dog Years*, six and a half pages of learned footnotes act as acid commentary, glossing 600 pages of text. In this shaggy dog story to end all
shaggy dog stories, the narrator is again hidden—this time under the name
of Brauxel or Brauksel or Haksel or Weichsel, after a river ('the river
which the Romans called the Vistula'), latterly nicknamed Goldmouth.
As in *Die Blechtrommel*, where Oskar has two fathers, one Polish (good),
one Nazi (bad), doubts are cast on paternity. 'Everybody has at least two
fathers. They aren't necessarily acquainted with each other. Some fathers
don't even know. Sometimes fathers get lost.' Heidegger is not quite Hitler
(the Other), though their birthplaces are perilously adjacent. 'In the end
every father becomes a sort of porter to every son.'

The plant of Brauxel & Co. is situated underground; with Hitler's
Alsatian Blondi renamed Pluto as guard-dog. Some of the jokes, sour as
saurkraut, are concerned with changes of name, Polish endings; and the
vexed matter of paternity comes up again, going back to pre-Neolithic
times to get the facts right; or wrong, as the case may be. 'Was it your
Neolithic system to keep us men in the dark?'

The Flounder was always 'hooked on culture.' From the dazed condition of man in Neolithic times, with all history before him, up to the
'thunder-hurling hair-splitting' of our own times, is a fearful jump; but
Herr Grass can manage it.

A comparison with Rabelais is not too far-fetched; even the chap-
terheads have a Rabelaisean ring to them—'How the Flounder was
prosecuted by the Ilsebills.' Disgust-engendering knowledge and self-
knowledge—this morbid modern condition, or migraine, is not entirely

confined to Germans, apparently. Melancholy, as he argued elsewhere, is part and parcel of progress. Gluttony (German-style) is a form of fear; over-eating a form of angst. Ideas engender their own forms of life, such as the three-breasted Neolithic woman.

Grass doesn't create characters by a laborious assembling of details as did Balzac; he *wills* them into being. Aphorisms become animated, take on life; the result is a sort of good-natured *Gulliver's Travels*. And, as with Swift, the real heroes and villains are ideas, translations of states of mind: Balnibarbi, Luggnag, Gludddudrib. His philological fancies are still running away with him.

The 'history-charged' original version—'The Fisherman and his Wife' by the Brothers Grimm—from the narrative of the little old woman, was burned in an excess of fear by the transcribers in the presence of the writers Arnim and Bretano. Time's tyrannical little caprices are examined with a fairly leery eye. Women's Liberation Movement and Neolithic cook consort in the oddest conjunction.

Towards the end of the Stone Age, a fisherman (another self-effacing Grass narrator) catches a talking flounder in the Vistula estuary in a basket-trap invented by the triple-breasted matriarch Awa. Jump-cut to Lubeck Bay in our time. Three 'hard-boiled' ladies in their early thirties, using a walking-stick (symbol of male domination?), string and nail-scissors, cast for and catch the talking flounder. He is tried in Berlin in an abandoned cinema in Steglitz, formerly the Stella but now known as The Pisspot. He quotes Ernst Bloch in his defense: 'The male cause is washed up . . . They've run out of inspiration and now they're trying to rescue capitalism by means of socialism, which is absurd.'

The Vistula, as ever with Grass, is invoked with love. As is Mottlava-Radure, the always hazy moors, the ridge of dunes, the white beaches; human destiny, German or Polish, is another kettle of fish.

The poems are on the theme of the manifestations we casually refer to as Culture, and in English are somewhat meaningless; 28 new poems have been added to the *Selected Poems* with German facing the English text; the herbalist and cook being much in evidence, not to mention the humanist.

Hibernia, 15 September 1979

113

Lebensraum

Günter Grass, *Headbirths, or, the Germans Are Dying Out*, translated from the German by Ralph Mannheim (Secker & Warburg)

He wrote his best work first: the great Danzig trilogy. This most untypical of Germans, the swarthy Kashubian, when away from Danzig and the Vistula (for him as useful a metaphor as the Mississippi for Mark Twain), becomes cantankerous. Langfuhr, come back! One misses the high jinks of the storyteller. Venom against *Bundesrepublik's* 'colossal piggishness' is a poor substitute.

As a diarist Max Frisch is more illuminating; his two-volume diary written in German may have prepared the way for Grass's success. For what French or English reader, let alone an American reader, would have accepted a large guilty *Bildungsroman* from Luchterhand Verlag in 1959?

In Mannheim's translation, the defeated speak in the argot of the victor. Exams are 'flunked,' a 'program' flawed. The manic (or exalted) side of Grass is suppressed; polemics move away from fiction. Now he, who could write about anything under the sun, writes about bores. Conscience-ridden Starusch, student Scherbaum, the spitz in the Berlin kennel. History is always German history, the absurdity of the normal. It's always wartime. His polemics are admittedly more interesting than the polite English fictions of a Golding or a Drabble; but he has given us nothing but polemical writing since *Ortlich Betaubt* of 1969, Englished into American idiom by Mannheim as *Local Anaesthetic*, a year later. The 'subsidized imbeciles' get it in the neck again.

The plot came into his head in Shanghai—'bicycle riders repeating one another *ad infinitem* in dress and bearing'—when on a sponsored tour for the Goethe Institute, with Volder Schlondorff, director of *The Tin Drum* movie. What if the world had to face up to the existence of 950 million Germans, whereas the Chinese nation numbered barely 80 million, or the combined populations of the two Germanys? An appalling thought. In Nuremberg there was a parade ground commodious enough to accommodate two million Germans in uniform.

> I was confronted with the image of a hundred million Saxons and a hundred and twenty million Swabians emigrating to offer the world their tight-packed industriousness.

Or something over two billion, two hundred million Germans by the end of the present century. Herr Grass, who likes turning thoughts on their heads, had arrived at this alarming notion from statistics that showed the German population is declining.

Kopfgeburten was written late in 1979, twenty years after the publication of *Die Blechtrommel*, or shortly after his trip to China and India and just before the German elections of 1980. The idea was offered to Schlondorff for a possible movie script, over a jug of Franconian wine at Marktheidenfeld.

I encountered him once at a Book Ball in Amsterdam, saw him bare his teeth in a wolfish grim for some prearranged 'happening,' some public disturbance involving a porker to be slaughtered and a kitchen maid dismissed, blood in the Dutch kitchen. He and Mary McCarthy were guests of honour at a banquet where a whole series of soups were served up by mistake, but no main course.

I was invited to participate, discuss the equation Literature and Politics. I said there was no connection. Ah, but that's a political comment, they said. Not my cup of tea, I said, thanks all the same.

It must be difficult to be a public man in Central Europe and not show concern for life gone wrong, missile bases everywhere, Baader-Meinhof, the abnormal become the norm.

> To be present again, I often have to take a running start from remote centuries. There once was: there once is. There will have been once again. I'm curious about the eighties: a meddling contemporary . . . All right, I whistle in the woods. I dream heroic dreams.

'There was always some Christ, always a different one, looking at me.' Glass beads feature again, but denims are worn above the knee with fringes this summer. Sandals and bras are out. Feathers are in. Girl students read Mao as their mothers did Rilke. 'With all its displays of realism, this younger generation is looking for a new myth. Watch your step!' Gutsmuthstrasse Guerilleros, Pragerstrasse Partisanen; *Theorie und Praxis.* Communes. Grass, who is doing for Danzig what Joyce did for Dublin, is rightly sceptical. 'Outside, it was snowing from left to right on Hohenzollemdamm':

> 'What are they talking about?'
> 'Oh well, themselves.'
> 'But what do they want?'
> 'Oh, change. To change the world.'

The New Statesman rejected this review as being 'Incomprehensible.'

114

Prophylactic Laughter

Günter Grass, *Local Anaesthetic*, translated from the German by Ralph Manheim (Secker & Warburg)

You must jump a chasm (the *Auschwitz Caesura*) from *Das Glasperlenspiel* to *Die Blechtrommel* (1959), moving away from the bees and glass bead games to a grimmer reality. Herman Hesse, who belonged to an earlier Germany as surely as Grass, along with Bonhoeffer, is a product of the Hitler era, died between the publication of the second and third volumes of Grass's Danzig trilogy, or around the time when the church of Maria Regina was erected as a memorial for those who had lost their lives because of their beliefs during the years 1933-45 and the building of the Berlin Wall around Grass's adopted city.

And whereas Hesse in Switzerland had averted his eyes from Germany and what was happening there and created a never-never land called Castalia (circa A.D. 2400) that would be popular with the Hippies, Herr Grass makes jokes about German firemen, the fathers of his generation, burnt by fires not so remote in time.

Local Anaesthetic, drawn from his play about dog-burning, is his first novel in four years; written in the time when he was not campaigning for Brandt's SPD. Perhaps he was tempted to rewrite Rousseau's *Social Contract*; he has spared himself the trouble and written a German *Candide*.

A Berlin dentist likes to quote Seneca to his patient—the Stoic is in this work as Socrates in *Dog Years*. Colonel Krings comes home from internment in Soviet Russia. A familiar compound ghost named Marxengels gibbers offstage. Günter Grass is as suspicious of the students as they are of him, Brandt's right-hand man. A gaudily dressed Che, that regular man of sorrows, parades on Hauptstrasse.

Seneca once, Malthus now; and Grass, ex-hewer of tombstones, where is he now? He passes through a border control at Friedrichstrasse Station with Nicholas Born, *en route* to a reading at Kopenick. Following an epileptic fit, Rudi Dutschke drowns in a bathtub. The interminable debates go on, the gluttony (a form of fear). Down in Bavaria, Franz Josef Strauss is bellowing. Chancellor Schmidt smokes a slim cigar, reels off statistics, is everywhere at once.

Flying into West Berlin I noticed the weedy, untended graveyards of the DDR; some ex-Germans didn't wish to be buried in soil no longer Germany. A thought for the ex-engraver of Dusseldorf tombstones, whose recent *falsch* fictions require more and more footnotes.

Write on, Maestro!

Hibernia, 17 November 1979

115

The Corpse in the Vault

Heinrich Böll, *The Safety Net*, translated from the German by Leila Vennewitz
(Secker & Warburg)

In a divided Germany, home of stout Prussians and the *Brüders* Grimm, security has become a branch of terrorism. Terrorists and their apologists are eloquent as the dead Rudi Dutschke or Baader-Meinhof, that unslaughterable hydra. To act, to behave, is to demean oneself.

The plot here is thick as tar—*Buddenbrooks* brought forward into *Bend Sinister* land, *Invitation to a Beheading*. 'Now you will belong even less to yourself, and even less to your family.'

The assassin's targets have become hostage to their own security forces; the abnormal becomes the norm. Even the birds of the air are suspect, flying bombs booby-trapped, the presentation birthday-cake may explode, and the cigarette packet primed, the bicycle is loaded. 'We're coming with the bucket'; the translation discharges authentic bile.

The turbulence of his speculations seem stronger than the main narrative when offered as dialogue; perhaps due to an imbalance in translation which veers from American slang ('the slammer' for gaol) into slack Anglo-Sax-*sprach* ('he was pretty sure') and back again ('shacked up'); these conflicting idioms intermarry awkwardly on the page, unlike Mannheim's all-American idiom when translating Grass, working out his own virile and modern German into the equivalent ironbound English.

Böll the Catholic sees no future in a strange theology that would ban sin in the confessional; the churches are emptying. 'Would it be the first time in recent centuries that the bell didn't ring in Hubreichen at a quarter to seven?' The Church accordingly is given a lower case 'c.' The subplots have ramifications that are frequently more interesting than the plot, and the words *Trauerigkeit* (sadness) and *Furcht* (fear) recur and recur, particularly the latter, as Böll shows his age. The moated manor is undermined with brown-coal seams to be mined all the way to the

---

Dutch border; powerstations manufacture their own bad weather on the horizon.

Subscribers request to have their private phones monitored; the trans-receivers buzz and whisper vile things in the shrubbery; microphones are planted under the beds of practicing pederasts. The young punks by the telephone booth call out abuse; to speak privately, husband and wife must hang their heads out of a bedroom window, in the rain, their bedroom bugged.

On the *autobahn* heavy traffic goes 'grinding, grinding, grinding, day and night; that grinding that sometimes turned into a roar.' The man on the station platform is thinking of something else; police dossiers accumulate. A flashback lurid as lightning reveals the ex-Nazi Bleibl associating with Bangers the American Army Major, together looting the *Reichbank* at Doberach.

German prosperity, seen in this jaundiced light, is just another wave of invasion, the land torn up once more, for building; the young become outlaws. The 'stinking cleanliness' of *Bunte* and *Stern* packed,with deodorant and detergent advertising, gives off a bad smell. The old wolves are crawling out of their cages again:

> A stupid bitch, perhaps a poor bitch who even had stupid hands, warped, and probably slipped into hash and rock as a school kid . . . had gone to the dogs, part of a generation that apparently couldn't live without music, if it could be called music.

Tolmshoven is failing down; Hornnauken, Trollschied, Breterheiden; Hubreichen is about to be levelled. Security Chief Holzpuke is only doing his duty.

> In his dreams eagles came, vultures with enormous wingspan, flying straight and hard at him, exploding breast to breast against him, in fire and smoke . . .

The Irish Times, 22 March 1982

SELECTED DALKEY ARCHIVE PAPERBACKS

PETROS ABATZOGLOU, *What Does Mrs. Freeman Want?*
PIERRE ALBERT-BIROT, *Grabinoulor.*
YUZ ALESHKOVSKY, *Kangaroo.*
FELIPE ALFAU, *Chromos.*
   Locos.
IVAN ÂNGELO, *The Celebration.*
   The Tower of Glass.
DAVID ANTIN, *Talking.*
DJUNA BARNES, *Ladies Almanack.*
   Ryder.
JOHN BARTH, *LETTERS.*
   Sabbatical.
DONALD BARTHELME, *The King.*
   Paradise.
SVETISLAV BASARA, *Chinese Letter.*
MARK BINELLI, *Sacco and Vanzetti Must Die!*
ANDREI BITOV, *Pushkin House.*
LOUIS PAUL BOON, *Chapel Road.*
   Summer in Termuren.
ROGER BOYLAN, *Killoyle.*
IGNÁCIO DE LOYOLA BRANDÃO, *Zero.*
CHRISTINE BROOKE-ROSE, *Amalgamemnon.*
BRIGID BROPHY, *In Transit.*
MEREDITH BROSNAN, *Mr. Dynamite.*
GERALD L. BRUNS,
   Modern Poetry and the Idea of Language.
GABRIELLE BURTON, *Heartbreak Hotel.*
MICHEL BUTOR, *Degrees.*
   Mobile.
   Portrait of the Artist as a Young Ape.
G. CABRERA INFANTE, *Infante's Inferno.*
   Three Trapped Tigers.
JULIETA CAMPOS, *The Fear of Losing Eurydice.*
ANNE CARSON, *Eros the Bittersweet.*
CAMILO JOSÉ CELA, *The Family of Pascual Duarte.*
   The Hive.
LOUIS-FERDINAND CÉLINE, *Castle to Castle.*
   Conversations with Professor Y.
   London Bridge.
   North.
   Rigadoon.
HUGO CHARTERIS, *The Tide Is Right.*
JEROME CHARYN, *The Tar Baby.*
MARC CHOLODENKO, *Mordechai Schamz.*
EMILY HOLMES COLEMAN, *The Shutter of Snow.*
ROBERT COOVER, *A Night at the Movies.*
STANLEY CRAWFORD, *Some Instructions to My Wife.*
ROBERT CREELEY, *Collected Prose.*
RENÉ CREVEL, *Putting My Foot in It.*
RALPH CUSACK, *Cadenza.*
SUSAN DAITCH, *L.C.*
   Storytown.
NIGEL DENNIS, *Cards of Identity.*
PETER DIMOCK,
   A Short Rhetoric for Leaving the Family.
ARIEL DORFMAN, *Konfidenz.*
COLEMAN DOWELL, *The Houses of Children.*
   Island People.
   Too Much Flesh and Jabez.
RIKKI DUCORNET, *The Complete Butcher's Tales.*
   The Fountains of Neptune.
   The Jade Cabinet.
   Phosphor in Dreamland.
   The Stain.
   The Word "Desire."
WILLIAM EASTLAKE, *The Bamboo Bed.*
   Castle Keep.
   Lyric of the Circle Heart.
JEAN ECHENOZ, *Chopin's Move.*
STANLEY ELKIN, *A Bad Man.*
   Boswell: A Modern Comedy.
   Criers and Kibitzers, Kibitzers and Criers.
   The Dick Gibson Show.
   The Franchiser.
   George Mills.
   The Living End.
   The MacGuffin.
   The Magic Kingdom.

Mrs. Ted Bliss.
   The Rabbi of Lud.
   Van Gogh's Room at Arles.
ANNIE ERNAUX, *Cleaned Out.*
LAUREN FAIRBANKS, *Muzzle Thyself.*
   Sister Carrie.
LESLIE A. FIEDLER,
   Love and Death in the American Novel.
GUSTAVE FLAUBERT, *Bouvard and Pécuchet.*
FORD MADOX FORD, *The March of Literature.*
CARLOS FUENTES, *Christopher Unborn.*
   Distant Relations.
   Terra Nostra.
   Where the Air Is Clear.
JANICE GALLOWAY, *Foreign Parts.*
   The Trick Is to Keep Breathing.
WILLIAM H. GASS, *The Tunnel.*
   Willie Masters' Lonesome Wife.
ETIENNE GILSON, *The Arts of the Beautiful.*
   Forms and Substances in the Arts.
C. S. GISCOMBE, *Giscome Road.*
   Here.
DOUGLAS GLOVER, *Bad News of the Heart.*
   The Enamoured Knight.
KAREN ELIZABETH GORDON, *The Red Shoes.*
GEORGI GOSPODINOV, *Natural Novel.*
PATRICK GRAINVILLE, *The Cave of Heaven.*
HENRY GREEN, *Blindness.*
   Concluding.
   Doting.
   Nothing.
JIŘÍ GRUŠA, *The Questionnaire.*
JOHN HAWKES, *Whistlejacket.*
AIDAN HIGGINS, *A Bestiary.*
   Bornholm Night-Ferry.
   Flotsam and Jetsam.
   Langrishe, Go Down.
   Scenes from a Receding Past.
   Windy Arbours.
ALDOUS HUXLEY, *Antic Hay.*
   Crome Yellow.
   Point Counter Point.
   Those Barren Leaves.
   Time Must Have a Stop.
MIKHAIL IOSSEL AND JEFF PARKER, EDS., *Amerika:*
   Contemporary Russians View
   the United States.
GERT JONKE, *Geometric Regional Novel.*
JACQUES JOUET, *Mountain R.*
HUGH KENNER, *The Counterfeiters.*
   Flaubert, Joyce and Beckett:
   The Stoic Comedians.
DANILO KIŠ, *Garden, Ashes.*
   A Tomb for Boris Davidovich.
ANITA KONKKA, *A Fool's Paradise.*
TADEUSZ KONWICKI, *A Minor Apocalypse.*
   The Polish Complex.
MENIS KOUMANDAREAS, *Koula.*
ELAINE KRAF, *The Princess of 72nd Street.*
JIM KRUSOE, *Iceland.*
EWA KURYLUK, *Century 21.*
VIOLETTE LEDUC, *La Bâtarde.*
DEBORAH LEVY, *Billy and Girl.*
   Pillow Talk in Europe and Other Places.
JOSÉ LEZAMA LIMA, *Paradiso.*
OSMAN LINS, *Avalovara.*
   The Queen of the Prisons of Greece.
ALF MAC LOCHLAINN, *The Corpus in the Library.*
   Out of Focus.
RON LOEWINSOHN, *Magnetic Field(s).*
D. KEITH MANO, *Take Five.*
BEN MARCUS, *The Age of Wire and String.*
WALLACE MARKFIELD, *Teitlebaum's Window.*
   To an Early Grave.
DAVID MARKSON, *Reader's Block.*
   Springer's Progress.
   Wittgenstein's Mistress.

FOR A FULL LIST OF PUBLICATIONS, VISIT:
www.dalkeyarchive.com

SELECTED DALKEY ARCHIVE PAPERBACKS

CAROLE MASO, AVA.
LADISLAV MATEJKA AND KRYSTYNA POMORSKA, EDS.,
 Readings in Russian Poetics: Formalist and
 Structuralist Views.
HARRY MATHEWS,
 The Case of the Persevering Maltese: Collected Essays.
 Cigarettes.
 The Conversions.
 The Human Country: New and Collected Stories.
 The Journalist.
 My Life in CIA.
 Singular Pleasures.
 The Sinking of the Odradek Stadium.
 Tlooth.
 20 Lines a Day.
ROBERT L MCLAUGHLIN, ED.,
 Innovations: An Anthology of Modern &
 Contemporary Fiction.
STEVEN MILLHAUSER, The Barnum Museum.
 In the Penny Arcade.
RALPH J. MILLS, JR., Essays on Poetry.
OLIVE MOORE, Spleen.
NICHOLAS MOSLEY, Accident.
 Assassins.
 Catastrophe Practice.
 Children of Darkness and Light.
 The Hesperides Tree.
 Hopeful Monsters.
 Imago Bird.
 Impossible Object.
 Inventing God.
 Judith.
 Look at the Dark.
 Natalie Natalia.
 Serpent.
 The Uses of Slime Mould: Essays of Four Decades.
WARREN F. MOTTE, JR.,
 Fables of the Novel: French Fiction since 1990.
 Oulipo: A Primer of Potential Literature.
YVES NAVARRE, Our Share of Time.
 Sweet Tooth.
DOROTHY NELSON, In Night's City.
 Tar and Feathers.
WILFRIDO D. NOLLEDO, But for the Lovers.
FLANN O'BRIEN, At Swim-Two-Birds.
 At War.
 The Best of Myles.
 The Dalkey Archive.
 Further Cuttings.
 The Hard Life.
 The Poor Mouth.
 The Third Policeman.
CLAUDE OLLIER, The Mise-en-Scène.
PATRIK OUŘEDNÍK, Europeana.
FERNANDO DEL PASO, Palinuro of Mexico.
ROBERT PINGET, The Inquisitory.
 Mahu or The Material.
 Trio.
RAYMOND QUENEAU, The Last Days.
 Odile.
 Pierrot Mon Ami.
 Saint Glinglin.
ANN QUIN, Berg.
 Passages.
 Three.
 Tripticks.
ISHMAEL REED, The Free-Lance Pallbearers.
 The Last Days of Louisiana Red.
 Reckless Eyeballing.
 The Terrible Threes.
 The Terrible Twos.
 Yellow Back Radio Broke-Down.
JULIÁN RÍOS, Larva: A Midsummer Night's Babel.
 Poundemonium.
AUGUSTO ROA BASTOS, I the Supreme.
JACQUES ROUBAUD, The Great Fire of London.

Hortense in Exile.
Hortense Is Abducted.
The Plurality of Worlds of Lewis.
The Princess Hoppy.
The Form of a City Changes Faster, Alas,
 Than the Human Heart.
Some Thing Black.
LEON S. ROUDIEZ, French Fiction Revisited.
VEDRANA RUDAN, Night.
LYDIE SALVAYRE, The Company of Ghosts.
 The Lecture.
LUIS RAFAEL SÁNCHEZ, Macho Camacho's Beat
SEVERO SARDUY, Cobra & Maitreya.
NATHALIE SARRAUTE, Do You Hear Them?
 Martereau.
 The Planetarium.
ARNO SCHMIDT, Collected Stories.
 Nobodaddy's Children.
CHRISTINE SCHUTT, Nightwork.
GAIL SCOTT, My Paris.
JUNE AKERS SEESE,
 Is This What Other Women Feel Too?
 What Waiting Really Means.
AURELIE SHEEHAN, Jack Kerouac Is Pregnant.
VIKTOR SHKLOVSKY, Knight's Move.
 A Sentimental Journey: Memoirs 1917-1922.
 Theory of Prose.
 Third Factory.
 Zoo, or Letters Not about Love.
JOSEF ŠKVORECKÝ,
 The Engineer of Human Souls.
CLAUDE SIMON, The Invitation.
GILBERT SORRENTINO, Aberration of Starlight.
 Blue Pastoral.
 Crystal Vision.
 Imaginative Qualities of Actual Things.
 Mulligan Stew.
 Pack of Lies.
 The Sky Changes.
 Something Said.
 Splendide-Hôtel.
 Steelwork.
 Under the Shadow.
W. M. SPACKMAN, The Complete Fiction.
GERTRUDE STEIN, Lucy Church Amiably.
 The Making of Americans.
 A Novel of Thank You.
PIOTR SZEWC, Annihilation.
STEFAN THEMERSON, Hobson's Island.
 Tom Harris.
JEAN-PHILIPPE TOUSSAINT, Television.
ESTHER TUSQUETS, Stranded.
DUBRAVKA UGRESIC, Lend Me Your Character.
 Thank You for Not Reading.
MATI UNT, Things in the Night.
ELOY URROZ, The Obstacles.
LUISA VALENZUELA, He Who Searches.
BORIS VIAN, Heartsnatcher.
PAUL WEST, Words for a Deaf Daughter & Gala.
CURTIS WHITE, America's Magic Mountain.
 The Idea of Home.
 Memories of My Father Watching TV.
 Monstrous Possibility: An Invitation to
 Literary Politics.
 Requiem.
DIANE WILLIAMS, Excitability: Selected Stories.
 Romancer Erector.
DOUGLAS WOOLF, Wall to Wall.
 Ya! & John-Juan.
PHILIP WYLIE, Generation of Vipers.
MARGUERITE YOUNG, Angel in the Forest.
 Miss MacIntosh, My Darling.
REYOUNG, Unbabbling.
ZORAN ŽIVKOVIĆ, Hidden Camera.
LOUIS ZUKOFSKY, Collected Fiction.
SCOTT ZWIREN, God Head.

FOR A FULL LIST OF PUBLICATIONS, VISIT:
www.dalkeyarchive.com